THE BOOK OF VMware

THE
BOOK OF
VMware

THE COMPLETE GUIDE TO
VMWARE WORKSTATION

Brian Ward

**NO STARCH
PRESS**

San Francisco

Printed in Canada

1 2 3 4 5 6 7 8 9 10 – 05 04 03 02

VMware, the VMware "boxes" logo, MultipleWorlds, GSX Server, and ESX Server are trademarks of VMware, Incorporated.

Trademarked names are used throughout this book. Rather than use a trademark symbol with every occurrence of a trademarked name, we are using the names only in an editorial fashion and to the benefit of the trademark owner, with no intention of infringement of the trademark.

Publisher: William Pollock
Editorial Director: Karol Jurado
Cover and Interior Design: Octopod Studios
Composition: 1106 Design, LLC
Technical Review: VMware, Inc.
Copyeditor: Nancy McLaughlin
Proofreader: Ruth Stevens

Distributed to the book trade in the United States by Publishers Group West, 1700 Fourth Street, Berkeley, CA 94710; phone: 800-788-3123; fax: 510-658-1834.

Distributed to the book trade in Canada by Jacqueline Gross & Associates, Inc., One Atlantic Avenue, Suite 105, Toronto, Ontario M6K 3E7 Canada; phone: 416-531-6737; fax 416-531-4259.

For information on translations or book distributors outside the United States, please contact No Starch Press, Inc. directly:

No Starch Press, Inc.
555 De Haro Street, Suite 250, San Francisco, CA 94107
phone: 415-863-9900; fax: 415-863-9950; info@nostarch.com; http://www.nostarch.com

Library of Congress Cataloging-in-Publication Data

```
Ward, Brian, 1972-
    The book of VMware / Brian Ward.
        p. cm.
        Includes index.
        ISBN 1-886411-72-7 (pbk.)
            1. Operating systems (Computers)  2. VMware.  I. Title.
QA76.76.063 W3653 2001
005.4'469--dc21
                                                              2001026610
```

ACKNOWLEDGMENTS

The author sincerely thanks:
Everyone at VMware, Inc. for their support,
Everyone at No Starch Press,
Everyone who has ever taught me
a thing or two about computers.

Brian Ward
Chicago, Illinois

BRIEF CONTENTS

Appendix A
Linux Display Parameters
229

Appendix B
Upgrading from VMware
Workstation 2
233

Index
237

CONTENTS IN DETAIL

1
INTRODUCTION

2
THE VMWARE VIRTUAL MACHINE

3
INSTALLING VMWARE WORKSTATION

4

VIRTUAL MACHINE CONFIGURATION AND OPERATION

5
WINDOWS GUEST SYSTEMS

6
LINUX GUEST OPERATING SYSTEMS

7

FREEBSD GUEST SYSTEMS

8

OTHER GUEST OPERATING SYSTEMS

9

HOST AND GUEST SYSTEM NETWORK CONFIGURATION

10

NETWORK SERVICES

11

NON-NETWORKED FILE TRANSFER

12

TROUBLESHOOTING

A

LINUX DISPLAY PARAMETERS

B

UPGRADING FROM VMWARE WORKSTATION 2

Index

1

INTRODUCTION

This book is about the VMware Workstation product: how to use it, how to set up its guest operating systems, and the things you can do with these systems once you have them up and running.

VMware Workstation functions as a computer *within* a computer, so that you can start up an entire operating system and run any programs for that operating system with it, while keeping your original operating system environment intact (and usable). For example, a Linux user who needs to use a Windows program not available for Linux (such as a map downloading system for a Palm's GPS) can fire up VMware Workstation in a window, start Windows NT there, run the mapping software, download the maps to the Palm using the virtual serial port (connected to the real serial port on Linux), and then put Windows away for another time. It can work the other way around, too—Windows users needing Linux applications can run them in a virtual machine. And that's just the beginning.

VMware is a *virtual machine* (*VM*) for an Intel Pentium-class or higher machine and is available for the Windows NT, Windows 2000, Windows XP, and Linux operating systems. Virtual machine software runs on a real machine and provides a virtual machine with the same basic *architecture* as the real machine. The architecture is based on the processor type—for example, the i686 (Intel Pentium II/III) and sun4u (Sun UltraSPARC) are two different architectures.

On the surface, VMware Workstation is similar to an *emulator* (a machine running only in software), but there is a crucial difference between a VMware-style virtual machine and an emulator. Whereas an emulator intercepts and interprets every last instruction for the target machine, a virtual machine passes most of the work down to the real machine sitting beneath it. Because the real machine is much faster than a software emulator, programs running on a real machine run much faster and efficiently than they do on an emulator. In addition, you needn't worry so much about compatibility issues as you would with an emulator—the real processor isn't likely to make a mistake.

A computer's processor is tightly coupled to its memory (RAM). VMware takes advantage of memory management techniques used in contemporary operating systems to keep this coupling in place on virtual machines.

However, there has to be emulation in a virtual machine at some level, or the virtual machine would just take over the whole computer. In VMware Workstation, the emulation comes in two places: peripheral hardware (disks, network cards, and so on) and certain privileged CPU instructions. However, even though VMware's hardware is at the software level, you can map your real hardware to the virtual hardware so that you can use the real hardware on the virtual machine just as you normally would. Of course, this takes a small bit of overhead because the communication between the real hardware and the virtual machine has to go through a few more layers, but this abstraction also enables certain features that more than make up for it. (A specific example is device disconnection and reconnection.)

1.1 Who Should Read This Book

This book strives to be a complete how-to and reference guide for VMware Workstation. Each chapter starts with a hands-on, step-by-step guide to getting one piece of the puzzle up and running. Then the material shifts into reference-style documentation. Because VMware Workstation runs such a wide range of operating systems, it's natural that some material will be a review to almost any reader. However, this material will be different for every user, depending on the operating systems with which the reader is most familiar.

Because VMware multiplexes a PC, this book discusses pertinent hardware and operating system elements. If you "sort of know" these concepts but are hazy on a few details (such as how a PC boots), you might pick up some of this information along the way. Remember, however, that this book is about VMware and doesn't stray from that theme.

This book is probably not for people who have never used any of the operating systems in the book, or for very advanced users who have used every single operating system ever produced.

1.2 Terms and Conventions

Now let's get to some terms and notation that you'll see throughout this book:

Host System: This is the computer and operating system that runs VMware—in other words, the computer you install VMware Workstation on. *Host operating system* refers to only the operating system side of your host system.

Guest System: The virtual machine and operating system running *inside* VMware. Under VMware Workstation, each host system may have several guest systems. *Guest operating system* refers to only the operating system on the guest system.

Boot and **Reboot**: The computer's boot procedure loads the operating system. Rebooting is simply shutting the operating system down and starting it up again. Some operating systems use the terms *start* and *restart* for these actions. We'll use the terms *boot* and *reboot* to avoid confusion because you can also start and restart processes on a running system. (The term *boot* comes from the metaphor of a system "pulling itself up by its bootstraps," though the computer sometimes doesn't do all the work by itself.)

Text in a monospaced typeface like this normally refers to something that you type at a Unix/Linux or DOS prompt, or something that you see on the screen. Sometimes it can be a file name on these systems. The important thing to remember is that monospaced text normally refers to something in a *command-line interface*.

On the other hand, *menu sequences* appear like this: **File • Save.** Menu sequences refer to a *graphical user interface*: For example, "pull down the File menu and select the Save option."

1.3 Book Layout

This book's organization follows the order of topics that a new VMware user encounters. Since there are many different combinations of host and guest operating systems, the information is laid out in such a way that you can skip ahead to another chapter when you've learned enough. For example, let's say you run VMware Workstation for Windows and want to run FreeBSD as a guest operating system. You can go over the information pertinent to Windows in Chapter 3, skip to Chapter 4, read about the Configuration Wizard and VMware's operation there, and then skip past the next two chapters to end up at the FreeBSD guest information in Chapter 7. After you become more familiar with VMware, you can go back to Chapter 4 and read about the Configuration Editor.

Before this book goes into much detail about how to use VMware Workstation, we discuss the virtual hardware in **Chapter 2**. Because not all users may be familiar with real hardware, each section briefly explains a PC's real hardware before describing what VMware provides. This chapter also discusses a few other topics, such as the PC BIOS.

Chapter 3 describes how to install VMware Workstation on your host system and the issues you may encounter in the process. Because VMware requires access to some of the host system's internal data structures, you may need to change your system's configuration. Although this discussion applies mainly to VMware Workstation for Linux, you'll find information about the Windows versions as well.

In **Chapter 4**, you'll learn how to set up a virtual machine configuration and get acquainted with VMware's user interface. VMware provides two configuration tools: the Configuration Wizard and Configuration Editor. You'll get started with the wizard and then learn how to operate the VMware controls.

This chapter also introduces a set of very important packages called the VMware Tools and tells you how to use the pieces common to all guest systems. Reference material in Chapter 4 also includes the Configuration Editor and the VMware BIOS.

Chapters 5 through 8 are devoted to guest operating systems. Most of the content in these chapters is devoted to device support—in particular, how to set up the devices in each guest system. Depending on the guest system, you may need to know something about the system beforehand. Although the Windows systems don't have many prerequisites, you'll need a little familiarity with the Unix shell interface for the Linux and FreeBSD chapters. Fortunately, VMware offers you the opportunity to learn as you go. If you install Linux as a guest on a VMware virtual disk, you can't damage your host system while you play around with the Linux system, and you can even set your virtual disk to an "undoable" mode.

You'll find information about Windows 95, 98, Me, NT, 2000, and XP in **Chapter 5**. Older Microsoft systems such as DOS 6 and Windows 3.1 also run under VMware; this book covers these as well. **Chapter 6** is devoted to Linux; **Chapter 7** describes FreeBSD under VMware. Other operating systems that work (to some degree, at least) with VMware Workstation are discussed in **Chapter 8**.

Networking is one of VMware's strong points, and **Chapter 9** goes into detail about how to set it up on your host and guest systems. Because there are many different possible configurations, the entire chapter is devoted to setup.

Once you get your network up, you'll want to do something with it. One of the most common network tasks with VMware is sharing the host filesystem with the guest system, and naturally, this book covers the procedure. However, there are many things you can do above and beyond simple file sharing; you'll learn which ones are of particular interest with respect to VMware in **Chapter 10**.

Chapter 11 is a small guide to transferring files between host and guest systems without the help of a network.

Finally, **Chapter 12** contains troubleshooting information. Since VMware Workstation acts like a real computer, it can have many of the same sorts of problems. This chapter discusses these potential problems following the same sequence as the rest of the book.

Appendix A provides hints on setting up video modes on a Linux host system. Because this is a somewhat tangled subject, and its relevance to VMware is tangential, it does not appear within the main text. However, if it did, it would be in Chapter 4, near the discussion of full-screen mode. **Appendix B** covers upgrades to VMware Workstation 3 from a previous version.

1.4   VMware Applications

The first use you may think up for VMware is gaining access to programs written for operating systems other than your native system. Many attempts have been made to achieve cross–operating system application support. Between Solaris and Windows, there are systems such as WABI; Linux has a module called iBCS (Intel Binary Compatibility Standard) to run other PC Unix flavors' binaries. However, all of these have their own little quirks because the underlying operating system is different. Since VMware Workstation actually runs the application's operating system in addition to the application itself, compatibility problems are rare.

However, VMware Workstation has many more uses beyond this. A few examples follow.

1.4.1 Quality Assurance (QA)

Because there are many possible versions and configurations of operating systems, testing software products can involve a large amount of overhead. Traditionally, quality assurance teams require several physical machines, each with a different operating system. Not only does this cost money, but the setup time for this infrastructure is substantial.

VMware eliminates the need for many physical machines. With virtual disks, you can fit many different operating systems onto the real disks of a single computer. You also have the option of running several of the operating systems simultaneously so that you can compare them side by side. There are many other benefits—for example, if your testing can somehow corrupt the operating system, you can take advantage of VMware's undoable disk mode and just go back to the machine's old state if something bad happens. On a real machine, you'd need to reinstall the operating system.

Due to its low cost compared to large hardware arrays, VMware Workstation helps to level the playing field in quality assurance for smaller software companies.

1.4.2 Network Programming and Testing

Because VMware's host-only networking mode doesn't require a physical network, you can experiment with networking without the hassle of running wires and setting up machines. If you have a peer-to-peer program, you can test it between your host and guest systems to your heart's content. Another advantage of this scheme is that you are isolated from your real network (if you have one). You won't have to bother your network administrator when you need a new IP address for experimentation, and if you saturate the host-only network, you won't have the network administrator knocking on your door.

Furthermore, you can test your network programs between different operating systems without any additional equipment. With host-only networking, your guest system isn't just limited to talking to the host system; you can run more than one guest system at the same time and have the systems talk to each other. For example, you can see how well a web server running on FreeBSD interacts with Internet Explorer on Windows NT, all on a Linux host system.

1.4.3 Operating System Development, Research, and Education

One of the most frustrating things about the first stage of writing operating systems is that operating systems take a lot of debugging. A common problem is how to get your compiled kernel onto a system for testing. It's hard to do your development on the same machine that you're writing the code on, because you have to reboot the machine all the time. Likewise, transferring your kernel to a test machine is also awkward: You can use floppy disks or some removable media. There are expensive hardware solutions to these problems, but VMware is an even more elegant answer that costs far less. You can simply manipulate your test kernels as images for guest operating systems and bring them up on the same screen as the rest of your development work.

Operating systems classes at the university level follow the same scenario. Any reasonable class provides absolutely no code beforehand—the students write everything from scratch. However, as mentioned, there is an initial, time-consuming hurdle. Instructors have responded with hardware simulator environments such as USLOSS and Yalnix that run most code in native mode, but have a home-grown system of CPU traps and simulated hardware. These latter pieces resemble true hardware to a certain degree, but they don't capture every detail. However, the instructor who wants to teach an intensive class (graduate level) to make students *really* work and get a true feeling for working with hardware can try the ultimate hardware simulator: VMware Workstation. Incidentally, VMware has some roots in these simulator environments.

1.4.4 Other VMware Products

This book is about VMware Workstation; however, VMware also offers several other products. Although this book doesn't discuss them, you may want to know a little about them.

VMware Server products are supercharged virtual machines. Their focus is on servers—that is, on running multiple operating systems at once. Although Workstation has this capability, the server products add features that make the operating system easier to manage, such as the web administration tool and remote virtual monitors. Furthermore, they offer performance improvements; they more closely replicate the underlying host operating system and support more than one processor.

There are currently two server products. **VMware GSX Server** is a mid-range product that runs on top of Linux or Windows NT/2000/XP. Like Workstation, it runs on almost any hardware that the host operating system does. On the other hand, **VMware Server ESX** pushes performance further by providing its own console operating system based on Linux. In particular, its network and disk devices have fewer levels of abstraction than any of the other VMware products and are therefore much faster. Both server versions are compatible with VMware Workstation; you can move virtual machine configurations around between the different products.

2

THE VMWARE VIRTUAL MACHINE

VMware Workstation provides virtual hardware on top of a host computer's real processor and memory. That hardware is the focus of this chapter. First, we'll take a short look at the hardware layout on a PC and show where the line between virtual and real is on VMware. An overview of each virtual device follows. To provide a base reference, a description of the real hardware accompanies each explanation of a virtual device.

The last two sections in this chapter are about the PC BIOS and boot process. You'll need to know the information there if you plan to use your disks in raw (direct) mode.

2.1 Processor, Bus, Memory, and Interrupts

A PC has three essential components: the CPU, memory, and I/O devices (which we'll just call devices from now on). CPU stands for *central processing unit* (or *processor*), and it is the heart of a computer. It not only runs the instructions that comprise a program, but it also supervises the rest of the system.

Because a CPU can't store all of the essential system data in its limited amount of storage space, the processor needs external memory, in the form of *random-access memory* (RAM). Because this storage is very important to the CPU's operation, the CPU has nearly direct access to it. Between the CPU and its RAM is an important layer called the *memory management unit* (MMU). This piece splits the RAM into many small pieces known as *pages*. The MMU has a map (called a *page table*) of the CPU-addressed memory to pages in real memory.

The memory that user programs see is called *virtual memory* (not a VMware term). When a CPU instruction asks for a certain address in memory, the MMU redirects the access through its page table to a place in real memory. (Note that this system is not hardware only; the operating system works with the MMU to get the job done. Some older systems, such as DOS, do not use the MMU.)

On the other hand, it's rare for a device to have a close connection to the CPU for two reasons. One is that devices vary so much that it would be almost impossible to create an interface inside the CPU supporting each device. Furthermore, devices often transmit data at irregular intervals, and several devices may try to talk to the CPU at once. It doesn't make sense for the CPU to bother with a device until all of its data is in order and in a format that the CPU understands, so the CPU has a common *bus* that connects the devices to the CPU. In addition, there are often extra controllers and interfaces between the devices and the bus; an example of this is the SCSI controller.

VMware has two virtual buses, resembling those in most modern PCs: PCI and an extension off the PCI bus called the *PCI-to-ISA bridge*. ISA is an old standard dating back to the first IBM PC. Though it is remarkably inferior to current technology, backward compatibility keeps ISA alive.

Although certain devices, such as serial ports, still use the ISA interface, hardware developers avoid it whenever possible because of its limitations. Some of those limitations have to do with *interrupts* and *I/O ports*. Devices send interrupts over the bus to the CPU when they're ready to transmit data or when they have something otherwise significant to say. The CPU notices this, stops its current activity, and processes the interrupt. ISA numbers its interrupts into *interrupt request* (IRQ) *levels* to differentiate them. Unfortunately, there aren't many IRQs, and if two devices try to share one number, serious conflicts result. Similarly, devices use I/O ports to communicate through the bus to the processor.

While ISA had fixed port numbers for every device, and you had to be very careful to avoid conflicts, PCI has neither of these problems. PCI interrupts have much more information, so several PCI devices can share an IRQ, and the chipset also automatically sets up the I/O ports when you turn the computer on.

Figure 2.1 shows an abstract map of the VMware Workstation PC. Notice the curious arrangement of the IDE disk interface (you can access it through the PCI or ISA bus).

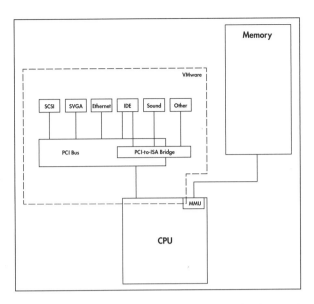

Figure 2.1: VMware Workstation virtual and real hardware—the virtual hardware is within the dashed box

2.2 The VMware Devices

Let's have a look at VMware's virtual devices. Each device discussed here corresponds to a real device on a PC. To ensure that you're up to speed, we'll first take a brief look at each real device before talking about VMware's virtual device.

2.2.1 IDE Disks and CD-ROM Drives

The most common type of disk in PCs is the Integrated Device Electronics, or IDE, disk. Traditional disk architectures had a disk *controller* somewhere on the main CPU board, with a dedicated data channel between the controller and any disks. However, these controllers tended to add cost to the machine. Also, they often did far more than a PC needed—a SCSI-I or II controller, for example, can handle up to seven disks or other devices. Because a PC rarely has more than one or two hard drives, and other components are usually in the form of Industry-Standard Architecture, or ISA, cards, PC designers decided that they might be able to reduce costs by removing this flexibility. They came up with IDE disks, where the controller is actually integrated into the disk itself, leaving only an ISA *interface* card on the PC's motherboard.

As PCs became popular, IDE disks quickly became the most common commodity disks, and prices dropped far below those of other disk types. However, the shortcuts taken in the design of IDE caused problems later, and every time a new difficulty arose, someone added a new "standard" to the specification. For example, the IDE interface didn't support CD-ROM drives, so hardware engineers squeezed ATAPI into the design. (ATAPI, or AT Attached Packet Interface, connects CD-ROM and tape drives to the IDE interface.) In modern PCs, it isn't even strictly true that the disks sit behind an interface anymore—it's hard to draw a clear line between the controller and the interface.

Like most PC motherboards, VMware Workstation has two IDE controllers, called the *primary* and *secondary* interfaces. The virtual hardware is the Intel 82371AB PIIX4 chipset. The IRQ (or interrupt request) and port assignments are as follows:

Interface	IRQ	I/O Ports
Primary	14	0x01f0 to 0x01f7, 0x03f6
Secondary	15	0x0170 to 0x0177, 0x0376

Like all IDE interfaces, each of these ports can support a maximum of two devices (sometimes called *master* and *slave* devices). Under VMware, they are limited to disk, CD-ROM/DVD-ROM, CD-R, and CD-RW drives that you can configure in a few different ways.

VMware stores *virtual* and *plain disks* as files on your host system. These files are images of a complete disk and are usually quite large. A *raw disk* is a mapping from one of your real disks to a disk under VMware.

VMware disks provide some added flexibility that you don't have with disks on a real machine, such as the ability to undo or make a disk appear as read-write without actually altering the data underneath. You may also configure VMware ATAPI CD-ROM drives as mappings to a real disk, or if you have a CD-ROM image on your host system (such as an ISO9660 file), you can point VMware to that. (See page 58 for more information on all of these modes and section 11.4 for a discussion of CD-ROM images.)

2.2.2   SCSI Disks

The small computer system interface, or SCSI, is a peripheral bus standard for small computers, meant for attaching various devices to a computer. The bus is independent of the computer's architecture, so you can, for example, exchange SCSI devices between PC and Sun systems, assuming that you have the drivers for those particular kinds of devices on those systems. The gateway between the SCSI bus and a computer is called a *SCSI host controller*, though it's often known as a SCSI adapter or SCSI card.

There are several types of SCSI buses: SCSI-I, SCSI-II, Fast SCSI-II, Ultra Wide SCSI, and so on. SCSI-I and II can have up to eight devices on a bus (this number includes the host controller). Wide SCSI can handle up to 16 devices. If you're interested in SCSI, a good place to look is *The Book of SCSI, 2nd Edition* (another No Starch Press publication; ISBN 1-886411-10-7).

VMware Workstation has virtual SCSI hardware. Its host controller is a PCI-based BusLogic BT-958 Ultra Wide SCSI adapter. You can configure up to seven disks or CD-ROM drives from VMware's controller, even though it shows up as wide (on real wide SCSI buses, you can have up to 15 devices). The special VMware SCSI disk modes and features are the same as for the IDE disks mentioned in the previous section. Because the virtual SCSI controller is a PCI device, the system dynamically configures the IRQ number and I/O ports when it starts.

In addition to SCSI disks, VMware Workstation 3 supports arbitrary virtual SCSI devices such as CD-R writers and SCSI scanners.

2.2.3 Floppy Drives

Probably the most primitive device that VMware supports is the PC floppy disk drive, and there isn't much hardware less intelligent than it. While floppy drives on other platforms have features such as automatic media detection and eject notification, everything is manual on a PC floppy drive. Like the actual floppy disks themselves, the hardware specification hasn't changed in years. The floppy controller on a PC can't even figure out whether a drive is present or what size drive it is. It just tries to access the media based on a predetermined configuration, and if it fails, it simply tells the operating system that it can't cope.

However, this design is something of a blessing for VMware Workstation, because you don't have to worry about guest system support. You can configure one or two virtual floppy drives as mappings to real floppy drives on your host system or as floppy image files on the host operating system, and as you work with floppy disks under VMware, you'll probably realize that the latter method is much more convenient. Floppy disks not only tend to be unreliable, but they're also slow. If you can just yank a floppy image off the disk at once and point VMware at the file you created, you'll get your work done quickly. You can also interact with floppy images on the host system. (You'll see how to do that in sections 11.2 and 11.3.)

The floppy controller resides at IRQ 6 on a PC, with I/O ports at 0x3f0 to 0x3f5 and 0x3f7.

To get around the deficiencies of the old floppy devices, vendors have started to offer USB and even IDE floppy disk drives. In addition to VMware Workstation's USB capability, a USB floppy drive on a Linux host system shows up as a SCSI drive, and you can map it to a virtual SCSI drive. The benefits are somewhat unclear though: If you're interested in getting something off a floppy disk, it's usually much faster to pull the entire image off at once from your host system and throw the floppy disk away afterward.

2.2.4 Ethernet Interfaces

A *network interface card* (NIC) is an adapter that intercepts the signals on a network, filters them, and sends them to the CPU for processing.

Ethernet is the most common type of local area network. Its low cost has led many PC manufacturers to include onboard Ethernet interfaces on their machines. VMware's virtual Ethernet interface is an AMD PCnet II based on the AMD 79C970A chip.

You can add up to three interfaces to a virtual machine, in three kinds of configurations. A *host-only network* exists only in the host operating system and is used primarily for communication between the host and guest. In contrast, *bridged networking* multiplexes the host system's real Ethernet interface in much the same way that VMware multiplexes the host's CPU, so a guest system can talk on the host's network. *NAT networking* is a host-only network that uses network address translation to communicate with outside networks.

Like the VMware SCSI controller, the virtual Ethernet interfaces are PCI devices, so the interrupts and I/O ports are automatic at system boot.

Networking support is one of VMware's gems. After enabling it on your guest systems, you open up many new possibilities for interaction between your host and guest systems. You aren't limited to just sharing files; you can use *any* feature that real networks offer, from SSH tunneling to remote print servers. Chapters 9 and 10 are dedicated to VMware networking and what you can achieve with it.

2.2.5 Serial Ports

An older type of peripheral interface, serial ports and lines transfer data between two devices one bit at a time. The most common type of serial interaction is between a computer and a modem; internal modems also show up as serial ports. The serial chip is called a UART (or universal asynchronous receiver-transmitter), and these are now integrated into motherboard chipsets.

PC UARTs have a long history of not being up to scratch. The original 8250 and 16450 chips didn't have adequate buffering to store incoming characters. This wasn't an issue with DOS, which didn't have multiple processes to worry about. But for real operating systems that were more than just program loaders, this became a problem at speeds over 2400 baud, because the UART often overwrote incoming data before the operating system kernel had a chance to pull the data out of the UART's buffer. To fix this problem, the 16550 UART came around with a first-in, first-out (FIFO) queue buffer. Unfortunately, this chip had a bug that rendered the FIFO buffer useless, and a replacement, the 16550A, was issued.

VMware Workstation has four serial ports with virtual 16550A UARTs. These ports are fixed at the PC default hardware configuration, shown here:

DOS Name	Linux Name	IRQ	I/O Ports
COM1:	/dev/ttyS0	4	0x3f8 to 0x3ff
COM2:	/dev/ttyS1	3	0x2f8 to 0x2ff
COM3:	/dev/ttyS2	4	0x3e8 to 0x3ef
COM4:	/dev/ttyS3	3	0x2e8 to 0x2ef

Under VMware, you can connect serial ports to actual devices, redirect output to files on the host system, or even attach serial ports to pipes and pseudo-terminals on the host system.

NOTE *Because the four ports share IRQs 3 and 4, you may run into trouble if you try to use the third or fourth port because some operating systems (notably, older versions of Linux) don't like to share serial port IRQs.*

2.2.6 Parallel Ports

Unlike serial ports, which send data one bit at a time to a device, parallel ports send eight bits at a time. The design was originally intended as largely unidirectional, which made it convenient for connecting a computer to moderate-bandwidth devices such as printers. As time went on, though, parallel ports gained greater bidirectional capability so that a device could talk back to the computer. Eventually, parallel ports became a sort of cheap alternative to SCSI. Though their bandwidth isn't very high and you can't really effectively use more than one device on a parallel port at once, they come on practically every PC, so parallel port Zip drives and the like popped up.

VMware Workstation supports two PC parallel ports in unidirectional and bidirectional modes:

DOS Name	Linux Name	IRQ	I/O Ports
LPT1:	/dev/lp0, /dev/parport0	7	0x3bc to 0x3be
LPT2:	/dev/lp1, /dev/parport1	5	0x378 to 0x37f

Similar to serial ports, you can redirect the output of a parallel port to a file instead of attaching it to a real device on the host system with VMware Workstation.

2.2.7 USB Interface

VMware Workstation 3 includes support for the universal serial bus (USB). A relatively new development, USB is a moderate-speed interface intended for small peripheral devices such as keyboards, mice, printers, scanners, and removable media readers. It is *hot-pluggable*, meaning that you can connect and disconnect devices without powering off the computer. One other advantage is that most devices also receive power from the bus, reducing cable clutter and power outlet overload. USB devices transfer data like a serial port, but USB also includes multiple device support, like SCSI. Unlike the SCSI bus, where the host controller and devices reside on a chain as equal peers, a USB host controller is the root of a device tree. This tree branches at hubs and has leaves at the devices. Many devices include built-in hubs.

VMware Workstation's virtual USB hardware emulates the universal host controller interface (UHCI), a specific hardware specification. Any USB-enabled operating system should support it; not only is it the most common kind of host controller on current motherboards, but there is only one other interface type in common use, so operating system developers generally choose to support all USB interfaces. VMware maps your host system's USB host controller to a virtual controller. Like other PCI devices, the virtual host controller's interrupt and I/O ports depend on the virtual machine's particular configuration.

2.2.8 Graphics

On a PC, the video card does more than connect your computer to the monitor; it holds the memory for the color value of each dot on the screen and has instructions for drawing complex structures. After going through a number of incompatible video adapter types, the PC industry settled on VGA (Video Graphics Adapter) as a base standard; all subsequent adapter types implement VGA and work around it. The VGA standard has *text modes*—for example, an 80-column by 25-row setting that displays only text—and a 16-color *graphics mode* that can display 640 *pixels* (dots) across and 480 pixels down (also called *VGA 16* mode). Almost immediately, vendors started to extend the graphics mode because it doesn't offer enough colors or resolution. These extensions tend to be called SVGA adapters, although standards are hard to come by. Consequently, to use the "special" modes (which any sane person would use; VGA16 output is simply painful to look at), you must load your vendor's special driver into your operating system.

VMware's virtual graphics adapter works in the same way. The adapter has the text and VGA16 modes, but it also has its own special SVGA extensions that enable any resolution at the exact same number of colors as your host system. To enable these extensions, you must install the *VMware Tools* for your guest operating system. Aside from adding graphics capabilities, VMware Tools also dramatically improve graphics performance because they talk directly to VMware on the host system, sidestepping many layers of virtual devices. We'll discuss how to install VMware Tools for each guest system in Chapters 5, 6, and 7.

Another graphics enhancement that comes with the VMware Tools is *full-screen mode*, which eliminates the VMware window around the guest operating system and maps it to the entire screen of your host system. It's easy to switch back and forth between your host and guest environments.

2.2.9 Mouse

The IBM PS/2 platform had a new port for the PS/2 Auxiliary Device. This eventually became the standard for PC mouse ports, and most new mice have PS/2 mouse capability of some sort. This device is at IRQ 12 and shares I/O ports with the PC keyboard (0x060 to 0x06f).

VMware takes mouse events from the host operating system's windowing environment and funnels them to its PS/2 mouse. Using the VMware Tools, you can play a few extra tricks with the mouse to make it operate seamlessly with your host system. We'll look at this in section 4.11.

Early mice normally connected to a computer's serial ports. Naturally, VMware Workstation supports this configuration, since it supports serial devices. Of course, you'll likely need to attach an extra mouse to your computer if you want to use this configuration.

2.2.10 Sound Cards

The state of PC sound cards is somewhat chaotic. There are many different varieties, all with their own proprietary hardware schemes. Nevertheless, they all have a few things in common, like the fact that they all have digital signal processors and mixers. VMware Workstation translates the host's sound device to a Creative Technology SoundBlaster 16 card, at the factory settings: IRQ 5, I/O ports 0x220 to 0x22f, DMA channel 1 (16-bit DMA channel: 5). Because these are the defaults for most drivers, guest system support shouldn't be a problem, though VMware may not support all SB16 features (such as the MP401 MIDI UART).

NOTE *Because this sound card uses IRQ 5, you may have problems in VMware Workstation if you try to configure a bidirectional parallel port on the second parallel port when sound is present, because that port also uses IRQ 5. Many guest systems don't bother with IRQs on unidirectional parallel ports and instead use a polling interface, so you may have some degree of success with this configuration. The only way to find out is to try it.*

2.3 PC BIOS

All PCs have a *BIOS* (or basic input/output system), which is a small piece of firmware on the motherboard. The BIOS knows how to talk to a number of devices on a PC in a very limited capacity.

Older operating systems such as DOS relied on the BIOS for communication with the hardware, but newer systems use it only for basic configuration and booting. The BIOS performs the memory and peripheral tests when you turn on a computer and is responsible for the beep you hear after the tests. The BIOS may also display all sorts of information about your computer.

Some vendors like to hide their BIOS screens from you, though there's always a key sequence you can use to display a setup utility. This setup tool is essential to any BIOS.

Each vendor's BIOS has its own degree of complexity. The basics include your floppy disk configuration, a few hard drive parameters, the boot sequence, and power management options. Some BIOS types offer a staggering degree of customization beyond this. But regardless of the number of bells and whistles, the BIOS must store these parameters somewhere so that the user doesn't have to enter them every time the computer is turned on. The BIOS normally stores its configuration in *nonvolatile memory*, or *NVRAM*, that stays in place either in flash memory or battery-operated memory.

Like a real PC, VMware also has a BIOS based on the Phoenix BIOS. You'll find a description of its configuration utility in section 4.14. VMware stores its BIOS NVRAM in a file on the host system.

NOTE *You can find way too much information about the PC BIOS at http://www.wimsbios.com/.*

Another component on a PC's motherboard closely related to the BIOS is the *real-time clock* (*RTC*). This is a small, battery-powered digital clock that operates when the computer is off, and it normally is used for setting the initial time and date when the system boots. VMware maps the host system's true RTC to a virtual device. If something else is using the RTC, VMware emulates it with date-stamps from the host operating system—but this is not the same as the RTC.

2.4 How a PC Boots

Before you begin working with an operating system on a VMware virtual machine, you should know how a real PC boots. The PC's BIOS oversees the first stages of the process. Since there are several ways that you can boot a PC (from the floppy drive, hard drive, CD-ROM, or even a network), the BIOS looks at the devices in a particular order. First it may decide to look at the floppy drive, and if there's nothing in the floppy drive, it sees whether the hard disk has a boot block, and so on.

The BIOS approaches each kind of device differently. Floppy disks are very simple and have a fixed boot sector that loads a program on the floppy. Since floppy disks don't normally have partition tables, this scheme works fine. CD-ROM drives are a little more complicated; you normally put an image of a bootable floppy disk somewhere in the CD-ROM filesystem and activate a special ISO9660 extension to point to this image.

Because they have partition tables, hard drives are more complex. You normally put a boot loader on the partition of the operating system. Then, with a program such as fdisk, you mark that partition as active in the partition table. However, at boot time, the BIOS loads sector 1 on the disk, which is called the *master boot record*, or *MBR*. The BIOS runs whatever it finds on the MBR. Normally, this is a tiny program that tries to find an active partition in the partition table, and if it is found, loads yet another boot sector from that partition (which is your operating system's boot loader, from above).

This can be a problem if you have multiple operating systems on the same disk, as you may with dual-boot configurations with VMware. Some boot loaders, such as Linux Loader (LILO) and the FreeBSD boot loader, are capable of loading the boot sectors on other partitions. This is fairly typical with Linux and Windows dual-boot systems. The BIOS first loads LILO from the active boot sector (normally on a Linux partition), and you can jump from there to the boot sector on the Windows partition.

You can circumvent the active partition by replacing the default MBR with your own boot loader. You'll often find this scheme in place when the disk is too large for the BIOS to handle. LILO makes circumventing the active partition easy; for example, just use /dev/hda instead of /dev/hda1 for the boot device. What is not so easy is to remove this custom boot sector once it is in place. You can use the DOS fdisk /MBR command or try to find the LILO backup of the original boot sector.

3

INSTALLING VMWARE WORKSTATION

Installing VMware Workstation on both Windows and Linux systems is straightforward, and VMware Workstation attempts to keep itself self-contained for easy administration. While there are naturally a few things on the system that VMware must slightly alter (for example, the host operating system startup sequence), the installation process doesn't try to hide this from you.

This chapter tells you how to install VMware. It also tells you the locations and significance of the files that the installation creates on your system.

You'll need to answer several questions during the installation process. Because installation is substantially different between the Windows and Linux platforms (and the Linux version has a few more components), this chapter is divided into two parts. Information about the VMware Workstation for Windows comes first. For Linux, just skip ahead to page 21 after reading the requirements in the next section—you won't miss anything. Also, because there are many more variables and more transparency in a Linux host installation than in the process for Windows, much of this chapter is devoted to the Linux version of VMware.

This chapter also includes a reference to the files that the VMware Workstation installation creates. If you're a VMware Workstation for Linux user, you'll also learn about an additional configuration script, `vmware-config.pl`, that you'll need to run from time to time.

3.1 Host System Requirements

VMware Workstation doesn't require too much hardware on your host system. Your processor must be a Pentium or better (any Intel or AMD chip made within the past few years should do). Technically speaking, it doesn't matter what speed of processor you have, but VMware, Inc. recommends 266 MHz at a minimum, and 400 MHz or more for the best performance. VMware Workstation warns you that your computer may not be powerful enough if you try to run it on a lesser machine.

Ultimately, however, the processor requirements boil down to the guest system: If you're running a guest that doesn't make much use of the CPU (for instance, a Linux system in text-only mode sitting idle most of the time), you may be able to get by with a system with a lower CPU speed.

Memory is another story. Your guest system will require about as much memory on a virtual machine as it does on a real machine, so add your host and guest system requirements together to get the amount you need. For example, if your experience running Windows 2000 on real hardware is painful with anything less than 128 MB, and your host is a Linux system that's okay with 64 MB, plan on at least 192 MB. The official VMware numbers are 128 MB minimum and 256 MB recommended. Again, this depends on which guest operating systems you plan to run. However, keep in mind that insufficient memory will devastate performance on all host and guest machines—unlike a slow CPU, which may slow things down by only a factor of two or so.

You should set your graphics mode to 16-bit color or better. In Windows NT/2000/XP, look at the **Settings** tab on the **Display** screen on the **Control Panel**. You should set the palette to 65536 colors or true color. On a Linux host system, this is not such a strict requirement, but if you're running in 8-bit mode, you're likely to be unhappy with the way your screen looks. Run xwininfo -root and look at the Depth line. If it's set to 8, see Appendix A for some pointers on how to change this.

Finally, if your host system is Windows NT, you must have Service Pack 3 or higher installed. Also, if you want the online help to work, your Internet Explorer version should be at least version 4. Linux host requirements are a little looser. All recent production Linux kernels should work—that is, those where the second digit of the version number is even (for example, 2.2.x, 2.4.x). The development kernels (2.1.x, 2.3.x, and so on) are risky to use even without VMware, and there's no telling whether any given one works or not. Also, you can't run VMware outside of the X Window System; you need XFree86 3.3.4 or higher.

That said, VMware Workstation supports most major Linux distributions. You'll find the most recent list in the support area of http://www.vmware.com/. If your distribution isn't on the list, it will probably work, but you may have to tweak a few things described in this chapter and Chapter 4.

Disk space requirements vary. The VMware Workstation software only uses about 20 MB, but if you're planning to create any virtual disks for your guest systems (rather than using one already installed on one of your disks), you'll need much more—plan on adding as much as the guest system requires. Furthermore, disk suspend operations require disk space roughly equal to your guest system's physical memory size, though you don't have to use disk suspends if you don't want to.

3.2 Installing VMware Workstation for Windows

If you're used to installing Windows packages, you won't be surprised that VMware Workstation uses a common commodity installer. There really aren't any surprises here; to install:

1. Log in as the Administrator user or a user with administrator privileges.

2. Download the newest VMware Workstation distribution from http://www.vmware.com/ and then click it. (As with most installation programs, avoid running anything else during the installation process.)

3. Read the end-user license agreement. This not only explains the license key that you pay for or get for evaluation, but it's also where you say that if VMware Workstation malfunctions and burns down your house, it's your fault and you can't sue anybody for it. Click **Yes**. You'll install the actual license key later.

4. Now you have a chance to change the installation location. The default is `C:\Program Files\VMware`. Keep this default unless you have a really good reason to change it (for example, if you want to run two different versions of VMware Workstation on your machine for some reason).

5. Select any folders where you want to place the VMware Workstation icon, and press **Next**.

6. Wait until the installer creates all necessary files on your system.

7. A system called AutoRun on Windows automatically starts programs on CDs as soon as you put the CD into your computer. Because this can seriously interfere with CD-ROM use on any running virtual machines, the VMware installer now asks you if you'd like to turn AutoRun off. While this means that you may have to make a few extra mouse clicks to install programs, it also has the pleasant side effect of speeding up initial CD-ROM access.

8. If you have any old virtual machines from previous versions of VMware Workstation, you now have a chance to rename them (see the next section). Also, if you would like a VMware Workstation icon on your Windows desktop, click **Yes** when prompted.

9. As with many Windows programs, you must reboot your computer after the installation process is complete.

You don't have to worry about network configuration during the installation process—see Chapter 9 for details.

Unlike VMware Workstation for Linux, the Windows version doesn't come with any software for making the host filesystems available to guest systems. If you have Windows guest systems, then you can use SMB (a network protocol for sharing files between computers). It's also possible to get a Linux guest system to access SMB shares. (See Chapter 10 for details.)

3.2.1   Upgrading from Version 2

Configuration and disk files changed format from VMware Workstation 2 to 3. Although newer versions of Workstation can read the old format, some features, such as redo logs, aren't available if you stick to the old format. The Workstation installer asks if you'd like to convert old files to new ones, and it searches your system for old files if you say yes. Unless you still need version 2, you should convert your files. If you'd like to use the new format but still have old versions of Workstation in use, just make a backup archive of your old .vmx and .dsk files before converting them.

See Appendix B for more information on upgrades from VMware Workstation 2.

3.3   Starting VMware for Windows

While you installed VMware as the Windows NT/2000/XP administrator or as a member of the Administrator group, you can run VMware Workstation as any user.

Recall that the installation process asks if you would like to create a VMware icon on the desktop. If you said yes, you can double-click that icon to start VMware. Otherwise, you'll find it on the **Start • Programs • VMware** menu.

Before you use VMware Workstation for the first time, you must enter a serial number. If you don't have a license yet, click on the Get Serial Number button on the serial number dialog box, or go to http://www.vmware.com. You can get a free temporary evaluation license or buy a full license.

After you enter the serial number, you'll see the main VMware Workstation window. Choose **New Virtual Machine** on this window and skip ahead to the next chapter to get started on a new VMware configuration.

3.4   VMware Workstation for Windows Files

From now on, we'll assume that you've installed VMware in the default location: C:\Program Files\VMware\VMware Workstation. In addition to a few shortcuts to Workstation, online help, and the uninstaller, you will find a subdirectory, Programs.

If you look in Programs, you'll find the VMware binary, as well as a number of utility programs and auxiliary files. Have a look at the VMInst.log file—this is a log of what the installer did. Because it persists over multiple VMware install and uninstall operations, it may contain information about any previous VMware installations or upgrades. If you forgot the answers you gave to the questions during installation, you'll find them here. This file also contains information about how the installer probed for a private subnet while using NAT networking.

Three files—linux.iso, windows.iso, and freebsd.iso—contain CD-ROM images for the VMware Tools for Linux and Windows host systems. You don't need to transfer these to actual CDs to use them; VMware automatically attaches them to the guest system when you perform the Tools installation. The details of this installation differ for each guest system; you'll learn more about the

VMware Tools in section 4.11 in the next chapter, and you'll learn how to install them for each guest system in Chapters 5 through 7.

There are also several networking programs in this directory: vnetconfig, vnetcfg, vmware_netinstall, vmnet-install, vnetsniffer, and vnetstats. VMware uses these during configuration and during network operation, and you can use them for internal network debugging. You'll learn more about these utilities in Chapter 9.

There are also a couple of dynamic link libraries (.dll files) and data files for uninstallation and some extra run-time support. There are a couple of system files in system32—mostly dealing with VMware's networking and its DHCP server, as well as some drivers in system32\drivers. Under normal circumstances, you won't have to worry about any of these files.

Documentation is a compiled HTML help file for Internet Explorer in the Workstation Programs folder: VMware.chm.

3.5   Uninstalling VMware for Windows

To remove VMware from your Windows system, go to the VMware Workstation directory in C:\Program Files\VMware and click the **VMware Uninstallation** icon. You'll navigate through a dialog box in several stages. One that you should pay attention to is removal of shared files: files that VMware may share with other programs. The uninstaller detects the ones that other programs may be using and asks you if you really want to get rid of them, one by one. If you know what you're doing, you can remove them, but it's safer to leave them in place.

NOTE   *Uninstalling VMware Workstation does **not** remove virtual machine configurations and files. If you have any big virtual disk files that you want to get rid of, you must delete them by hand.*

3.6   Installing VMware Workstation for Linux

To install VMware Workstation on your Linux machine, you'll need the following:

- About 15 MB of free disk space in the eventual installation location.
- Perl (this shouldn't be a problem).
- Superuser (root) access.

In addition, you may need the following to create some special VMware kernel modules, especially if your system has been customized in some way:

- A C compiler capable of compiling a kernel. On many systems, this is the default gcc, but on Red Hat 7, you want kgcc.
- The make utility.
- Kernel header files that match your current kernel. It's best to have the full kernel source code.

VMware Workstation for Linux comes in two forms: a `tar` archive and an RPM file. Both are available for download at http://www.vmware.com/. If you want to use the RPM file, become `root` and run this command on the `.rpm` archive you downloaded:

```
rpm -Uhv VMware-version.rpm
```

Then you must run `vmware-config.pl`. Skip to the next section, on page 24, for more information.

To unpack the `tar` archive, use a command like this:

```
zcat VMware-version.tar.gz | tar xvf -
```

Here, *version* is a version number. This command extracts all of the VMware installation files into a new directory called `vmware-distrib`. Use a `cd vmware-distrib` command to change to that directory, become `root` (with `su` or some other way), and run the installer program with this command:

```
./vmware-install.pl
```

This is a Perl script. If it doesn't run (with a `command not found` error or something similar), then either you don't have Perl installed, or it's not in /usr/bin. Locate the `perl` executable on your system if Perl isn't in /usr/bin and either make a symbolic link from /usr/bin/perl to the real location or change the first line of the `vmware-install.pl` script.

NOTE *If you choose the latter option, you must change **all** `.pl` scripts that come with VMware. This will be a hassle.*

The `install` script recognizes most major distributions and knows how to look for reasonable default values on other systems. If you're having trouble with the installation because your system is somewhat nonstandard, one option is to read the `install` script to see what it tries.

If you just want to go for it, you can answer yes or accept the defaults to all of the installer's questions. VMware knows about several Linux distributions and boot schemes and should have no difficulty figuring out your system. However, you'll probably want to know what the installer does and how to customize your VMware installation somewhat, so read on.

The installer then asks where you'd like to install the binary files:

```
In which directory do you want to install the binary files? [/usr/bin]
```

This is where the executable programs such as `vmware` and `vmware-config.pl` go. The default is /usr/bin, a directory containing most binaries on a Linux system. Instead, you may wish to install the binaries in /usr/local/bin, a conventional location for new programs that don't come with a Linux distribution. Because most distribution upgrade programs don't touch anything in /usr/local, this is fairly safe, but you may want finer control over the VMware files if you use a package control system such as encap to manage your local packages.

Next up is the library file location:

```
In which directory do you want to install the library files? [/usr/lib/vmware]
```

Try to make this location at least somewhat consistent with your answer to the previous question.

Next, you are asked where to install the manual pages:

```
In which directory do you want to install the manual files? [/usr/man]
```

Again, try to keep this in line with your previous answers.

The same goes for the rest of the documentation:

```
In which directory do you want to install the documentation files? [/usr/doc/vmware]
```

These are HTML files, used by VMware's online help; Workstation invokes Netscape to look at them as needed. (You do not need a web server running on your Linux machine to view them.)

The next question is where to put the VMware boot script and links, described in section 3.11:

```
What is the directory under which the init scripts reside (it should contain
init.d/, and from rc0.d/ to rc6.d/)? [/etc]
```

This is a somewhat misleading question because the init scripts aren't normally in this directory, but rather in the init.d directory below. VMware needs this information to start certain essential services at boot time. In any case, the default answer is usually correct; it's /etc on most standard systems and /etc/rc.d on many Red Hat systems.

After you answer these questions, the installer moves the entire set of VMware files into place, at which point this message appears:

```
Before running VMware for the first time, you need to configure it for your running
kernel by invoking the following command: vmware-config.pl. Do you want this script
to invoke the command for you now? [yes]
```

Type yes unless you really know what you're doing, and continue to the next section in this book.

NOTE *To remove VMware Workstation from your system, use the* **vmware-uninstall.pl** *script in the binary directory that you just created. Note that you must have an /etc/vmware directory for this to work.*

3.7 Configuring VMware Workstation for Linux

The program vmware-config.pl is an important configuration program that you must run after you complete the initial VMware installation. There are seven steps:

1. The first question this configuration program asks is about the end-user license agreement. This is the usual stuff about how if VMware Workstation opens up a black hole and sucks your computer and your dog inside, you can't sue VMware, Inc. (You'll have to enter your actual license key serial number later, after you install VMware.) Read the agreement and type yes.

2. vmware-config.pl fits a few system drivers to your current system and sets up VMware networking. To access certain parts of the Linux kernel, VMware needs to install a few kernel drivers, including a module named vmmon. This is the Virtual Machine Monitor.

    Because each Linux distribution installs its own version of the Linux kernel, VMware comes with precompiled kernel modules suitable for many common Linux distributions, and the vmmon module must match your current kernel. The installer prints the following message when attempting to locate a module for your system:

```
Trying to find a suitable vmmon module for your running kernel.
```

    If the installer is successful, you get a message to that effect. If it is not, see the next section, "Compiling VMware Kernel Modules" on page 26. Then skip back here.

    You'll have to go through the same process with the VMware vmnet module (for networking support), and if you're running a Linux kernel version less than 2.4.0, the configuration script also asks you about parallel port support. This is for bidirectional parallel port support only. The module here is called vmppuser. For it to work, you need the parport and parport_pc drivers either compiled into your Linux kernel or loaded as modules.

3. vmware-config.pl asks you if you'd like to enable networking:

```
Do you want networking for your Virtual Machines? [yes]
```

    Answer yes. Although we won't go into detail about networking in this chapter, it's safe to enable the network because it's simple to change later. vmware-config.pl tells you that it is configuring bridged networking on vmnet0 and NAT networking on vmnet8.

4. For the NAT network, you'll see this question:

```
Do you want this script to probe for an unused private subnet? (yes/no/help) [yes]
```

    Normally, you'll answer yes. The virtual network on a host-only network needs a block of Internet addresses, so vmware-config.pl looks on the predefined private subnets defined by RFC 1918 for one that you aren't currently using. You can configure this by hand; see Chapter 9 for more information.

When you answer yes, this appears:

```
Probing for an unused private subnet (this can take some time).

The subnet 192.168.14.0/255.255.255.0 appears to be unused.
```

Pay close attention to the subnet that the script chooses. If your host machine is on a private subnet itself, there is a chance of a conflict. For example, if the script chooses 172.16.37.0/255.255.255.0, but your corporate network uses all of 172.16.0.0/255.0.0.0, you don't want to accept the script's choice. In general, you can find out by entering ifconfig -a on your host machine and looking for the entry eth0. If the first number of your IP address matches the first number in the address that VMware chose, ask the configuration script to try again.

If, on the other hand, you answer no to the probe question, the script asks you to enter the IP address of your host machine on the private network to be and the netmask of that network.

5. Next up is host-only networking:

```
Do you want to be able to use host-only networking in your Virtual Machines? [no]
```

For now, keep the default of no; a host-only network is a somewhat more limited version of the NAT network. After you read through Chapter 9, you can decide if you need it or not. Host-only network configuration (on the host system) is identical to NAT networking.

6. The final stage is if you'd like to set up filesystem sharing from your host system to your guest systems:

```
Do you want this script to automatically configure your system to allow your Virtual
Machines to access the host filesystem? (yes/no/help)
```

This question refers only to virtual machines running a Windows-like guest operating system. VMware comes with a package called SAMBA that allows Windows to access a Unix host filesystem through network SMB shares. If you don't want to bother with this just yet, answer no, and you'll be finished with the configuration. Remember that you can always come back to it later. Chapter 10 has more details on SAMBA configuration.

7. The vmware-config.pl program starts the VMware services and finishes. You're now ready to run VMware Workstation—see section 3.8.

3.8 Compiling VMware Kernel Modules

If your kernel doesn't match any in the common Linux distributions, you'll need to compile the VMware Workstation modules for your current kernel. This is likely to be true if you're running a non-mainstream system like MOSIX, and it will definitely be the case if you always compile your own kernel. The vmware-install.pl or vmware-config.pl script builds the driver modules for you.

When compiling these modules, you must have make and a proper C compiler installed on your system (gcc on most systems except Red Hat 7, where you'll want kgcc), as well as the kernel header files for your current kernel, which come with the kernel source. Linux distributions often offer header files as separate packages because application development requires them.

For example, let's say that vmware-config.pl tries to find a vmmon module for your system, but can't. It then asks you this question:

```
None of VMware's pre-built vmmon modules is suitable for your running kernel. Do you
want this script to try to build the vmmon module for your system (you need to have
a C compiler installed on your system)? [yes]
```

Enter yes, and you'll see this in response:

```
What is the location of the directory of C header files that match your running
kernel? [/lib/modules/2.4.9/build/include]
```

Enter the full pathname of your kernel source code tree's include directory (normally it's located in /usr/src/linux-*version*). It's critical to get the answer right since the script makes a guess. Here, we're running a kernel in the Linux 2.4 series, which makes a symbolic link from /lib/modules/*version*/build to the kernel source tree, where *version* is the Linux kernel version number. (If you move or delete your kernel source, this link becomes invalid, and you'll need to point vmware-config.pl in the right direction.)

Once you've entered the include path, the script unpacks and builds the module, printing these messages as it does its work:

```
Extracting the sources of the vmmon module.

Building the vmmon module.

make: Entering directory `/tmp/vmware-config0/vmmon-only'
make[1]: Entering directory `/tmp/vmware-config0/vmmon-only'
make[2]: Entering directory `/tmp/vmware-config0/vmmon-only/driver-2.4.9'
make[2]: Leaving directory `/tmp/vmware-config0/vmmon-only/driver-2.4.9'
make[2]: Entering directory `/tmp/vmware-config0/vmmon-only/driver-2.4.9'
make[2]: Leaving directory `/tmp/vmware-config0/vmmon-only/driver-2.4.9'
make[1]: Leaving directory `/tmp/vmware-config0/vmmon-only'
make: Leaving directory `/tmp/vmware-config0/vmmon-only'
```

Then the script tries to load the module. Upon success, you see this message:

```
The module loads perfectly in the running kernel.
```

If the build fails, your kernel source tree probably wasn't set up properly with a command such as `make mrproper`, or you tried to build for a kernel that VMware doesn't support. (If your kernel is very new, the latter is likely, so check the VMware website for an update to VMware Workstation.)

If the module load fails, it will probably do so with numerous error messages about unknown symbols, a sign that the kernel header files you specified didn't match your current kernel.

There's a slim chance that inserting a module built with mismatched header files will cause a kernel `oops` (Linux for kernel crash), which may bring down the whole system. In any case, it's generally a good idea to reboot after an `oops`.

There's also a chance that your kernel version matches one of VMware's prebuilt modules but doesn't work correctly due to your customizations. In this case, you must force the script to compile the modules with `vmware-config.pl --compile`.

Aside from the `vmmon` module, you'll need the `vmnet` module to enable host-only or bridged networking for your virtual machines under VMware. The build procedure goes the same way. If the `vmmon` build works, `vmnet` will almost certainly work as well. Depending on your kernel version, you may also need `vmppuser` for bidirectional parallel port support.

3.9 Starting VMware Workstation for Linux

Assuming that the binary directory you specified in the `install` script is in your path, you may now start VMware with the `vmware` command, as a regular user.

When VMware starts, you'll see the main VMware window and a box asking you to enter a serial number (license key). You need a license to do any real work with VMware Workstation. If you try to start without a license, VMware disables the power on the virtual machine. Visit http://www.vmware.com/ to get a temporary evaluation license key or purchase a full copy.

After you have the license key out of the way, you have three choices: **Run the Configuration Wizard**, **Run the Configuration Editor**, or **Open an existing configuration**.

NOTE   *If this is your first time working with VMware Workstation, select the Configuration Wizard and skip to Chapter 4 to begin with the guest system configuration. The rest of this chapter is for reference.*

VMware has a few command-line options:

-x	Turn on the virtual machine's power automatically.
-X	Turn on the virtual machine's power and switch to full-screen mode. See the section on full screen mode in Chapter 4 for more information.
-q	Exit VMware when the virtual machine powers off.
-s*name*=*value*	Change the VMware configuration parameter *name* to *value*. The parameter can be anything in a VMware configuration file.
-v	Display the current release statistics.
-y *file*.vmdk	Check a virtual disk file (*file*.vmdk), but don't fix any problems if present.
-Y *file*.vmdk	Check a virtual disk file as above, and fix any inconsistencies.

Following any of these options, you can specify a VMware configuration file ending in .cfg (see Chapter 4 for information on how to use the VMware Configuration Wizard and Configuration Editor to create and edit configuration files), or you can provide a --, followed by an X toolkit option.

The most useful of the X Window System options is -geometry +x+y, which puts the window at certain x and y coordinates on the screen. (VMware disregards hxw -geometry directives for window size, along with many other X toolkit options.) For example, to start VMware in the upper-left corner on a configuration called vmware/debian/linux.cfg, setting the virtual machine's memory allocation to 32 MB, run this command:

```
vmware -smemsize=32 vmware/debian/linux.cfg -- -geometry +0+0
```

3.10 VMware Linux Executables

Aside from the main vmware binary, there are a number of other programs in the bin directory where you installed VMware.

vmware-config.pl

This program is used to reconfigure VMware (for example, if you upgrade your Linux kernel). It will ask you the same questions it did when you first installed Workstation.

vmware-uninstall.pl

This program completely removes VMware Workstation from your system.

vmware-wizard

This is the VMware Configuration Wizard (see Chapter 4). You should run it from VMware, not from the command line.

vmware-nmbd, vmware-smbd, vmware-smbpasswd, vmware-smbpasswd.bin

These programs are part of the SAMBA distribution that comes with VMware for use with host-only networking. (See Chapter 10 for more information.)

vmware-mount.pl, vmware-loop

The `vmware-mount.pl` program allows you to attach a VMware virtual disk to your host system. (See section 11.5 for more information. The `vmware-mount.pl` program uses `vmware-loop`.)

vmnet-bridge, vmnet-dhcpd, vmnet-natd, vmnet-netifup, vmware-ping

These utilities manage VMware's bridged, host-only, and NAT networking. The boot script described in the next section runs these utilities with the correct arguments; normally, you won't need to run them manually.

vmnet-sniffer

This is a packet sniffer for virtual networks. See section 9.11 for more information.

3.11   VMware Linux Library Directory

Recall from section 3.5 that the `install` script for the `tar` format asked you where you want to put the libraries, and it creates a `vmware` directory underneath this location. If your library directory is `/usr/local/lib`, the installer creates `/usr/local/lib/vmware` and puts program data there. Here's a quick rundown of the library content:

configurator	DHCP and SMB settings for host-only networking.
isoimages	ISO 9660 CD-ROM images for installing VMware Tools for guest operating systems.
modules	Predefined kernel modules for several Linux distributions, as well as their source code for use when none of the modules match.
smb	NLS codepages for use with SAMBA.
licenses	Sitewide and user license data.
help	Online help files (in HTML format).
config, xkeymap	Miscellaneous configuration data.
bin	Auxiliary programs (don't run these on the command line).

3.12   VMware Workstation for Linux Boot Script

When you reboot your machine, the running kernel has no modules until the automatic module loader or some other mechanism loads them. Since VMware needs the vmmon module and can't load it when you're running as a user, a script loads it automatically at boot time. For networking features, the script activates the vmnet module and starts the DHCP and SAMBA host-only utilities.

If your Linux system uses the System V init program, your boot scripts are in /etc/init.d or /etc/rc.d/init.d. The VMware installer places a new vmware script in this directory. To start the services manually, become root and (assuming that your init.d directory is /etc/init.d) run the following:

```
/etc/init.d/vmware start
```

To stop the services, use this command:

```
/etc/init.d/vmware stop
```

To get the current status of the VMware subsystems, including the number of virtual machines currently active, enter

```
/etc/init.d/vmware status
```

NOTE   *For a Red Hat system, use /etc/rc.d/init.d/vmware instead of /etc/init.d/vmware.*

To enable automatic startup of boot scripts, Linux has several *runlevels*, and you can customize your boot sequence for each. The runlevel directories are in /etc/rcN.d or /etc/rc.d/rcN.d, where N is a number between 0 and 6. Look at /etc/inittab to find your default runlevel; it's under the initdefault keyword.

The VMware installer looks for the default runlevel directory and places a S90vmware link there to the vmware script in your init.d directory. With this link in place, init runs the vmware script with the start parameter so when your system boots, your VMware services start. Similarly, the installer looks for your system shutdown runlevel (usually 6) and places a K08vmware link there, shutting off services in an orderly system shutdown.

Because the installer uses the init.d/vmware system boot script on an upgrade, this boot script looks a little different than a normal init.d script. The init.d/vmware script also defines several utility functions before actually starting or stopping the VMware subsystems.

If you don't know much about the Bourne shell, you probably won't want to change (or even look at) the boot script. All you need to know is that it loads the vmmon, vmnet, and vmppuser modules and then starts VMware's version of dhcpd and SAMBA on the host-only or NAT networks.

3.13   Additional Files in /etc/vmware and /dev

The VMware installer creates a directory called /etc/vmware on your system, which holds all configuration information specific to your host machine.

locations

The locations file records all files and directories that the VMware installer creates, moves, or deletes; vmware-config.pl may append to this file if it needs to add something such as a new kernel module. In addition, locations contains configuration data for the VMware boot script (see section 3.11 on page 30), including all network settings. Don't confuse this with parameters in the config file (below).

The uninstaller program uses locations to determine what it needs to delete for a clean uninstall. This file also provides a handy way to determine whether a file on your system came from the VMware installation, to move VMware from one machine to another, or to distribute a VMware installation over several machines.

config

The config file primarily contains the full pathnames of VMware binaries and libraries and also contains some default parameters. The vmware executable program loads these values as defaults for all configurations. You normally won't need to change this file.

installer.sh

The installer.sh file is a utility program normally run by the VMware install, configuration, and uninstall utilities. Though you normally won't need to bother with this file, since it's just a shell script, you can skip to the end of it to see what its arguments do.

/etc/vmware/vmnet Directories

If you configured VMware with host-only or NAT networking, you may have one or more vmnet directories in /etc/vmware. These directories contain the configuration files for the utilities that run on each vmnet host-only network interface. We'll talk more about this in Chapter 9.

not_configured

You may have a not_configured file in /etc/vmware, a flag telling VMware service startup programs that you need to run vmware-config.pl before running VMware. This file may appear if you choose not to run vmware-config.pl during the installation process, or if the VMware boot script (/etc/init.d/vmware) failed to run any of its components. It may also appear if you abort the vmware-config.pl program.

You would typically remove not_configured by running vmware-config.pl, though if it was created because you were testing a new kernel (or booting from an emergency backup) and caused the boot script to fail, you can remove the file after going back to your old kernel.

Device Files

The VMware installer also creates a number of special files in /dev. The vmmon module controls the /dev/vmmon device, and the vmnet module maintains /dev/vmnet*. In addition, you may not have the /dev/parport* devices required for bidirectional parallel ports on your system; the installer creates these if necessary.

3.14 Upgrading VMware Workstation for Linux

To upgrade VMware Workstation for Linux, use the vmware-install program that comes with the VMware tar archive, or if you're using .rpm archives, use the Red Hat rpm program). When you run the installer, you should see messages like the following:

```
A previous installation of VMware has been detected.
The previous installation was made by the tar installer (version 2).
Keeping the tar2 installer database format.

Uninstalling the tar installation of VMware.
```

At this point, the installer looks for the older installation and attempts to remove it before proceeding. It may spit out some diagnostic messages like this:

```
This script previously created the file /lib/modules/2.2.14/misc/vmppuser.o,
and was about to remove it. Somebody else apparently did it already.
```

In this particular case, someone probably upgraded the Linux kernel and removed the entire /lib/modules/2.2.14 directory. (This kernel upgrade may be why you're upgrading VMware in the first place.)

Then, during an upgrade, the installer runs through all of the questions about which directory to use to store the binary, library, manual, and documentation files. You may remember these questions from the first time you installed VMware Workstation; the installer uses the answers you gave for the previous installation. Finally, the installer runs the vmware-config.pl program.

NOTE *For those users upgrading from VMware Workstation 2, see Appendix B for further information on upgrading your virtual machines.*

VIRTUAL MACHINE
CONFIGURATION AND OPERATION

In this chapter, you'll learn how to get a guest operating system up and running under VMware Workstation. To do so, you'll first need to create a configuration. Then you'll become familiar with VMware's user interface, and learn how to modify and maintain a configuration.

Once you have a guest system working, installing VMware Tools can improve performance; you'll see why in this chapter, but we won't cover the details for each guest system until Chapters 5 through 8.

This chapter finishes with a discussion of the VMware BIOS.

4.1   Getting Started

Before you can run a guest operating system under VMware, you must create at least one VMware *configuration*. (You'll create a separate configuration for each guest system.) A configuration includes a set of disk information files, a data file for the VMware BIOS, and a configuration file that binds everything together.

VMware's **File** menu operates on configuration files. When you change files, you're going to a different configuration. You should use one directory for each configuration, although you may want to relocate larger data files (such as virtual disks) later.

You can work with configurations in three ways. If you're interested in creating a configuration quickly, use the *VMware Configuration Wizard*. You can run this program when you start VMware, or you can run it with the **Wizard** option on the VMware **File** menu. This program only creates new configurations; you can't use it to edit one that already exists.

The *VMware Configuration Editor* gives you complete control over each piece of the virtual machine, and you'll need it to add certain hardware, such as parallel ports. To find the editor, choose **Configuration Editor** from the VMware **Settings** menu.

Although you normally won't need to, you can edit configuration files manually with a text editor. Configuration files have a `.vmx` extension on a Windows host and end with `.cfg` on a Linux host. Just remember that if your manual modifications to the configuration file corrupt it, VMware may not be able to repair it.

4.2 The VMware Configuration Wizard

Use the VMware Configuration Wizard when you first configure a guest operating system under VMware. The term *wizard* is just a fancy name for a program that attempts to simplify a larger program's setup the first time through by boiling down the steps to series of questions. But the wizard doesn't always get everything right—after using it, you may need to enter the more powerful Configuration Editor to fix things.

Once you start VMware and get the licensing out of the way, you'll have the option of starting the VMware Configuration Wizard right away. If you choose it, a new greeting window appears with a number of buttons along the bottom: **Help**, **Cancel**, **Prev**, **Next**, and **Finish**. To begin, click **Next**. If at any point you feel that you messed up something, click the **Prev** button to go to the previous screen. Some screens also have an **Advanced** button to bring up more settings.

The wizard is slightly different between the two kinds of host system. Under Windows, it's also called the New Virtual Machine Wizard.

To bring up the wizard in a Windows host system, click the New Virtual Machine icon or select the **New Virtual Machine** option from the **File • New** menu. The first thing the wizard asks you is how you want to configure the machine. For a Windows host system, there are three options: **Typical**, **Custom**, and **VMware Guest OS Kit**. Typical gives you only the most basic options, and Custom adds several more configuration screens. Guest system kits, on the other hand, not only create the configuration but also install the guest operating system on the virtual machine.

The Linux Configuration Wizard operates much like the Windows wizard in Custom mode, but some of the screens are in a different order.

The next section takes you through the rest of the VMware Configuration Wizard.

4.2.1 Stepping Through the VMware Configuration Wizard

Here are all of the hardware configuration questions that the VMware Configuration Wizard can ask you.

Windows	Select a Guest Operating System
Linux	Guest Operating System

The wizard asks you which **Guest Operating System** you plan to run on this virtual machine. You'll need to select one before continuing.

Windows	Name the Virtual Machine
Linux	Virtual Machine Display Name and Directory

The wizard now wants to know the virtual machine's name and its directory, which is where the files associated with this virtual machine will be stored. Be sure that the directory doesn't already exist, since you may accidentally overwrite an existing configuration or otherwise clutter it up. Click **Next** after the guest operating system and directory configuration; the next screen depends on your host system and on the configuration option you chose. For a Windows host, if you chose a **Typical** configuration, the questions stop here, and you'll see a final confirmation screen. For **Custom**, the questions continue. If you're using a Linux host system, the wizard asks you about the disk, CD-ROM, and floppy drives before the networking steps.

Windows	Memory for the Virtual Machine
Linux	(Not present)

Here you specify the amount of memory for the virtual machine. If this is your first time through, keep the default value.

Windows	Select a Network Connection
Linux	Networking Setting

There are several options here: **No networking**, **Bridged** networking, **Host-only** networking, **NAT** networking, and combinations. Bridged networking sets up a virtual Ethernet interface just like the one already inside your computer (that is, if you have an Ethernet interface). Host-only networking creates a virtual network inside your machine, meant only for communication between the guest and host operating systems. NAT networking is like host-only networking, but enables connections from guest systems to an external network. We'll go into much more detail about networking in Chapters 9 and 10.

If you've never done any network setup before, choosing an option may seem difficult, but any selection is safe because you can always use the Configuration Editor to change it later, and it's easy to remove unwanted interfaces in a guest operating system.

Windows	Select a Disk
Linux	Disk Type Setting

Next is the **Disk Type Setting**, which refers to the kind of disk you want to attach to the virtual machine. You have three options: **New virtual disk**, **Existing virtual disk**, and **Existing physical disk**.

If you choose the virtual disk, the virtual disk appears as a file on your host operating system (by default in the directory you chose in the previous question). Next, you're asked how large the virtual disk should be. The size can be up to 128 GB (128,000 MB) for an IDE disk on a Windows host, or 64 GB on a Linux host. If you don't have that much free space on the partition you chose for the virtual machine directory, the wizard warns you about it, but still lets you create the virtual disk, because the virtual disk size is initially small and grows as needed. (You can later move the virtual disk file to a larger partition on your host system and update this configuration with the Configuration Editor.)

An existing virtual disk is a virtual disk file that you created earlier and want to use with a new virtual machine.

If you choose an existing physical (or *raw*) disk, the wizard presents a list of available hard disks on your host system, and you have to navigate through tables of disk partitions and permissions. Because raw disks are an advanced option, you should read the "Physical (Raw) Disks" section on page 56 if you want to proceed with this option.

Once you complete all of the questions, the wizard displays a summary of the new configuration. Just click **Finish** or **Done** to finish and create all necessary files and directories (the wizard displays this information).

You're now ready to turn on your virtual machine.

Linux-only Questions

There are two wizard questions that only appear in VMware Workstation for Linux. In the **CD-ROM Device Setting** option, you can choose to disable the new virtual machine's CD-ROM, or pick a drive on the host system that you want to use for the virtual machine's CD-ROM. Under Windows, the wizard lets you choose from a list, but if Linux is your host operating system, you may need to type something. (Most distributions create a symbolic link /dev/cdrom to the CD-ROM device, so the default will probably work.)

NOTE *Choose **Start with the CD-ROM connected** if you want the drive to be immediately available when you power on the virtual machine. This setting is useful if you're installing a new guest operating system.*

The **Floppy Device Setting** screen works just like the CD-ROM settings. Linux floppy devices are normally /dev/fd0 and /dev/fd1. As with the CD-ROM drive, you can keep the floppy drive disconnected when you activate the virtual machine.

4.3 VMware Operation

Figures 4.1 and 4.2 show VMware's main window before you turn the power on. Many of the buttons and options are disabled because the virtual machine is off—like a PC with the power off. As in many other applications, the top of the window is a system of pull-down menus.

The row of buttons below the menu items is called the *VMware Toolbar*. These are shortcuts for items on the **Power** menu.

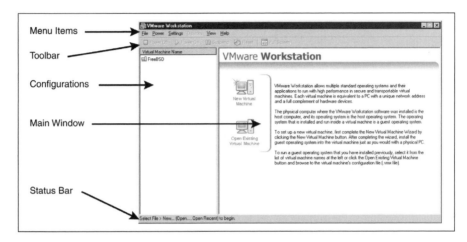

Figure 4.1: Initial VMware screen (Windows host)

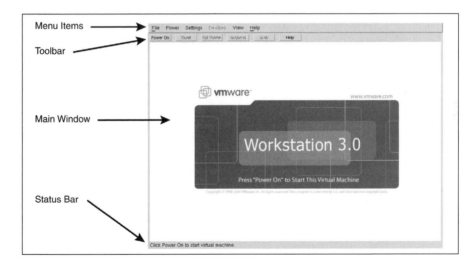

Figure 4.2: Initial VMware screen (Linux host)

The *status bar* is at the bottom of the window. With the power off, it displays only a help message, but after you activate a virtual machine, it also shows the device status, as shown in the right-hand corner of Figure 4.3.

Figure 4.3: VMware power-on self-test

4.4   Power On

To get started, click the **Power On** button at the upper left. Just after you turn on the power, the VMware window may resize itself and flash a couple of times. This is normal. Then the *power-on self-test* (POST), shown in Figure 4.3, begins, much like the POST that a real PC runs on startup. Notice that all of the menu options and buttons are now active, and that there's a new row of pictures at the lower right, on the status bar; these represent the devices on your virtual machine. For example, the machine in Figure 4.3 has one floppy disk, one hard drive, a CD-ROM drive, and an Ethernet interface. Disconnected devices show up as inverted grayscale pictures.

After the POST screen, VMware tries to load a guest operating system. If you configured your machine with a new virtual disk, there's absolutely nothing on the disk to load, and you'll get an `Operating System not found` error message. However, if you have a dual-boot system and told VMware to boot from an existing partition with an operating system, that system may boot.

If you don't have a guest operating system on your VMware disk, you'll need to install it, usually from a CD. Make sure that your CD-ROM device is connected; if not, go to the **Devices** menu and connect it right away.

If you start typing in the guest operating system, VMware grabs the input focus, and you won't be able to move the mouse pointer outside the VMware window. Use CTRL-ALT to free your mouse and return your input devices to the host system.

4.5 Toolbar Buttons

The toolbar provides a handy way to access frequently used actions in VMware and resembles the front panel of your PC. Some of the buttons, like Power and Reset, are familiar. The buttons may show up as text or icons, and each is also available as a menu item. You can remove the whole toolbar if you like (choose **View • Toolbar**).

Power On turns on the virtual machine. On a Linux host, when the power is on, this button changes to **Power Off** (Windows hosts have both buttons on the toolbar). These buttons are the same as the **Power • Power On/Off** menu selections.

Reset switches the virtual machine off and then on again. It isn't available when the virtual machine is off. This button is the same as the **Power • Power Reset** menu item.

Full Screen switches VMware to full-screen mode, making the guest system take up the entire screen. Because some extra configuration may be needed on your host system to use full-screen mode, we'll talk more about it later in this chapter. Full Screen is not available when the virtual machine is off. This button is the same as the **View • Full Screen** menu selection.

Suspend stops the virtual machine and saves the entire state of the guest operating system to the host system. After you suspend the system, the button changes to **Resume**, which loads all of the data back into the virtual machine and starts it running again where it left off. Suspend isn't available when the virtual machine is off. These buttons are the same as the **Power • Suspend VM/Resume VM** menu selections.

Grab (Linux host only) gives VMware complete control of the host system's mouse and keyboard until you press CTRL-ALT. Grab is not available when the virtual machine is off. This button is the same as the **Power • Grab** menu item.

Help (Linux host only) brings up VMware's online help system (in a web browser). This button is the same as the items in the **Help** menu.

4.6 VMware Menu Items

The six pull-down menus at the top of the VMware window provide access to nearly every feature you need on the host system side.

4.6.1 File Menu

The **File** menu items pertain to the opening and switching of configuration files.

For Windows hosts:

New contains a submenu with two items. **New Virtual Machine** creates a new virtual machine configuration with the VMware New Virtual Machine Wizard. **New Window** brings up a new VMware Workstation window.

For Linux hosts:

New creates a new VMware configuration with the Configuration Editor.

Wizard creates a new VMware configuration with the VMware Configuration Wizard.

For all hosts:

Open allows you to switch to any VMware configuration on your system. When you select this option, a file browser pops up. Remember that a configuration file ends with .vmx in Windows and .cfg in Linux.

Open Recent, a submenu with a list of frequently used configurations, provides the fastest way to get to a configuration.

Instant Restore is a submenu listing all of the virtual machines you suspended. When you select one, VMware opens the configuration and resumes it from where it was suspended. See section 4.8 on page 46 for more details on suspending virtual machines.

Exit terminates the current VMware window.

4.6.2 Power Menu

Use the **Power** menu options to start and stop the virtual machine.

Power On turns the virtual machine on. On Linux hosts, this changes to a **Power Off** item when the virtual machine is on; on Windows hosts, **Power Off** is a separate menu item.

Power Reset performs a virtual power cycle, turning the virtual machine off and on. As with a real system, this is a harsh way to reboot a machine and should be used only when the machine freezes, since guest filesystems may become corrupt if you don't shut down and reboot properly. Also under most guest systems, if you use Power Reset, your machine will take longer to boot after the reset.

Suspend (virtual machine) stops a virtual machine and saves its entire memory to the host system.

Resume (virtual machine) loads the memory from a suspended virtual machine and starts it running again. (We'll talk more about Suspend and Resume later in this chapter.)

Send Ctrl-Alt-Del sends the CTRL-ALT-DELETE key sequence to the virtual machine and is not the same as **Reset**. In MS-DOS, this key sequence performs a soft reset. Modern operating systems disable or reroute this sequence; for example, in Linux, the key sequence sends a message to the init program.

Grab (input) is the same as pressing **Grab** in the toolbar (note that the toolbar button doesn't exist on a Windows host, but the function is the same). You probably won't use this much; it's easier to click on the VMware Workstation window.

4.6.3 Settings Menu

The **Settings** menu gives you fine-control options for a virtual machine configuration, with different options for Windows and Linux host systems. In particular, Linux doesn't have a **Preferences** option, though many of the options are available on the **Input Preferences** submenu on VMware Workstation for Linux.

Configuration Editor starts the VMware Configuration Editor for the current configuration, which gives you complete control over the virtual machine's devices. (See "The Configuration Editor" later in this chapter.)

Show All Hints resets the VMware hints. As with many programs, VMware may pop up a window from time to time to warn or remind you of something. You can prevent this window from appearing again by checking **Don't show this hint again** in the window before you dismiss it. However, if you feel like you went too far, you can select this menu option to restore *all* hints.

Input Preferences is a submenu on Linux host systems only, but all options here are present in the Windows host's Preferences window. See section 4.7 for a description of these options.

Hot Key Modifiers is present only on the **Settings** menu on a Linux host. It's identical to the **Hot Keys** tab in Windows Preferences; see page 42.

Host Reserved Memory brings up VMware's memory settings for the *host* system. See the "Host Memory Requirements" section 4.13 on page 66 for more information. On VMware for Windows, this setting is on the **Memory** tab, under **Preferences**.

VMware Tools Install prepares the virtual machine for installing the VMware Tools on a currently running guest operating system. Selecting this option temporarily replaces your virtual machine's CD-ROM drive with an image containing the Tools for your guest system (these images come with VMware). When you're finished, VMware restores the drive to its original state. We'll go into more detail about what the Tools are and why they're important later in this chapter. The full installation procedure for each applicable guest system is covered in Chapters 5 through 7.

Upgrade Virtual Hardware (Windows) and **Upgrade Disk** (Linux) convert configuration and disk files from previous versions of VMware Workstation to the current version. Upgrading old disks is necessary if you want to continue using certain disk features, like undo.

Local and **Global Priority** (Windows host only) are shortcuts for setting VMware's precedence in the host operating system's scheduler. This determines the amount of CPU time that VMware receives. See the "Priority" section on this page for a full description of these settings.

Preferences (Windows Host Only)

The Preferences window has six tabs.

Input contains items relevant to input focus. Its options are identical to those on the Linux host's **Input Preferences** submenu; see section 4.7.

Hot Keys allows you to change the first part of hotkey sequences. Normally, you use CTRL-ALT to start a hotkey, but if this interferes with your guest operating system's user interface, you can change this to CTRL-SHIFT-ALT or to any combination of CTRL, SHIFT, and ALT.

Display sets the refresh rate for the guest display.

Priority sets a default scheduling priority for all virtual machines as described in the "Priority (Windows Host Only)" section that follows.

Memory is described in the Host Memory Requirements section (4.13) on page 66.

Workspace controls the maximum number of recently used and suspended virtual machines under the **Open Recent** and **Instant Restore** menus under **File**. You can also change the default location for virtual machine configurations here by choosing **Default Path for virtual machines**.

Priority (Windows Host Only)

The *priority* of a program in a multiprocessing operating system like Unix or Windows NT determines how often that program gets to use the CPU. The operating system can give all programs an equal chance at system resources, or it can give more time to certain processes with higher priorities.

Normally, VMware is on equal footing with other running applications, but this setting on VMware Workstation for Windows allows you to tip the scales somewhat if you feel that it's taking up too much CPU time or that it's not getting enough. (There is no priority setting for VMware Workstation for Linux, not just because Linux does a fine job at scheduling processes and you'd normally never think of such a thing, but also because you can use the `renice` command to change VMware's priority, just as with any other process.)

You can set different priorities for when VMware has control over the mouse and keyboard (input focus, also known as *grabbed* input) versus when it doesn't. There are three priority levels: *high* for preferred treatment over other processes, *normal* for the same treatment as other processes, and *low* to allow other processes more time to run than VMware. There are four settings to choose from: **High - Normal**, **High - Low**, **Normal - Normal**, and **Normal - Low**. The first priority (e.g., the "High" in High-Normal) on each setting is active when VMware has the input focus; the second is active when VMware is running as a background process.

4.6.4 Devices Menu

You can use the **Devices** menu to activate, deactivate, and change certain devices from within VMware while the machine is in operation. If a device is connected, you can use **Disconnect** or **Disconnect and Edit** to disconnect or disconnect and edit it; these selections bring up the Configuration Editor for the device after it is decoupled from the virtual machine. For already disconnected devices, you can use **Connect** to connect the device or **Edit** to edit it with the Configuration Editor. See "Connecting and Disconnecting Devices" in section 4.10 for more information.

4.6.5 View Menu

The **View** menu manipulates the display on the current virtual machine.

Full Screen turns on full-screen mode. See "Full-Screen Mode" in section 4.9 on page 48 later in this chapter for more details.

Fit resizes the VMware window to accommodate the full size of the guest system. This option has an effect only when the guest system doesn't fit within the entire window, meaning that there are scrollbars at the bottom and right sides of the VMware window. **Fit** does nothing if you have **Autofit** turned on.

Autofit is an on/off item. When this option is active, the VMware window automatically expands or contracts when the guest system resizes its display, for example, when the VMware POST process completes right after you turn on a virtual machine and the boot screen appears. If you turn off this option, you'll need to manually resize the window.

Toolbar (Linux host only) turns the VMware toolbar on and off. When it is off, you save a small amount of space.

Status Bar toggles the information display at the bottom of the VMware window (the little pictures representing the devices as well as any hints at the lower left). As with **Toolbar**, turning off this option can free up some screen space.

Icons (Linux host only) switches the toolbar buttons between text and pictures.

Toolbar Buttons (Windows host only) alters the appearance of the VMware toolbar buttons. You can choose **Picture**, **Text**, both, or none. When you turn both off, VMware hides the toolbar.

4.6.6 Help Menu

VMware's help system is split between program documentation stored locally and the VMware website at http://www.vmware.com. All information is in HTML, and VMware runs a web browser to show it to you. (On Windows systems, you'll need Internet Explorer version 4 or later.)

On a Windows host, you can start looking for help in the **Contents** or **Index**, or you can use **Search**. If you have a Linux host system, you can go straight to the table of contents with **Built-in Help**. The online help is in the **VMware software on the web** submenu, where you'll not only find links to the help web pages, but also licensing information and online technical support.

4.7 Input Options

The input options are on the **Input** tab of a Windows host system's **Global Preferences** screen and the **Input Preferences** menu on a Linux host.

NOTE *When we say that a window has the focus or input focus, we mean that it is the target of all keyboard and mouse input.*

Grab On Key Press and **Grab On Mouse Click** affect input focus—that is, VMware takes command of the keyboard when you type or click in the virtual machine window. (Note that VMware does not pass the first mouse click to the virtual machine, but *does* pass the first keystroke.)

The following options are best used in conjunction with VMware Tools. Some options won't work without the Tools; the others tend to be annoying without the Tools.

Release input focus when the mouse leaves the virtual machine: If you check this box, VMware releases the mouse pointer (and all input focus) back to the host operating system when you move the mouse pointer past the edge of the VMware window. Without the VMware Toolbox, you must press CTRL-ALT to free the cursor once you are inside a VMware guest system. Try it for yourself: When you're not running VMware in full-screen mode, check the box and move the mouse past the boundary of the VMware window and watch the host system cursor pop out from the edge of the window. Then move the mouse back and deactivate the check box. If you try this again, you won't be able to get back to the host system unless you press CTRL-ALT.

Capture input focus when the mouse enters the virtual machine: If you check this, when you move the mouse into the virtual machine, VMware grabs it. This option works best when **Release** is active. If **Release** is inactive, you may casually move the mouse over the VMware window while trying to get to some other window, and VMware will grab it, refusing to release it when the mouse pointer on the virtual machine goes past the edge of the VMware window. This can be annoying, to say the least.

If another application on your host system has absolute input focus when you move your pointer across the VMware window, this option won't override that. On Windows systems, you get this kind of focus with some dialog boxes; on Linux systems, certain window manager functions have absolute focus.

Scroll when mouse nears edge of the virtual machine works only when the guest operating system's display is larger than the VMware window. If this option is checked, when you move the mouse pointer close to the edge of the VMware window, the entire guest system display scrolls (unless there's nothing hidden past the edge of the window, of course), as shown in Figure 4.4. Notice that the host system is larger than the window and that there are scrollbars at the right and bottom. If the **Scroll when mouse...** option were not checked, you'd need to press CTRL-ALT to release the cursor and use the scrollbars to see the obscured part of the screen. But since it is checked, you can simply move the mouse right and downward to see the rest of the guest system screen.

*If **Scroll when mouse...** is off, you can turn it on just for a moment by clicking a mouse button, holding it down, and moving the pointer near the edge of the VMware Workstation window. This is primarily useful for drag-and-drop operations.*

Figure 4.4: Guest system doesn't fit into the VMware window

Hide cursor when the virtual machine loses input focus makes the mouse pointer disappear when you're outside the VMware window and using your host system. Try this option by unchecking it and pressing CTRL-ALT. Notice that there are now two mouse pointers. If you choose this option to make the guest system's pointer disappear, you'll get only one. This is especially handy when your guest system is the same (or has the same type of pointer as) your host system.

Bring the virtual machine to top when it gets input focus: If you have several windows open in addition to the VMware window and at least one is partially covering VMware, this option causes the VMware window to pop up to the top of the screen when you give VMware control of the mouse and keyboard. For some users, this can be annoying. (However, some windowing environments do this to all windows by default.)

Allow copy and paste to and from the virtual machine is a particularly useful option. You can use the host and guest operating systems' cut-and-paste systems seamlessly; they act as they normally would. For example, if Linux is the host system and Windows is the guest, you can use CTRL-C to copy a segment of text within Windows to put it into the text buffer, and then drag your mouse to some xterm window on your Linux host and press the middle mouse button to paste the copied text.

4.8 Suspend/Resume

One handy feature of VMware is its ability to suspend and resume a virtual machine. When you suspend a virtual machine, VMware freezes the guest operating system in the current session and saves it. Everything, including memory, video display, and interrupt vectors, goes to a storage area. Later, when you resume the session, VMware checks to see if enough memory is available on the host system and, if so, loads everything back into the virtual machine and sends the guest system back on its way, precisely where it left off.

Suspend/Resume has several uses. One is avoiding the long boot sequence of certain guest systems. Windows, for example, has a tendency to take a painfully long time to start. Instead of shutting down the machine every time you want to get out of Windows, suspend it. A resume operation can take a little time depending on where the state was saved, but it's normally a bit faster than waiting for the whole guest system to boot, especially if the boot process involves a lot of repetitive disk access.

Another reason you may want to use resume is to save memory and/or CPU resources on the host system. In addition to the memory that all guest systems use, operating systems also consume a certain amount of processor time even when they're not doing anything for the user, because they're performing memory management, system upkeep, and other important tasks. (One side benefit is that if you suspend a virtual machine on a notebook, it conserves power, so your battery lasts longer.)

VMware stores the suspended state of a guest operating on the host system's disk. You'll find this file in the same directory as the virtual machine's configuration file, ending with .vmss. Depending on the amount of memory you configured for the guest system, this file can get fairly large, so it's a good idea to reserve some space on your host system's disk. With disk suspend operations, you can exit VMware after suspending and resume at a later time. You can even resume the virtual machine after you reboot your host machine, a common situation with notebooks.

VMware's suspend feature is similar to suspend on a notebook and on some desktop machines, except that it doesn't need to talk to the advanced power management (APM) interface of the BIOS or guest operating system. In fact, the default setting for APM in the VMware BIOS is off. You can use APM if you like (there's an option in **Misc** in the Configuration Editor), and when you do, the **Suspend/Resume** button acts like a real Suspend/Resume button. Be careful about using APM on dual-configuration systems, though, because it may cause the guest system to save its state to a certain partition on your hard drive that may clash with the host system. In this case, if you press the VMware **Suspend** button and then press the real Suspend button on your real computer, the host system may overwrite the guest system's state, and when you try to restore, something unpleasant will happen. Therefore, you should leave the APM features off unless you really know what you're doing.

4.8.1 Performance Notes

Sometimes, a suspend operation may take some time and may even temporarily freeze your host system while VMware writes all the state data to the disk. The time involved depends on several factors. One is the amount of information that changed on the guest system since the last suspend operation. Suspending takes longest if you haven't performed a previous suspend operation on the system. State changes include the virtual machine's disk as well as its memory; VMware caches disk operations and must write its cache to disk during a suspend operation.

The second major factor affecting the time it takes to suspend is the amount of physical memory you configured on the virtual machine. The more memory, the more time it takes to write that memory to a state file.

Finally, the speed of the disk and filesystem on your host machine can affect performance. If the disk holding your VMware data is on a different interface or controller than your system disk, your host system will be less vulnerable to a temporary freeze during a suspend operation. Modern SCSI disks tend to be faster than IDE/ATA disks because they are meant for server applications. And notebook disks are always slower than their desktop counterparts. However, you can get better performance on suspend operations with an IDE/ATA disk by tweaking your device drivers. For Windows host systems, make sure that the host system has all applicable high-bandwidth drivers installed and enabled. For Linux host systems, use hdparm to enable multiple-sector transfer mode and 32-bit transfer mode. Here's an example that turns on 16-sector transfers and 32-bit transfers for the primary master drive:

```
hdparm -m 16 /dev/hda
hdparm -c 1 /dev/hda
```

Note that -c 1 won't work for all IDE chipsets; if it fails, try -c 3 instead. If you're particularly obsessed about trying to squeeze a little more performance from an IDE disk, have a look at the hdparm manual page.

4.9 Full-Screen Mode

When the main VMware window comes up, and you power on a virtual machine, you can interact with the virtual machine inside that window. However, it's also possible for you to maximize the guest operating system display—that is, make it take up your entire screen—by switching to *full-screen mode*.

To switch to full-screen mode, click the **Full Screen** button on the toolbar or select **Full Screen** from the **View** menu. To get back to your host system and return VMware to its usual window mode, press CTRL-ALT. With no extra configuration, your host system should support full-screen mode in text mode and in the generic 640x480 VGA mode. However, to get better resolution, you must install the VMware Tools on your guest system to get the special VMware display driver. (The VMware Tools are currently available for Windows 95/98/Me/NT/2000/XP, Linux, and FreeBSD.)

Superficially, implementing full-screen mode may seem no different than maximizing any other window; however, there are significant differences that require a certain amount of host and guest operating system configuration to get the best results. Specifically, both systems must support the same screen resolutions. If they do not, you can still use full-screen mode, but it will look awkward. If your host system's resolution is greater than that of the guest display, and the host's resolutions aren't fully enabled, the guest display shows up centered on the host system and surrounded by a big black border. In this case, the results are not much different from running VMware within a window because the pixel size is still the same.

Your host display operates at a certain *pixel resolution*, *bit depth*, and *refresh rate*. The pixel resolution determines the number of dots on the screen; for example, 1024x768 is 1024 pixels across and 768 pixels high. The bit depth determines the number of colors available at any time. Eight bits per pixel gives you 256 colors, 16 bits gives you 65,536 colors, and 24 bits gives you a maximum of 16,777,216 colors. The refresh rate is the number of times the screen repaints itself per second. You should try to make this at least 72 Hz (72 times per second) on your host system since anything less causes eye strain. (This applies only to CRT screens. If you have an LCD panel display, you needn't worry about this.)

Your host system's range of resolutions should match that of your guest system. We'll talk about how to set up the VMware driver—from the VMware Tools—for each guest system in Chapters 5 through 7. But first, you need to make sure that the host system's display is correct. If Windows is your host, you probably won't need to do anything. However, if Linux is your host, you may need to fine-tune your display, because it's easier to overlook things in a Linux display configuration.

4.9.1   Windows Host Display Configuration

If Windows is your host system, check whether the pixel depth is correct. To do so, open **Display** on the **Control Panel**, click the **Settings** tab, and look at **Color Palette**. Also, if your driver doesn't get monitor information through the display data channel (DDC), make sure that you've installed the correct monitor information file on your system. (These files usually end in `.icm`.) Once you've installed the appropriate drivers, you'll be able to choose from a list of resolutions on the Display screen of the Control Panel. You can set the guest system resolution to any of these values, and full-screen mode should work fine.

4.9.2   Linux Host Display Configuration

To get full-screen mode to work properly on a Linux host system, make sure that your X server configuration supports all of the desired modes on your guest system. Although a number of tools, such as xconfig, XF86Setup, and xf86cfg, are available to help you to do this, they often don't do a very good job.

Instead, check other video modes by pressing CTRL-ALT-PLUS and CTRL-ALT-MINUS (where PLUS and MINUS are the + and – keys on the numeric keypad). If the screen switches between several resolutions, you may be able to use full-screen mode without further configuration.

Run

```
xwininfo -root
```

from the command line to see the current settings. Note the bit depth as indicated by Depth: (you want 16 or 24), and the numbers after -geometry, your current resolution. The geometry does not change when you cycle through the resolutions.

You'll find some information on how to set up different resolutions in Appendix A. If you still can't get different display modes to work, your display drivers may not work, and you should disable mode switching by placing

```
gui.fullScreenResize = false
```

in your VMware configuration file.

In addition to having a suitable configuration file, your X server must support direct graphics access (DGA) for full-screen mode to work correctly. For XFree86 3.3.*x*, check your server's release notes—not all drivers support it. Most drivers for XFree86 4.1.*x* and higher work. Stay away from XFree86 4.0.*x*; DGA has bugs in these versions. DGA does not work in multimonitor mode (the Xinerama extension).

4.10   Connecting and Disconnecting Devices

VMware offers an additional layer of functionality with CD-ROM drives, floppy drives, sound devices, serial ports, and parallel ports. Rather than keeping real devices (or files) connected to the virtual devices at all times, VMware can ignore the real devices and just fake the virtual device for the guest operating system. This is called *disconnecting* a device.

An easy way to understand this is to consider a CD-ROM drive. A CD-ROM drive doesn't always have a CD inside, and disconnecting it in a virtual machine is like ejecting a CD. If a guest operating system asks to see a disconnected CD-ROM drive, VMware tells it that there's no CD in the drive (just the way a real CD-ROM drive would).

Furthermore, if the CD-ROM is connected and the guest system has locked its door, VMware won't let you disconnect the drive until the guest operating system unlocks it.

To connect or disconnect a device, use the **Devices** menu (or the VMware Toolbox). Each item in the menu is a submenu with options: **Connect**, **Disconnect**, and **Edit**. The submenu label indicates the device, its status, and, if it is connected, where on the host machine it is connected. For example, on a Linux host, `ide0:1 -> /dev/hdc` indicates that a CD-ROM at `/dev/hdc` is connected as the primary slave on the virtual machine. `RTC -> /dev/rtc` means that the real-time clock is active and attached to `/dev/rtc`. On the other hand, `floppy0 (not connected)` means the current configuration includes a floppy drive that's currently disconnected.

In addition to disconnecting a device, you can also reconfigure one while it's disconnected, which can be handy when dealing with floppy disks and CD-ROM drives. For example, if you have a floppy image that you want to use temporarily on your virtual machine but normally have the floppy connected to a real drive on your host system, you can disconnect that floppy, switch its configuration to the image file, reconnect the floppy, and start using the image.

VMware supports disconnection on most of its devices. For removable media devices, a disconnect simply looks like a device with no disk inside. Others, such as the sound device, act as if there were a virtual device present, but throw away any data received instead of sending it to the host system. You can't disconnect a hard drive (if you could, and the guest operating system were using it, the guest system would more than likely crash horribly).

You can choose to start a device as disconnected when you turn on the virtual machine. Also, if VMware can't access an underlying device on the host system when you power on the system, it switches the device to disconnected mode and warns you.

Starting disconnected is a handy way to get around problems where the real device is actually disconnected from the host machine, as is common on notebooks with detachable floppy and CD-ROM drives. In some cases, a notebook may even freeze if you try to access a floppy drive that's not physically connected.

4.11 VMware Tools

The VMware Tools are bundled with VMware; you don't need to download any additional packages. You won't need much free disk space on your guest system to install the Tools, but your guest system does need the ability to talk to a CD-ROM drive.

For optimal performance on a PC, your operating system must support the PC's devices and all of their features. Not only do you want to make use of any hardware speedups, but you want to make sure that any extras actually work. For example, if you bought a three-button mouse, you probably want to make use of each button.

VMware is like a regular PC in this regard. It works fine if you install an operating system without extra support. Some devices, such as the Ethernet and serial interfaces, already operate at a fairly good speed. However, the 16-color VGA graphic mode is sluggish and doesn't operate at higher resolutions. To fix this on a real PC, you'd install the device driver for your video card. On VMware, you install VMware Tools for your guest operating system.

The VMware Tools contain a device driver for VMware's SVGA modes, giving you higher resolutions and a larger range of colors, up to your host system's maximum. This enhances the capability of full-screen mode, where you can use the entire screen for the guest system without the host system getting in the way. In addition, you'll be able to access a number of new features, many dealing with interaction between the host and guest operating systems. In particular, you can:

- Move the mouse between host and guest system without a key sequence.
- Connect or reconnect a device within the guest system (useful when in full-screen mode).
- Allow cut and paste between the host and guest operating systems (and between guest systems, if more than one is running).
- Reduce the size of virtual disk files on the host system.
- Set the guest system's clock to the host machine's clock.

To use most of these features, you must run your guest operating system in graphics mode rather than text mode, though the VMware Tools for some operating systems (such as Linux and FreeBSD) also come with a few other utilities that work fine in text mode.

NOTE *You may wonder why VMware can't do these extended mouse operations without the help of VMware Tools. The reason is that VMware can't guess the mouse pointer location in the guest system because it can't reliably look inside the guest system's window environment.*

4.11.1 VMware Tools Properties (Toolbox)

Each set of VMware Tools comes with a small application capable of turning on some extra features when the guest operating system runs under VMware. This is called the *VMware Tools Properties* on Windows guests and the *VMware Toolbox* on Linux and FreeBSD guest systems. One feature you'll immediately appreciate is the ability to move the mouse off the edge of the VMware window and have VMware release the mouse pointer to the host operating system without the need to press CTRL-ALT.

How you access the Properties/Toolbox depends on the guest system. Under Windows, it's a little application that you add to your taskbar, and you can click it to bring up a main window with several settings (see Figure 4.5). On Unix-like systems, the Toolbox is an application for the X Window System called vmware-toolbox. The installer for VMware Tools for Windows automatically activates the Properties, but for other guest systems, you must enable it manually (as we'll discuss in Chapters 6 and 7).

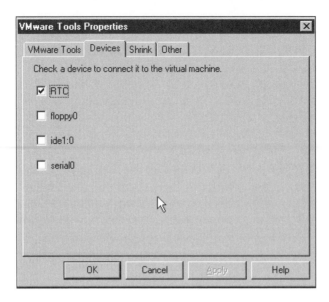

Figure 4.5: VMware Tools Properties (Windows guest)

There are four tabs in the main window: **VMware Tools**, **Devices**, **Shrink**, and **Other**. **VMware Tools** tells you about the current VMware Tools version and its status. **Devices** provides you with a list of VMware devices with disconnect capability (for example, CD-ROM drives and floppy disks). You can connect and disconnect devices here without leaving the guest system. **Shrink** is for virtual disk shrinking. Here, you can analyze any filesystem on a virtual disk and, if possible, reduce the virtual disk file size on the *host* system. **Other** contains miscellaneous options.

Devices

When you click the **Devices** tab, a list of devices appears in the window. You'll only see the devices that you can connect and disconnect, including removable devices such as floppy and CD-ROM drives, the real-time clock, the sound card, and parallel and serial ports. Checking a device connects it to the guest system, and unchecking it disconnects it. For example, if you're running Windows as a guest system and its sounds annoy you, a quick fix is to disconnect the sound device.

This tab duplicates the function of VMware's **Devices** pull-down menu (at the top of the VMware window). However, it's much more convenient to use this tab to connect and disconnect devices while in full-screen mode.

Shrink

At times, you'll be able to contract the virtual disk files on your host operating system by *shrinking* them, a two-step process that you initiate through the Toolbox. When you click the **Shrink** tab, you get two lists: **Supported partitions** and **Unsupported partitions**. You can shrink partitions only on virtual disks; unsupported partitions include CD-ROM drives and other removable media.

To shrink disks, check the ones you want to shrink on the list of supported partitions and click the **Prepare to shrink** button. A progress bar appears, and after a while, a dialog box pops up, asking you if you want to shrink your disks now. If you click **Yes**, VMware freezes the virtual machine and starts the second stage, where it scans the disk files for free space (which may take a while). Then VMware Workstation tells you how much space the process will save and asks if you want to proceed. Click **Yes**, and the shrink process starts, which may take some time. Your virtual machine resumes normal operation after the shrink operation is complete.

Shrink support varies between guest systems. Windows support is fairly good, but under Linux, the Toolbox may not be able to determine where the virtual disks are. One fix is simply to remove all hard drive devices other than virtual disks from your VMware configuration.

How Virtual Disk Shrinking Works

Shrinking is not an aggressive form of compression. It doesn't actually convert any real data into a smaller form; it simply reclaims unused space on the disk. Due to performance considerations, it's practical for VMware to compress blocks of zeros.

When you delete a file, normal operating systems don't overwrite the actual data, at least not right away. Instead, they just update the filesystem data structures to reflect the fact that the file is no longer there and the space it was using is now free. Therefore, old data from removed files hangs around on virtual disks. To get VMware to reclaim this space, you first need to zero out old data, a step best done by the guest operating system. Once this step is complete, VMware can run through the partition on the virtual disk and rebuild it without the old data.

Other

Time synchronization between the virtual machine and the host operating system forces the guest system's clock to match the host system's. On some guest systems, such as Unix, you can't perform this synchronization unless you're running the Toolbox as the superuser (`root`). Moreover, you should use this option only if there are serious problems with the time on the guest system.

Show VMware Tools in Taskbar is only on VMware Tools for Windows. Disabling this box turns off the VMware Tools icon on your taskbar. This is useful if your taskbar is cluttered; you can always access the Tools setup from the control panel on a Windows guest system.

4.12 The Configuration Editor

Unlike the Setup Wizard, VMware's Configuration Editor permits fine control over each piece of hardware in your virtual machine, allowing you to install and uninstall devices, switch disk mappings (in some cases, even when a machine is running), and change VMware's preferences.

To reach the Configuration Editor, select **Configuration Editor** from VMware's **Settings** menu. Most options pertain to VMware's virtual hardware, as shown later in Figures 4.6 and 4.7, showing the Configuration Editor for Windows and Linux, respectively. Although the two Configuration Editor versions have somewhat different interfaces, they are identical in function.

NOTE *The Configuration Editor's preferences are on a per-configuration basis; for example, full-screen mode options won't carry over from one virtual machine configuration to another.*

4.12.1 Windows Configuration Editor

Figure 4.6 shows the Configuration Editor in VMware Workstation for Windows. The **Hardware** tab's display shows the virtual machine's current devices on the left. When you click one of them, the device configuration appears on the right. You can alter the device there. All device-specific options are described in section 4.12.3. (Keep in mind that you can't change most options when a virtual machine is on.) The **Options** tab pertains to settings unrelated to hardware; see section 4.12.4 for a description of these.

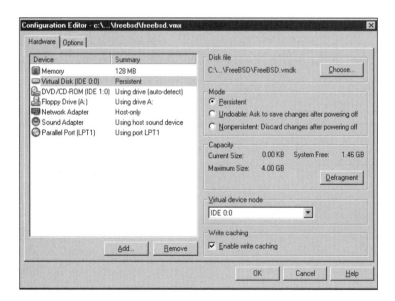

Figure 4.6: VMware Configuration Editor (Windows)

To add a new device, click the **Add** button. The Add Hardware Wizard dialog box appears, asking you which kind of device you want to install. Pick one and click **Next** for the device configuration; then click **Finish** to add the new device to the virtual machine. Don't worry about getting all the settings right in the Add Hardware Wizard, because you can always change them afterward (or remove the devices and add them again). To remove a device, click the device icon to highlight it, then click the **Remove** button.

4.12.2 Linux Configuration Editor

In VMware Workstation for Linux, the Configuration Editor contains a complete map of existing and possible devices on the left (see Figure 4.7). When you click a device, its configuration appears on the right. These settings are identical to those in the Windows Configuration Editor; for explanations of each device, see section 4.12.3.

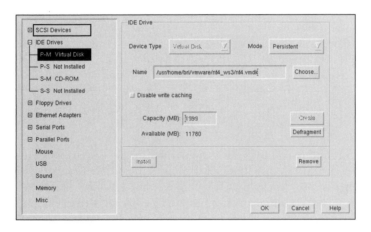

Figure 4.7: VMware Configuration Editor (Linux)

Empty slots in the configuration have a **Not Installed** label. To add a device, click an empty slot and then click the **Install** button. You can change the device's configuration at any time. To remove a device, select the device and click the **Remove** button.

To open a configuration category, click the + symbol next to it. A number of options appear for the category; choose one to bring up the specific configuration (which appears on the right side of the Configuration Editor display).

4.12.3 Configuration Editor Options

Here are the options available under the Configuration Editor. Most pertain to devices.

IDE Drives

You can install up to four IDE drives on a virtual machine, on primary (P) and secondary (S) IDE interfaces, and there are two disks per interface, the master (M) and slave (S); thus, you'll find the abbreviations **P-M**, **P-S**, **S-M**, and **S-S** in the Linux Configuration Editor. On a Windows host, these are disks **0:0**, **0:1**, **1:0**, and **1:1**. Selecting one makes the disk parameter settings appear.

Device Type refers to the kind of disk you want to use for this IDE disk. To create a disk, first give it a unique file name in the **Name** box. This file usually resides in the same place as the rest of the VMware configuration files, but you can change the location if you like—for example, if there isn't enough space for a virtual drive on the partition with the rest of your VMware files.

The next sections explain the different device types and their options.

Virtual Disks

A **Virtual Disk** is a VMware disk within a file on your host operating system. Its size is dynamic; that is, the space it requires depends on how much the *guest* operating system uses. A virtual disk is the only type of disk you can shrink, and its maximum sizes are 128 GB (Windows host), and 64 GB (Linux host).

When you create a virtual disk on either host operating system, you must give it a new and unique file name and a capacity. On a Windows host system, the Add Hardware Wizard also has an Advanced button that you can use to choose between an IDE and SCSI virtual disk. On Linux systems, you make this choice by clicking empty slots in the device map. Also on Linux systems, before you click the **Install** button, you must choose **Create** to create the disk if it doesn't exist already.

Enable/Disable write caching turns VMware's write buffer for the virtual disk files on or off. If you turn caching off, all writes to a disk go immediately to the files. This hinders performance somewhat, but you may need to do this if you exchange a disk between the host and guest operating systems frequently. You can also disable write caching on plain and raw disks.

The **Defragment** button straightens out the blocks in a virtual disk file. VMware writes each new block to the end of a virtual disk file. However, because guest operating systems do not write blocks in the order that they would appear on an actual disk, blocks get scattered about. This may affect performance to a certain degree if your guest operating system makes assumptions about the characteristics of contiguous disk blocks. Defragmenting a virtual disk puts its blocks in the same order as they would appear on a real disk (it does not change the size). You can only defragment a virtual disk when its virtual machine is off.

Physical (Raw) Disks

The **Physical Disk** (Windows host) or **Raw Disk** (Linux host) device type offers an entire real disk to the guest operating system. This is useful primarily for a dual-boot machine, where you installed Linux and Windows on different disks and/or partitions. Raw disks are an advanced feature of VMware Workstation intended for experienced users.

NOTE *VMware has safety features for raw disks, including the ability to mark certain partitions as read-only or unreadable, so that you can protect yourself from accidentally wiping out something on your host system.*

Adding a raw disk on a Windows host involves these steps:

1. In the Add Hardware Wizard, choose **Use a physical disk** and click **Next**.

2. On the next screen, pick the appropriate disk on your host system and click **Next**.

3. Customize the raw disk's partition access. See "Partition Access" on page 58 for a description of this screen. After you're done, click **Next**. (You can change the partition access later, so don't worry about making a mistake here.)

4. Choose a unique new name for the raw disk map file on the host system. The default should be fine. The **Advanced** button on this screen allows you to connect the raw drive to any place on the virtual machine, though you can change this later. Click **Finish** when everything is ready.

To add a raw disk to your system on a Linux host, follow these steps:

1. Specify a new file in the **Name** box, keeping it in the same directory as the rest of the guest operating system configuration files. (This is a small map file, not the disk device in /dev.) Click **Create**.

2. A new window appears, gives an overview of what you're about to do, and asks which disk you want to use. In Windows, there's a menu of devices to choose from. Under Linux, VMware wants you to type in the disk device file name. Since IDE disk devices start with /dev/hd in Linux, you'd use /dev/hda for the primary master drive. (Don't use a partition number, like /dev/hdb3.) Click **OK** when you're ready.

3. The partition access screen appears, similar to the one shown in Figure 4.8. (See page 58 for an explanation.)

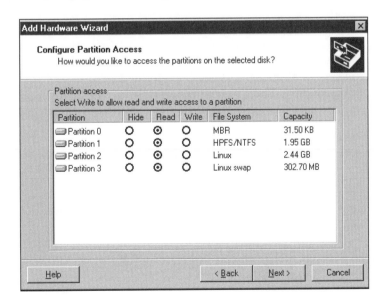

Figure 4.8: Raw disk partition access (Windows host, Add Hardware Wizard)

4. Click **Save** when you're happy with the permissions. The pop-up window disappears. You can now click **Install** to attach the new raw disk to the VMware configuration.

Partition Access

The *partition access screen* (Figure 4-8) includes a matrix of partitions and access permissions and types. (The master boot record, or MBR, appears as partition 0.) The permissions pertain to the guest operating system. If you choose **No Access**, the guest system won't be able to read or write to the partition. **Read Only** write-protects a partition; the guest system will have no problem reading, but if it wants to write to a partition, VMware warns you and gives you the option of rejecting the write operation. **Read/Write** gives full permission on the partition to a guest operating system. You'll almost certainly need to choose this for the guest system's primary partition (such as / on a Unix system or C: on a Windows system).

Plain Disks

A **Plain Disk** is like a virtual disk, except that when you create it, it immediately takes up its true capacity on the host operating system's disk. Plain disks were a feature of VMware Workstation 2; they were designed to get around the limitations of virtual disks in that release and are now obsolete. Later versions of VMware Workstation support existing plain disks; however, the creation of new ones is no longer supported.

To use an existing plain disk, choose **Plain Disk** as the device type and enter the pathname of the plain disk map file (it should end with .pln). Plain disk map files refer to pieces of the disk called *extents*.

VMware Disk Modes and Names

You can use **Mode** to set the disk mode any time after you create a disk for your virtual machine. These modes are available because all disk access on a virtual machine goes through VMware first, making a few extra tricks possible.

Persistent mode makes all disk writes immediate and final. This is the fastest mode and works no differently than a real disk on any other computer.

Nonpersistent mode makes the actual disk device or file read-only, but it offers it as a read-write file to the guest system. VMware intercepts writes from the guest system to the disk and puts them in a *redo log file* instead. VMware throws away a nonpersistent disk's redo log file after you power off the virtual machine, leaving the original data intact. Therefore, any files or changes you make on the guest system disappear after you power off. If you want the chance to keep the changes, use undoable mode.

Undoable mode adds extra features to nonpersistent mode. Instead of throwing away the redo log when you power off the virtual machine, VMware can merge the changes from the redo log back into the disk or just keep the log available to use when you restart the machine.

Turning off a virtual machine with disks in undoable mode results in a dialog box with three options. You can choose **Commit** to incorporate all changes to the original disk device or file, **Discard** to get rid of them, or **Keep** to retain them for later. If you choose to commit, you may have to wait a little while for VMware to write all of the changes back, especially if you made some large software installations on your guest system. Discard is like an undo button, except that you can't redo the changes once you delete the log.

Whenever you turn on a virtual machine with undoable disks, VMware looks for a redo log. If the log file exists (for example, if you pressed the **Keep** button mentioned above), a pop-up window appears with four options: **Commit** and **Discard** to merge or throw away the changes (just as when powering off), **Append** to continue using the log, and **Cancel** to abort the session and halt the virtual machine power-on until you figure out what you want to do with the log.

On both Windows and Linux hosts, disk files associated with each kind of disk have different names. It's important to know where these files are because they have a tendency to get large, using resources on your host system. You may want to move them if you have more than one disk or partition on your host system and you're running out of space.

NOTE *By default, virtual disk files end with* `.vmdk`, *plain disk control files have a* `.pln` *extension, the plain disk extents described in the control file have a* `.dat` *suffix, and raw disk control files use* `.raw`. *Under Linux, you don't necessarily need to follow these conventions, though doing so is always helpful for quick identification. VMware normally stores a disk's redo logs with the rest of the virtual machine's configuration, as files ending in* `.REDO`. *For resource- and performance-related reasons, you can change the location of these files in the Configuration Editor by entering a new path in* **Redo Log Directory***, under* **Misc**. *Because VMware stores an entire disk block in its log, if you modify anything in the block, your log files can get large, even if you write only a relatively small amount of data to the disk.*

CD-ROM/DVD-ROM

You can configure a **CD-ROM** device type as IDE (ATAPI) or SCSI. Keep in mind that ATAPI CD-ROM drives enjoy the best support in most guest operating systems.

When you install or modify a drive, a Windows host provides you with a list of CD-ROM drives to choose from; under a Linux host, you must enter the device file for your CD-ROM drive in the **Name** box. For an ATAPI drive, this name is the same as for the hard drive device. For example, /dev/hdb is the primary slave. You might also have a link /dev/cdrom pointing to the correct device, which will work fine as well. If you don't know the name, run the dmesg command and check for a line like this:

```
hdc: ATAPI 24X CD-ROM drive, 128kB Cache
```

Since you can disconnect and reconnect CD-ROM drives under VMware, you can choose to make the CD-ROM drive start disconnected. Once you have a guest operating system configured and installed, you may want to keep the drive disconnected until you need it. (Since a CD-ROM drive is read-only, the host and guest operating systems won't clash over the device file, though the guest system will attempt to access the CD-ROM at boot time, which can cause an extra seek, adding some time to your guest system's boot sequence.)

You can also connect an ISO9660 image file to the virtual CD-ROM drive instead of a real device. To do this, choose **CD-ROM Image** from the **Device Type** menu and type the file name of the image file in the **Name** box.

NOTE *CD-R and CD-RW drives show up as CD-ROM drives in virtual machines. If you want to use their CD-writing capability in a virtual machine under a Linux host, you can try to use the ide-scsi emulation made on your host system.*

SCSI Drives and Devices

The **SCSI Drives** section has a maximum of seven disks, corresponding to targets 0 through 6 of the virtual SCSI bus. Configuration is identical to that for the IDE devices in the previous section, with **Virtual Disk**, **Plain Disk**, **Raw Disk**, **CD-ROM**, **CD-ROM Image**, and **CD-ROM (raw access)** types.

Virtual SCSI disks are one means of adding more drives to a guest operating system if you're out of IDE devices; but if you do, be sure that your guest system fully supports the BusLogic controller (Windows and Linux systems do).

In addition, you can configure a SCSI target using the **Generic Device** option. This option translates all SCSI commands to and from a real SCSI device on your host machine to a SCSI device on your virtual machine, regardless of the device's actual type. You can use this to attach scanners and CD-RW drives to your guest operating system.

NOTE *Although you can connect and disconnect generic SCSI devices during virtual machine operation, you should only do so if you're certain that a driver isn't using it. Otherwise, your guest operating system may crash. SCSI wasn't meant to be hot-pluggable.*

To add a generic SCSI device to a Windows host, follow these steps:

1. In the Add Hardware Wizard, choose **Generic SCSI Device**; then click **Next**.

2. Select the desired SCSI device on the host machine, choose its target on the virtual machine, and click **Finish**. You can change the settings later if you want.

To add a generic SCSI device to a Linux host, follow these steps:

1. Select an empty device slot in the Configuration Editor; then choose **Generic Device** as the device type.

2. Determine the source device file on your host system. All generic SCSI devices start with /dev/sg on a Linux system. The first device is /dev/sg0, the second is /dev/sg1, with the number progressing first by SCSI host controller and then by target—much like SCSI disks on a Linux system. If you're using a Linux 2.4 kernel, look at /proc/scsi/sg/device_strs to see the progression on your host system. If you're using Linux 2.2, you're stuck with /proc/scsi/scsi, which is a bit more verbose. Note that some Linux systems use the letters a, b, c, . . . instead of numbers, for example /dev/sga.

3. Type this device name in the **Name** box and click the **Install** button to finish.

If you don't configure any SCSI devices, VMware doesn't attach the SCSI controller to the virtual machine.

Floppy Drives

VMware supports two regular floppy disk drives. In addition to the host system's real disks, you can also use a file containing a floppy disk image. Since a floppy is a removable medium, you can disconnect and reconnect floppy drives during guest operating system operation. You can even disconnect, change the underlying device or file in the Configuration Editor, and then reconnect the device without rebooting the guest system.

When configuring a floppy disk drive, you can pick the first (A:) or second (B:) disk drive in the **Floppy Drives** section of the Configuration Editor. For **Type**, choose **Device** for a real disk or **File** for an image file.

On a Windows host, you choose a real device from a list. On a Linux host, you must enter a device name in the **Path** box for the device: /dev/fd0 or /dev/fd1 for a real floppy drive. On both hosts, you can also opt for a floppy image file (for a blank image, enter the desired file name and then click **Create**). Click **Install** to add the drive to the VMware configuration.

Use **Start Connected** if you're sure that you want VMware to see the drive when you activate the virtual machine (for example, if you're booting the system from a floppy drive).

Start the VMware floppy drive disconnected if your host system has a removable drive, as many notebooks do; asking for a nonexistent floppy drive may cause your host system to hang. Also, VMware takes exclusive use of some devices (such as floppy drives) when connected, making them unavailable to the host system unless you disconnect them.

Ethernet Adapters

You can install up to three virtual Ethernet interfaces on a guest operating system. When you configure an interface, you must select a type from the **Connection Type** options.

Bridged networking makes the host system act as if it has another network interface. That interface is for the guest system running under VMware, and you'll need to configure it under the guest system. Your network address on the guest system differs from the one on the host system or any other machine on the network. At many sites, you can simply configure it with DHCP.

Host-only networking attaches the virtual network card to an entire virtual network running entirely within your host system.

NAT networking is like host-only networking with a connection to the outside world. It uses VMware's built-in network address translation to transform your host operating system into a gateway.

We'll talk more about the **Custom** option and go into detail on networking in Chapter 9.

> **NOTE** *For all network modes to operate correctly, you must enable special support on your host system—for a Linux host, a special kernel module called* vmnet *provides the virtual network support—and activate this network at boot time. If you don't have the* vmnet *module, the* vmware-config.pl *script can try to find one or can compile it for you.*

Serial Ports

You'll find the standard PC COM1 through COM4 port assignments under **Serial Ports** in the Configuration Editor. The following port options are available:

Connection (Windows host) or **Type** (Linux host) indicates where the serial port resides on the host system. **Physical Serial Port** or **Device** refers to a real serial port. Under Linux, you'll need to type a device file name in the **Path** box; these files are in /dev (for example, /dev/ttyS0 is the file for the first serial port). Under Windows, you can pick from a list of available ports (for example, COM1). If you choose **File** for the output, you can redirect the virtual serial port's output to a file on the host operating system (the port won't get any input from your virtual system). Under Windows, you can pick a named pipe. Under Linux, you can choose **TTY**, which allows the host operating system to talk to the guest's serial port though a pseudo-TTY.

Start Connected activates the serial port at power on. If you're using the port for a mouse, you should probably keep it connected all of the time.

Parallel Ports

There are two available **Parallel Ports** for a virtual machine. Configuration is similar to that of serial ports:

For **Connection** (or **Type**), you can choose **Physical serial port** (**Device**), to specify a port on the host machine, or **File**, to specify an output file. If your host system is Windows, you can choose an available port from a list. Under Linux, you need to type a path to a file in /dev. If you use bidirectional mode, you'll want to enter /dev/parport0 or /dev/parport1 in the **Path** box. Otherwise, you can use the unidirectional ports, which are normally at /dev/lp0 and /dev/lp1. Use the dmesg command to see what's available.

Bidirectional mode is for parallel port devices, such as Zip drives, that talk back to the operating system. Some printers are also bidirectional.

Check **Start Connected** if you want the parallel port available when the guest operating system starts. This option is important because some guest systems may be unable to recognize a device if it's not present at boot time.

*If you pick **File** as the device type, VMware redirects the guest operating system's parallel port output to a file on the host system (enter a file name in the **Path** box). This option offers a good way to capture printer output for drivers that don't have a print-to-file option. (Since this is a one-way data transfer from guest to host, you can use only unidirectional mode with **File**.)*

Mouse (Linux Host Only)

Normally, you won't need to bother with the settings for **Mouse**, since the host operating system normally supplies everything VMware needs. You should usually leave the **Host Mouse Type** and **Host Mouse Device** options set to **Autodetect**.

But because Linux allows access to multiple mouse devices through different device files, you can add a separate mouse device manually. For example, you can plug a Logitech serial mouse into your host machine's second serial port, select **MouseMan Serial**, and specify /dev/ttyS1 as the device.

USB

VMware Workstation supports the universal serial bus (USB) on all host systems except Windows NT. On a Windows host, you can add a USB controller in the Configuration editor. For a Linux host, you can click the **Enable USB** option in the Configuration Editor's **USB** section.

Once a USB device connects to a kernel driver in an operating system, the kernel must have exclusive access to the device. Since you may run several operating systems at once with VMware Workstation, it's important to understand how virtual machines get control of USB devices. The mechanism is simple: If the virtual machine has input focus (that is, it has control over the keyboard and mouse), the guest operating system running in that virtual machine gets complete control of the device. Therefore, both your host and guest systems can use different USB devices at the same time, but they can never share one device. You can temporarily prohibit VMware from taking over new devices with the **Automatically connect new USB devices** option.

VMware Workstation for Linux has a **Path to usbdevfs** box; under normal circumstances, the entry here should be /proc/bus/usb. As with everything else in /proc, the Linux kernel creates and maintains this directory, but only if you have the appropriate kernel support. When configuring a kernel, look for this option in the USB support configuration section. (You may need to turn on the experimental options.)

Sound

Click **Sound** to configure a sound card for your guest system. On a Windows host, you can pick from a list of currently installed cards, though you probably have only one. If Linux is your host system, enter the name of your DSP device (your sound card). If you have one sound card, enter /dev/dsp into the box labeled **Device**. (If you have more than one, pick one of your /dev/dsp* devices.)

Check **Start Connected** if you want sound active when the system boots; disabling this option is handy for silencing the annoying noises that certain operating systems make after they boot.

Memory

The **Memory** setting regulates the guest system's use of random-access memory (RAM). The box indicates the RAM currently available to the guest system, in megabytes; adjust this value up or down by clicking the arrow buttons or entering a number in the box. Due to performance considerations, you won't be able to set the guest memory higher than that of the host, even if your host has ample virtual memory.

The optimal value here depends on how efficient your guest system is, and what applications you use under it, just as it would on a real machine. VMware Workstation also gives a recommendation based on the guest system. In general, Windows needs more memory than other operating systems, and older operating systems require less than newer ones. A setting of 16 to 64 MB may be fine for Windows 95, 98, and NT, but you'll want 96 MB or more for systems like Windows 2000, Me, XP, and newer releases, or for older systems with big software packages. (Unix systems running in text mode only are normally fine with as little as 16 MB, but when you run an X server, figure on at least 32 MB.)

NOTE *The VMware-recommended values for the older Windows guests tend to be on the high side—for example, VMware recommends 96 MB for Windows NT. Unless you plan to run every single application installed on your guest system at the same time, you can pare this down a little.*

To avoid using virtual memory on the guest system, consider adding more memory to the configuration. While operating systems like Unix manage memory fairly efficiently, they go through at least one additional layer of access to get to the disk (to use virtual memory) when running under VMware.

NOTE *Adding memory to a virtual machine configuration slows down VMware suspend operations.*

4.12.4 Nonhardware Options

The **Options** tab on VMware Workstation for Windows and the **Misc** section of the Linux Configuration Editor offer several additional options. These settings have little to do with the virtual hardware.

Display Name is the window name on your host operating system. If this field is left empty, VMware uses the full pathname of the configuration file.

Guest OS is the operating system you plan to use for the current configuration. Remember that this setting not only tells VMware which set of the VMware Tools to install on a guest operating system, but also tweaks a few hardware parameters for the best performance. VMware Workstation knows about various quirks in guest operating system kernels, and when you tell it which kernel you're using, it can bypass features on the CPU that the guest operating system never uses. Don't pick the wrong operating system—these same optimizations may cause the guest system to malfunction when misapplied.

Power on after starting the application (Windows host) or **Power on when program starts** (Linux host) turns on the power as soon as you start VMware and open a configuration, so you don't need to click the power button when you start the machine. You can also enable automatic virtual machine startup scripts on your host system with this option.

Exit the application after powering off (Windows host) or **Exit at power off (also at suspend to disk)** (Linux host) terminates VMware Workstation when the power goes off or when you suspend operation.

Use APM features of guest OS when suspending makes VMware interact with the advanced power management interface of your guest operating system. Normally, VMware uses its own scheme, contained entirely within the host system, for suspend operations. (See "Suspend/Resume" in section 4.8 on page 46 for details.)

Hide partition type of read-only partitions masks any read-only partitions on a raw disk. Each one has a type, and operating systems try to identify which partitions they can use through that type. If you choose this option, the guest system sees the type of all read-only partitions except for the master boot record as unknown, and VMware catches any attempt to change the master boot record.

Windows 95 and later systems (but not Linux or FreeBSD) assume that they need to access any partitions that they can identify. If you have several types of Windows partitions on a raw disk and two are running (either as guests or the host), a guest could see another unmasked partition currently in use by the other and try to access it. Because that partition is in use, its current state is "dirty," so the guest will try to fix its filesystem, which will probably do the opposite of fixing: corrupt the filesystem.

Some third-party boot loaders deal with this problem by setting partition types to unknown when needed. If this is the case, you won't need the **Hide partition type of read-only partitions** option (in fact, your system may not boot correctly if you use it).

Find best resolution in full-screen mode (Linux host only) tells VMware to look at your host system's video mode and to try to change it to best suit the guest system in full-screen mode.

The **Redo Log Directory** field indicates where you should put the log file for the persistent and undoable disk modes. (See "VMware Disk Modes and Names" on page 58 for more information on disk modes and the log files.) If you leave this field blank, VMware sets the redo log directory to the same as the guest system's configuration file.

Run with debugging information (on the Windows host only) turns on debugging information. Look for the `.log` file in your virtual machine's configuration directory; you'll need it when contacting VMware technical support.

Logging level (Linux host only) controls the type and number of messages sent to the diagnostic log (these log files also have a `.log` suffix on Linux systems). There are two settings: **Normal** and **Debug**; the latter generates more information. As with Windows host logging, as mentioned earlier, you'll normally need to adjust the logging level only when VMware technical support investigates a problem.

4.13   Host Memory Requirements

The **Memory** tab under **Preferences** (for a Windows host) or the **Reserved Memory** option on the **Settings** menu (Linux host) give you finer control over the host system memory dedicated to VMware. Figure 4.9 shows the screen that appears.

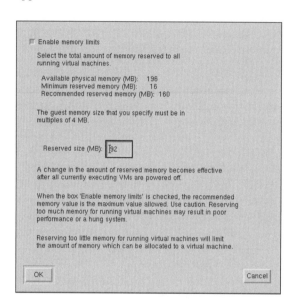

Figure 4.9: VMware host reserved memory settings (Linux host)

The panel tells you how much real memory your host has (196 MB in this case), the minimum required for any operation (here, 16 MB), and how much VMware recommends (half or more of the host memory: 160 MB in this case). On VMware Workstation for Windows, you can adjust the amount of memory with the arrow buttons, and on the Linux version, all you need to do is enter the number in the **Reserved size** box. You can also turn off the memory limit checks by unchecking the **Enable memory limits** box.

Your settings here depend on the type and number of your guest operating systems, as well as on how much RAM you have on your host system. If you use the recommended value for the amount of host reserved memory and do not change the **Memory** setting in the Configuration Editor for your virtual machine, you probably won't run into trouble. However, if you have problems with memory performance, your virtual machine won't power on (because it doesn't have enough memory), or if you feel like you're wasting too much host memory, do some calculations and experimentation.

First, find out how much memory (in MB) each of your guest systems use by viewing the **Memory** setting in the Configuration Editor. Then determine how many guest systems you'll ever run at once—call this number n. Look at all of the memory figures together and add the top n numbers. Then take this sum and add n times 10 MB to it. (This extra 10 MB per guest system is typical overhead.)

The number you get is the maximum amount of memory VMware should ever need, and to be on the safe side, you can set the host reserved memory to this amount. However, because other processes on your host machine can't touch this memory when it is occupied by virtual machines, you may feel you're wasting resources (and reserving this memory may severely degrade your host's performance). Therefore, consider setting the reserved memory to less than your theoretical maximum.

Because guest operating systems ask for memory in small chunks called *pages*, VMware doesn't need to give out all of its reserved memory at once. However, if VMware Workstation runs out of reserved memory, it powers off the virtual machine that asked for more.

VMware doesn't lock the reserved memory on the host right away. When a virtual machine requests a page, VMware goes out to the host system and locks a page. If any other program on the host is using that page, the host operating system will probably kick that program's data on the page to the swap area on disk. This operation is costly to the host system and will probably slow down the program with the displaced page.

Be careful not only of asking for too much reserved memory, but also of disabling the memory limits. If VMware asks for more memory than your host has, your host system will *thrash*. In other words, it will continuously send memory pages back and forth between memory and disk as processes ask for their pages (or your system may just start terminating programs that ask for more memory, or just hang). If you're considering turning this safety check off, consider installing more memory.

4.14 The VMware BIOS

Every PC has a basic input/output system, or BIOS, a small program in a motherboard and its hardware. In addition to storing a few parameters such as the current time, the BIOS also knows a little bit about the attached hardware. Your computer uses the BIOS to read the boot sector from a disk so that your operating system can load successfully.

Systems such as MS-DOS used the BIOS during operation. However, since using the BIOS in this way tends to slow things down (a BIOS knows very little about hardware, especially with regard to newer, faster modes), modern operating systems generally ignore the fact that a BIOS exists and talk directly to the hardware.

NOTE *When you turn on a PC, it beeps, and you usually see a screen with a memory test and some other stuff before the operating system boots. This is the BIOS in action. Some PC makers (notebook vendors in particular) try to hide this screen from you, but even if they do, it's still there (you may have to press a weird key sequence after powering on to actually see the evidence).*

VMware has a BIOS, just like a real PC. Its BIOS is a Phoenix utility; one of the simpler BIOSs. To access the BIOS screen, press F2 during the memory test, right after you power on the virtual machine, and then wait a couple of seconds for the main BIOS screen (Figure 4.10) to appear. (Under VMware, you won't normally need to change anything other than possibly the boot sequence, but it never hurts to know how.)

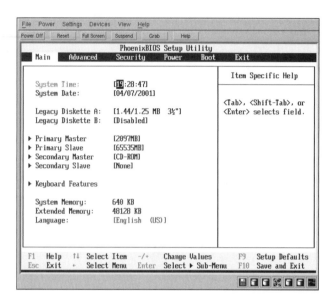

Figure 4.10: VMware main BIOS screen

Use your keyboard to navigate the BIOS settings; the keyboard commands appear at the bottom of the screen.

The BIOS configuration has six sections: **Main**, **Advanced**, **Security**, **Power**, **Boot**, and **Exit**. You begin in the **Main** section. (Note that the keyboard commands may vary between sections.)

Use the arrow keys to move through the BIOS configuration, the LEFT and RIGHT ARROW keys to flip through sections, and the UP and DOWN ARROW keys to move between individual settings within a single section. Some items with a little triangle next to them, like **Keyboard Features** in Figure 4.10, indicate that you can access a submenu by pressing ENTER. Pressing ESC takes you out of a submenu.

To change a parameter, use the – and + keys. To exit, press ESC within a section; you'll go directly to the **Exit** section, where you can save any changes you made and exit the BIOS setup. Here, you can also undo your changes and return the settings to the way they were before you entered the BIOS screen, or load the default values (probably not a good idea, unless you *really* messed up your system).

The **Main** section has settings for the time and date, as well as information about disk hardware. You probably won't need to change anything here other than the time or date if they're wrong and/or the guest system doesn't know how to get the correct time and date. You won't normally need to touch the disk information; VMware provides this information automatically to its BIOS. (The **Keyboard Features** submenu has a few interesting parameters such as the key repeat rate.)

You also probably won't need to change anything under **Advanced** because VMware provides consistent mouse and IDE device support to the virtual machine. You may need to change **Large Disk Access Mode** to suit your guest system, though; some guest systems aren't smart enough to ask the disks about their geometries.

Security provides a rudimentary form of access control for a computer. You can set a supervisor password to restrict access control to the setup utility and set a user password, which will be required for booting. (This is somewhat pointless, however, if you're running VMware, since you can always configure another virtual machine with the same disk devices, easily defeating the password protection.)

Under **Power**, you'll find options pertaining to the BIOS power management features. Again, these aren't worth much with VMware because your host operating system should take care of power management for you (remember that you can't really spin down a virtual disk). Still, there may be some quirks in your guest operating system that require you to make some changes here.

Boot is probably the most important section on this screen. When you power on a real or virtual machine, the BIOS looks at a number of devices in a particular order, called the *boot sequence*, to determine where it will load the operating system. The BIOS loads the operating system from the first bootable device it finds in the sequence. By default, the VMware BIOS looks at floppy drives, then hard drives, and then a CD-ROM, and if all of these searches fail, it searches the network for a boot record. You'll see this process in the **Boot** section as follows:

```
+Removable Devices
+Hard Drive
 ATAPI CD-ROM Drive
 Network boot
```

A + next to a name means that this is a category of devices, and that there are several devices inside. To see what they are, highlight the category and press ENTER. For example, you'll find **Legacy Floppy Drives** under **Removable Devices**. To view everything at once, press CTRL-ENTER.

To change the sequence, highlight the entry you want to move and press + to move it up or - to move it down. For example, if you're replacing the operating system on a VMware disk, you'll want the BIOS to look at the CD-ROM drive before the hard drive, so use the arrow keys to highlight **ATAPI CD-ROM Drive** and then press + to move it above **Hard Drive**.

In general, you cannot move devices outside a category. To move a particular hard drive, do so within **Hard Drive**, or move the whole category—that is, except for removable devices. If you have an IDE Zip drive, you might be able to move it between **Removable Device** and **Hard Drive**. But since VMware doesn't support removable IDE disks (yet), this is currently impossible—no such IDE drives will appear on the **Boot** menu. (Remember that the VMware BIOS was developed for real PCs.)

The **Exit** section has a couple of options for exiting the BIOS setup utility. If you choose **Exit Saving Changes**, the BIOS saves any changes you made and resets the virtual machine. If you choose instead to exit and discard your changes, things go back to the way they were before you entered the utility and the machine resets. (This is a good way to exit if you were only looking around.) There are also options for saving and discarding changes without leaving the setup utility.

You can also choose **Load Setup Defaults**. Be careful with this option, because it erases many of the custom options. It's not quite as dangerous as it is on a real machine because VMware provides a certain amount of information to the BIOS, but it's still not a great idea to take a chance here (especially if you have a configuration that works).

5

WINDOWS GUEST SYSTEMS

VMware Workstation supports Windows guest systems from version 3.1 on. Though there are quite a few versions of Windows, they fall into three categories. The oldest are the 16-bit DOS-based systems and their extensions, such as Windows 3.1. Next are the newer 32-bit single-user systems such as Windows 95, 98, and Me. Finally, there are 32–61+ multiuser offerings based on Windows NT, including Windows 2000 and XP.

This chapter has four main parts. First, we'll go over the Windows NT family and look at how to examine the VMware devices and get them to work under those systems. Next we'll do the same for Windows 95–like guest systems. We'll round off our discussion of the 32-bit systems with coverage of VMware Tools for Windows, dual configurations, and the Cygwin utilities. Finally, we'll talk about DOS and Windows 3.1.

5.1 Windows Driver Compatibility in a Guest System

Most of the drivers that Windows needs to run under VMware come with the base operating system. To get the most out of a Windows guest system, though, you should install VMware Tools for Windows to get a video driver optimized for VMware and the VMware Toolbox, as described in section 4.11. The Tools come with VMware, but are available only for Windows 95 and later. (Depending on your system, you may also need additional drivers for VMware's sound card.)

As with other guest systems, you can choose to install Windows from scratch under VMware or to run an installation already on one of your hard disk's partitions using VMware's raw disks. You can also make one of these systems into a dual-configuration system that runs fine on your real hardware as well as under VMware, as you'll learn in section 5.43.

When you create a new virtual machine with a new virtual disk with the New Virtual Machine Wizard, you'll get an IDE disk if you choose MS-DOS, Windows 3.1, 95, 98, Me, or XP, and a SCSI disk for Windows NT or 2000.

5.2 Windows NT, 2000, and XP

Windows NT is a 32-bit protected-memory operating system that was built mainly with network use in mind. There are two main versions, NT Workstation and Server, but they don't differ much in terms of actual base implementation. Workstation is a "smaller" version for desktop machines; Server needs more memory because it normally runs more network services at once.

NOTE *Windows NT has gone through several service pack updates to get rid of security holes and other bugs. It's always a good idea to get your installation at the highest service pack possible.*

Windows 2000 is NT's successor. The underlying system isn't radically different from NT's, but the user interface and administration tools depart somewhat from NT's in look and feel. As with NT, 2000 comes in different versions: Professional, Server, and Advanced Server.

The latest in the Windows NT family is Windows XP, which consists of Windows XP Home Edition, Professional, and Server. The operation of all versions is similar to that of Windows 2000.

5.2.1   Navigating the Control Panels

You perform most Windows NT/2000/XP administration through **Control Panel** items, located off the **Start • Settings** menu. Although you'll have no trouble pointing and clicking, finding all of the drivers can be a challenge, and some configuration files are distributed throughout the system.

There are a lot of control panels, and they differ between NT and 2000/XP. For example, you'll find hard drives under **SCSI Adapters** in Windows NT and under **Device Manager** in Windows 2000 and XP.

NOTE *If you're using Windows XP, set your control panel to **Classic View**. This switches the panel to a view consistent with Windows 2000.*

If you have to work with NT and 2000/XP at the same time, it can help to remember which control panels pertain to low-level hardware and which pertain to higher-level protocols. For example, the **Internet** settings won't tell you anything about your actual network interfaces; you have to look in **Network** or the Windows 2000/XP **Device Manager** for that, as discussed later.

Windows NT's **Devices** control panel gives an overview of all device drivers that your system knows about. (Windows has probably disabled most of them because you don't have them installed in your system.) This panel is useful primarily for looking at all of your device drivers at once and for manually starting and stopping them. You can also control the startup behavior of the devices here if you want to disable some devices at boot time.

Windows 2000 and XP have a unified configuration editor for devices, called the Device Manager. To access it, open the **System** control panel and click **Device Manager**. A list of categories and devices, as shown in Figure 5.1, appears. When you double-click a device, some additional information and controls come up, such as the driver information. (You can also change the driver here.)

Figure 5.1: Windows 2000 Device Manager

5.2.2 IDE Devices

Windows NT channels its IDE device driver through its SCSI subsystem, essentially pretending that IDE drives are SCSI drives. You'll find VMware's virtual IDE disk and CD-ROM drives in the **SCSI Adapters** control panel on the **Devices** tab. If you have devices installed under more than one IDE interface, each interface shows up as a separate adapter in the list. You can't change any individual drive settings here (and it's unlikely that you'd want to), but you can remove an IDE interface from your system if you really want to.

NOTE *IDE disks show up in the Windows 2000/XP Device Manager under **Disk drives**, but there aren't many options there.*

Disk Partitioning

To partition a new disk under Windows NT (such as a new VMware virtual disk), follow these steps:

1. Choose **Disk Administrator** from the **Start • Administrative Tools (Common)** menu.

2. Right-click the disk you want to partition and select **Create**.

3. Choose a size and layout; then select **Commit Changes Now** from the **File** menu.

4. Right-click the partition on which you want to place the filesystem and select **Format** from the menu that appears to format the partition. When formatting is complete, the disk should show up on the system under a new drive letter (such as E:).

To partition a disk under Windows 2000 and XP, follow these steps:

1. Open the control panel and choose **Administrative Tools**.

2. Double-click **Computer Management**, click **Storage** in the right pane, and then choose **Disk Management (Local)**.

3. The right pane splits in two; in the lower part, you'll see a list of disks. An empty disk without a partition table should have a red and white "do not enter" symbol (like the street sign) on it, as in Figure 5.2. Right-click an empty disk and choose **Write Signature** from the menu that appears; confirm your action in the dialog box, and the "do not enter" symbol should go away.

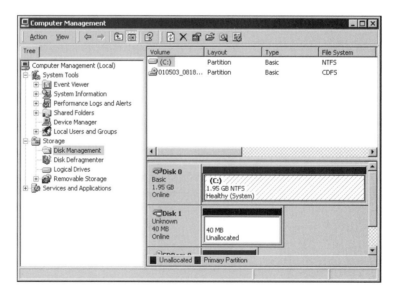

Figure 5.2: Windows 2000/XP Disk Management

4. Right-click the unallocated space to the right and select **Create Partition** from the menu that appears. You'll proceed through a series of Partitioning Wizard dialog boxes and eventually end up with a new partition and a new drive letter.

5.2.3 SCSI Devices

Configuring SCSI drives under Windows NT/2000/XP is much like the procedure for configuring an IDE disk, but you may need to go through an additional step to install the SCSI host adapter driver.

Under Windows NT, you'll find the SCSI device settings in the **SCSI Adapters** control panel. If you add a SCSI drive to a VMware configuration that has no SCSI drives yet, then you must add the SCSI driver in this control panel. To do so, click the **Drivers** tab, select **BusLogic** from the list of manufacturers, and choose **MultiMaster PCI SCSI Host Adapters** (the only option that works) from the list (you may need your NT CD-ROM). Then reboot your guest system, which may take quite a while.

For Windows 2000/XP, just add the device and log in as a user with administrator capability. Log-in will take a little while. As you log in, Windows goes through a process of detecting new hardware, including the SCSI host adapter. Once the process finishes, the virtual BusLogic SCSI controller should appear in the Device Manager.

To put a filesystem on a SCSI disk on either an NT, 2000, or XP system, use the Disk Manager as you would for an IDE disk, as described previously.

For miscellaneous SCSI devices such as scanners and obscure removable-media drives, you will probably need drivers from the device manufacturer. Windows NT/2000/XP include support only for common devices such as disks and CD-ROM drives.

NOTE *To get the VMware Workstation's virtual BusLogic SCSI host controller working under Windows XP, you must download a driver for it available at the VMware website.*

5.2.4 Floppy Drives

Neither Windows NT nor 2000/XP let you change many settings for floppy drives. If you installed a floppy device with the Configuration Editor or Configuration Wizard, both the VMware BIOS (see section 4.14) and Windows should see it, unless you turn it off in the BIOS.

NOTE *Floppy devices are very primitive, sitting at fixed addresses. Windows performs a quick check at boot time to see if a floppy controller is present, but that's about it; it won't look at a floppy disk unless you specifically ask it to. Under Windows NT, you won't see much information, and about the only additional information you'll see under the Windows 2000/XP Device Manager is the driver name.*

5.2.5 Ethernet Interfaces

A VMware Ethernet card shows up as **AMD PCNET PCI Ethernet Adapter** on the **Adapters** tab on Windows NT's **Network** control panel. In Windows 2000 and XP, an Ethernet card shows up under **Network adapters** in the Device Manager and should also appear under **Local Area Connection** in the **Network and Dial-up Connections** control panel. You may have more than one Ethernet adapter if you chose to configure more than one type of VMware networking.

In NT, if you select an adapter and click **Properties**, you won't get much useful information—and you should leave the settings at their default values. Windows 2000 and XP are a little more verbose, but you needn't change anything once the operating system detects the device. Furthermore, Windows NT/2000/XP should automatically detect any new adapters that you add to the system at boot time, so you should have no reason to add anything. However, when this autodetection process occurs (if you're adding one of VMware's network adapters for the first time), you may need your Windows installation CD handy, because it contains the driver for the interface.

We'll go into more detail on how to make the network interface actually talk to something in Chapters 9 and 10.

5.2.6 Serial Ports

To change the configuration of a serial port on your system, use the **Ports** control panel. Remember that VMware shows all four ports to the guest system even if they aren't configured, so you'll get a list of COM1 through COM4. When you choose a port, you'll see the baud rate, parity, and other information that most programs accessing serial ports should use. VMware will automatically adjust the settings on the host system if it is necessary. To experiment with different port assignments, click the **Advanced** button.

In the Windows 2000 Device Manager, six ports may appear, even though VMware provides only up to four. If you have a Linux host operating system, your serial ports probably don't work. Look at page 221 in Chapter 12 for a fix.

5.2.7 Parallel Ports

Windows NT hides the parallel ports on your system until you configure a device that uses one. For example, if you want to use a printer and you know that it's sitting on the first parallel port (LPT1), before you can send a file to the port at the command prompt with the copy *file* LPT1: command, you must configure the printer. To configure a printer, click **Printers** on the control panel, select **Add Printer**, and then add a local printer using port LPT1.

Under Windows 2000/XP, a parallel port shows up in the Device Manager as soon as you configure one under VMware. For **Port Settings**, you have three options dealing with interrupts; the default **Never use an interrupt** is fine for mostly unidirectional devices such as printers, but you should use an interrupt if you're using a bidirectional port device such as a Zip drive.

5.2.8 Sound Card

The drivers for VMware's sound card come with Windows NT, 2000, and XP, but the operating system installer may not automatically detect the sound card. To see if a sound device is present, open the **Multimedia** control panel and click the **Devices** tab. If nothing is listed under **Audio Devices**, then Windows didn't find the sound card.

To add the sound card in Windows NT, follow these steps:

1. Click the **Add** button on the **Devices** tab of the **Multimedia** control panel.

2. In the dialog box that appears, choose **Creative Labs Sound Blaster 1.X, Pro, 16** and click **OK**. (You may need your NT installation CD at this point.)

3. A dialog box asks you about the card's hardware addresses. The defaults should work under VMware: base I/O address 220, interrupt 5, DMA 1, 16-bit DMA 7, and MPU401 address 330.

4. Reboot your system.

   For Windows 2000/XP, follow these steps:

1. Open up the **Add/Remove Hardware** control panel. This brings up the Add/Remove Hardware Wizard.

2. Keep the default **Add/Troubleshoot a Device** and click **Next**.

3. Click **Add a new device** and then click **Next**.

4. Choose **No, I want to select the hardware from a list** and click **Next**.

5. Scroll down to **Sound, video and game controllers**, choose it, and click **Next**.

6. Click **Creative Technology Ltd** in the left box, then **Sound Blaster 16 or AWE32 or compatible (WDM)** in the right box, and then **Next**.

7. Click **Next** to use the default settings and click **Finish** when this button appears. You will not need to reboot your computer. The device should now appear on the **Hardware** tab of the **Sounds and Multimedia** control panel.

NOTE *Depending on your host system's sound card and processor, sound on a Windows 2000 or XP guest system can be choppy. See page 220 in Chapter 12 for possible remedies.*

NOTE *Remember to turn the volume all the way up when using Windows as a guest system under VMware (use the speaker icon in the taskbar for this). You can also turn off all of the annoying sounds that you just enabled with the **Sounds** control panel, or just disconnect the sound device under VMware until you actually need it.*

5.2.9 USB Controller

Open the Windows 2000/XP Device Manager. You'll see **Universal serial bus controllers** and the hardware attached to the controllers. When you plug in a USB device, it shows up here (and possibly other places, depending on the device—for example, a flash memory reader/writer appears in the list of disks). When you first insert a USB device, Windows looks for an appropriate driver. If it can't find one, it runs a wizard to install a new driver, giving you the options of looking on the system disk, CD-ROM drives, and floppy disks. If it can't find the driver in any of these locations, the wizard gives you a choice of either leaving the device unconfigured or deferring the driver installation. You should defer it so that you can install the drivers later. If you choose to leave the device unconfigured, Windows tends to ignore it even if you install drivers. (To fix this, you must remove the unconfigured device: Unplug the device, right-click its entry in the Device Manager, and choose **Uninstall**.)

Because Windows 2000 and XP classify USB devices as removable, a new **Unplug or Eject Hardware** icon appears in the system tray when a device connects. Use this to eject media in USB devices and to safely disconnect before you manually eject flash memory cards and other removable media.

> **NOTE** *Microsoft does not support USB in Windows NT, but there are several third-party drivers for it. The best way to look for current driver support for NT is to first check with the device's manufacturer. If the manufacturer doesn't offer a driver, type* `windows nt usb` *into a web search engine.*

5.3 Windows 95, 98, and Me

Like the Windows NT–based systems, the Windows 95 family operates in 32-bit protected mode. However, because they are meant more for individual use, these systems don't have any real notion of users or system administrators. They generally require less memory, processor resources, and disk space than their NT-based cousins.

5.3.1 Installation under VMware

The installation procedure for Windows 95, 98, and Me is fairly straightforward, though the procedure under VMware requires some patience: Not only does the installer reboot the machine several times during the process, but Microsoft's use of animation and special text effects can slow to a crawl in VMware's VGA16 mode. For example, when you are finally at the end of the installation process and boot the guest system normally for the first time, the Welcome to Windows 98 window that appears has an opening animation that takes several minutes to play in this mode. Furthermore, you can't permanently close this window until the animation completes. Just hang tight and install the VMware Tools right after you boot.

5.3.2 VMware Devices under Windows 95, 98, and Me

Windows 95, 98, and Me have a utility, called the Device Manager, for viewing all hardware on the current system. To get to it, open the **System** control panel (either by choosing it from the **Control Panel** or right-clicking **My Computer** and selecting **Properties**) and select the **Device Manager** tab. The display resembles the Device Manager in Windows 2000 (shown earlier in Figure 5.1). It is useful primarily to see whether Windows recognizes that a certain device is attached to your system and, if so, whether that device has a working driver.

The Device Manager divides devices into categories, and if you double-click a device in a category (or select one and click the **Properties** button), a new window with information about the device and its driver appears. In addition, you can find configuration settings for the device on the **Settings** tab, though you generally will not need to change these when running the system under VMware.

The Device Manager displays its devices in two ways. The default is **View devices by type** (at the top of the Device Manager). This display categorizes devices by their general purpose, such as CD-ROM drives, fixed and removable storage, and communications ports. This display normally provides the fastest way to find a device because there is only one level of categories. Furthermore, many intermediate devices that don't concern most users are set off in a miscellaneous **System devices** category.

If you choose **View devices by connection**, you can track down a device by its location in the computer. You'll find most of VMware's devices under **Plug and Play BIOS / PCI BUS**, though some of the more primitive ones, such as floppy drives and serial ports, are at outer levels of the device hierarchy.

5.3.3 IDE Disks

VMware's virtual IDE disks show up in Windows 95/98/Me under **Disk drives** in the Device Manager. A disk should have a name like **GENERIC IDE DISK TYPE0x**, where *x* is some number.

Unfortunately, the Properties display doesn't show the disk's interface and configuration, so you can't tell what the **Current drive letter assignment** (on the **Settings** tab) actually corresponds to it unless you rearrange the display somewhat. In the Device Manager, switch the display to **View devices by connection**. Open **Plug and Play BIOS** and then open **PCI bus, Intel 82371AB/EB Bus Master IDE Controller**. The primary and secondary interfaces should be listed, and your virtual IDE disks (and CD-ROM drives) should be beneath them.

Adding and Partitioning a New Disk

When you add a new, blank disk such as a VMware virtual IDE or SCSI disk, it doesn't show up under **My Computer**, and the drive letter doesn't appear anywhere, because the disk contains no partition table or filesystem. To create a partition table on the disk and mark one of the partitions as usable by Windows (by changing its partition ID to a filesystem type that Windows can handle, such as FAT16 or FAT32), use a tool such as FDISK. Here's how:

1. Bring up an MS-DOS prompt by choosing **Start • Programs • MS-DOS Prompt**; then run FDISK in the new MS-DOS window to start the disk partition program in interactive mode.

2. When asked whether to enable large disk support, answer Y.

3. You should see the screen shown in Figure 5.3. The current fixed disk drive is probably your system disk. Change it by typing 5 and pressing ENTER.

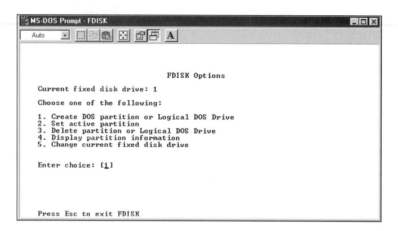

Figure 5.3: FDISK main menu

4. You should see a list of drives on your system; your new disk should also appear, though lacking a drive letter assignment. Type its number and press ENTER.

5. You should now be back at the main menu shown in Figure 5.3. Type 4 and press ENTER to display the partition information. For a new VMware virtual disk (or other brand-new, unformatted disk), you should see the message "No partitions defined." (If there are partitions, this may not be your new disk—try some other ones.) Press ESC to return to the main menu.

6. Type 1 to create a DOS partition. FDISK asks if you want to create primary or extended partitions. You'll probably want a primary partition. To do so, type 1 and press ENTER.

7. You're asked whether to fill the entire disk with the partition. Type Y and press ENTER if this is okay, or pick a size.

8. Once you confirm the size, you'll see a message saying that FDISK created the partition and did something with the drive letters. Press ESC twice to leave FDISK.

9. Before it exits, FDISK tells you that you must reboot your system for the changes to take effect. (Press ESC again, this time to *really* make FDISK go away.) Then reboot. (Rebooting will take a bit longer than normal.)

10. You should now have a new disk under **My Computer**, but you still need to put a filesystem on it (also called formatting the disk). Click *once* on the new drive in the **My Computer** display and then select **Format** from the **File** menu.

Be careful here. Windows may have reassigned your drive letters (such as you're the assignment for your CD-ROM drive).

11. A new window pops up. Verify the options here and click **Start**. When warned that this operation will wipe out whatever is on the drive, confirm that you're working with the right drive and click **OK**.

12. If you choose **Quick format**, just before the formatting starts, a message about mismatched drive capacity may appear. This is *not* an error message— it's just a diagnostic warning, and it also indicates that full formatting will be performed instead if you click OK. Click **OK**.

13. Once the formatting is complete, you'll see a summary of the new filesystem and a window telling you to run ScanDisk (as well as the help browser). Run **ScanDisk**, and you're done.

5.3.4 CD-ROM Drives

A VMware virtual CD-ROM drive appears in the **CDROM** category in the Device Manager, with a name like **NECVMWar VMware IDE CDR10**. As with IDE disks, you can't do much with **Settings**, under **Properties**. However, even though an ATAPI CD-ROM drive is an IDE device, it has a **Target ID** value in addition to its drive letter assignment.

Though you may have to search the devices by their connections to determine a CD-ROM's IDE interface, you can determine whether a CD-ROM drive is the master or slave by whether the target is 0 (for master) or 1 (for slave). You can assign a specific drive letter to a CD-ROM if you don't want another device to use that drive letter, under **Reserved drive letters**.

5.3.5 SCSI Devices

Because VMware's virtual SCSI controller is a PCI-type card, Windows 95 and 98 detect it as soon as you add a SCSI disk through VMware's Configuration Editor. The autodetect process will likely ask you to load the Windows CD-ROM. Although the SCSI controller shows up under **SCSI controllers** in the Device Manager, the disk shows up under **Disk drives**. (You can put a partition table on a disk the same way that you would for an IDE disk.)

A VMware SCSI disk should have a name such as **VMware Virtual hard dri**. You can verify that it is a SCSI disk because parameters such as **Target ID**, **Sync data transfer**, and **Disconnect** appear on the **Settings** tab of the disk's Properties screen. Furthermore, you can also determine which Windows drive letter corresponds to the target without looking at the device hierarchy as you would have to do for an IDE disk.

As in the Windows NT family, drivers for devices such as SCSI scanners and tape drives don't come with the operating system; you'll need drivers from the manufacturers.

5.3.6 Ethernet Interfaces

Network interfaces show up under **Network adapters** in the Windows 95 and 98 Device Manager. VMware devices have an **AMD PCNET Family Ethernet Adapter (PCI-ISA)** label. Because Windows automatically detects these devices, you will not need to add them manually to your guest system after you configure new devices with VMware's Configuration Editor. Windows should see the new virtual Ethernet card right after you boot your guest system, and it should then try to load its driver. (Have your Windows CD handy because you may need to insert it so that the system can get the driver files.)

Though the driver configuration shows up in the Device Manager, the actual protocol settings for network interfaces are on the **Network** control panel. We'll talk more about how to set this up in Chapter 9.

5.3.7 Serial Ports

In Windows 95/98/Me, you can view the serial ports with the Device Manager from the **System** control panel. Under VMware, six ports appear: **COM1** through **COM6**. Ignore the last two.

5.3.8 Parallel Ports

The Windows 95/98/Me Device Manager also shows parallel ports under **Ports**, though you can't really do much with a parallel port here except disable it. To use a port, you need to add another driver on top of it, by adding a printer or another removable device.

To add a new VMware parallel port under Windows 95/98/Me, follow these steps:

1. Open **Add New Hardware** on the control panel. After plug-and-play detection, select **No** ("the device is not in the list") and then click **Next**.

2. On the next screen, keep the default option **Yes** (to search for new hardware) and click **Next**.

3. When detection is complete (which may take a while), click **Details**; you should see a new printer port. That's it—you're done.

5.3.9 Mouse

You change the mouse tracking speed and buttons on the **Mouse** control panel; the Device Manager shows information about the mouse driver. The mouse should appear as a generic three-button mouse on the PS/2 mouse port, even if your real mouse only has two buttons.

5.3.10 Sound Card

Configuring a sound card under Windows 95, 98, and Me is similar to configuring one for Windows 2000/XP:

1. Click **Add/Remove Hardware** on the control panel to start the wizard.

2. Click **Next** twice, after which you will be asked whether the device you want to install is on the screen. Select **No** and click **Next**.

3. On the next screen, select **No** (select the hardware from a list) and click **Next**.

4. Scroll down to **Sound, video, and game controllers**, select this, and click **Next**.

5. On the next screen, click **Creative** in the left list box and **Sound Blaster 16 or AWE-32 or compatible**. Then click **Next**.

6. The dialog box asks whether you want to use the factory default settings. Since these are also the settings for VMware, click **Next**. (You may need to insert your Windows CD in the drive.)

7. Windows should report that it's done. Click **Finish** and reboot.

NOTE *Remember to turn the volume to its maximum level on your Windows guest system so that it plays at a normal level on your host system. (You can turn the system sounds off from the **Sounds** control panel.)*

5.3.11 USB Controller

As with Windows 2000/XP, you'll find two entries under **Universal serial bus controller** in the Windows 98/Me Device Manager: the controller itself and the USB root hub that it connects to. As you add USB devices, they show up here. Windows automatically detects USB hardware at boot time. However, you may need a driver—USB devices often require firmware and other things to work properly.

If you insert an unrecognized USB device, Windows declares that it doesn't know what to do with it and prompts you to install a driver. If you go through the entire process without installing a driver, Windows ignores the device until you explicitly add one. If you run a driver installation program, Windows should properly detect the new device when you reboot the Windows guest system. However, if the drivers are in a directory without an installation program, you need to do this:

1. Choose **Add New Hardware** in the control panel, click **Next** twice, and wait for Windows to identify the plug-and-play devices.

2. The USB device should show up in a list with a question mark next to it. Click it to highlight it and then click **Next**.

3. The Add New Hardware Wizard will report that there's a problem with the device. Click **Next** and then **Finish** to bring up a driver troubleshooting dialog box.

4. On the **General** tab, click **Reinstall Driver**.

5. On the screen that appears, click **Next** until you get to a screen where you can enter an explicit path. Enter the full pathname of the directory containing the driver's .INF files and proceed until you can click **Finish**.

Support for USB in Windows 95 depends on the release version. Release OSR 2.1 and later support USB. To check for USB support, open the **Add/Remove Programs** control panel and look for **USB Supplement to OSR2** on the **Install/Uninstall** tab.

5.4 VMware Tools for Windows

To get the most out of a Windows guest system, install the VMware Tools described in section 4.1. Don't put off the Tools installation. You'll make up for the time you spend installing the Tools almost right away.

As with other VMware Tools sets, there are two main components: a graphics driver to enable SVGA and full-screen video modes and the VMware Tools Properties. The graphics driver is of particular importance with Windows because your full-screen mode options are severely limited without it.

NOTE *A further incentive for installing the VMware graphics driver is that Microsoft embellishes almost every dialog box and menu action with some sort of animation. Your guest system takes much longer to perform animations in the default VGA16 graphics mode—and they get excruciatingly more tedious with every new release of Windows. For example, while Windows NT didn't have much in the way of bitplane-scrolled menus and alpha blending, Windows 2000 uses these effects heavily. Although you can turn off most of this stuff under the **Effects** tab on the **Display** control panel, there's little you can do about the animations.*

The Tools Properties described in the next section and in section 4.11 offers a number of handy features, such as the ability to move the mouse pointer out of the VMware guest operating system window by pushing it off the edge of the VMware screen. The VMware Tools software set for Windows is not large; you should be able to find its relevant files by searching for vm*.

To install the VMware Tools for your Windows guest system, follow these steps:

1. If the control panel window is open, close it.

2. Select **VMware Tools Install** from VMware's **Settings** menu. This temporarily replaces your virtual machine's CD-ROM drive with an image of the VMware Tools.

3. If your virtual machine has AutoRun enabled, the install program starts automatically. If it does not, then open **My Computer** on your desktop and double-click the VMware Tools CD-ROM icon.

4. Click **Next** numerous times to go through the installation process. The installer gives you the option of changing the install directory. Depending on your version of Windows, you may need to reboot your guest system after the installer completes.

IMPORTANT *If you're upgrading VMware Tools from a release prior to Workstation 3, see Appendix B for information on upgrading virtual hardware for information on how to upgrade the display drivers.*

5.4.1 Windows NT Only

If your guest operating system is Windows NT, you must perform some extra steps in order to use the new VMware graphics drivers. Do this just after step 4 (above):

4a. Click the **Display Type** button, and a new Display Type window appears. Click **Change**.

4b. A new window, Change Display, should appear. Click **Have Disk** and then type `d:\video\winnt` and press ENTER.

4c. The dialog disappears, and the Change Display window should now contain **VMware SVGA II**. Click **OK** and then **Yes** in the warning dialog box that follows.

4d. Close the **Display** control panel and reboot your NT guest system.

5. Your display should be noticeably faster now, and you're ready to tailor the display to your taste. Open the **Display** control panel again and select the **Settings** tab. Choose the resolution you want with the **Screen Area** slider. VMware sets the number of colors automatically from the host system.

5.4.2 VMware Tools Properties for Windows

When you install the VMware Tools on a Windows guest system, the Tools Properties go in your `Program Files\VMware` directory, and a **VMware Tools** item appears on your control panel. This brings up the VMware Tools Properties, described in section 4.11. However, you normally won't have to look for it here, because the installation process tries to put a shortcut in the system tray—it's a picture of the VMware logo. When you double-click this icon, the VMware Tools Properties window appears.

5.4.3 Dual Configurations and Hardware Profiles

If you choose to set up a Windows NT, 2000, XP, 95, 98, or Me guest system installed on a raw disk to boot both under and outside VMware, you'll need to set up different hardware configurations. Windows calls these *hardware profiles*. The idea is to have one profile for VMware that includes the VMware Tools graphics driver, and another profile suitable for your real hardware. When you boot your machine, you select the proper hardware profile. (Unlike with the dual configurations on Linux and FreeBSD, VMware Tools for Windows can't select a configuration for you at boot time; you must choose one manually at boot time.)

NOTE *If you're not quite sure how PCs boot, or if you have LILO on your boot block but don't know what it does, see section 2.4 for a brief explanation.*

Because some hardware and drivers are picky, you should create the new hardware profiles for VMware before you try to boot Windows as a guest system for the first time. To create the new profiles, follow these steps:

1. Open the **System** control panel. If you're using Windows NT, 95, 98, or Me, select the **Hardware Profiles** tab (Figure 5.4 shows the panel under Windows NT). If you're using Windows 2000 or XP, select the **Hardware** tab and click **Hardware Profiles** to bring up a new window with the same name.

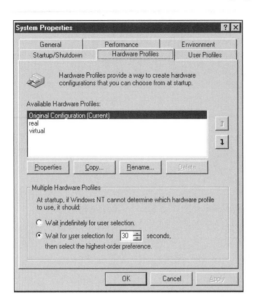

Figure 5.4: Windows NT hardware profile settings

2. Select **Original Configuration (Current)**, then click **Copy**.
3. When the dialog box for the new profile appears, name it real. You'll use this profile when you boot the system natively, and it can also serve as a backup for your original configuration.
4. Select the original configuration and click **Copy** again, but this time, name the copy virtual.
5. Click **OK** to close the Hardware Profiles window. When you bring up this window again, the new profiles appear.

Now is a good time to learn how to boot with a different hardware profile. See if you can boot from the **virtual** profile as follows:

Windows NT
After you select the default mode (not VGA mode) from the first boot menu, a screen appears for a few seconds that says "Press spacebar NOW for Hardware Profile/Last Known Good Menu." Press the spacebar before this screen disappears to see the Hardware Profile/Configuration Recovery menu. Move the cursor down to **virtual** and press ENTER.

Windows 2000/XP

At the initial text boot screen (the screen that says "Starting Windows 2000/XP"), press F8 to bring up an Options menu. Move the cursor down to Last Known Good Configuration and select it to activate the Hardware Profile/Configuration Recovery menu mentioned in the preceding section. Choose **virtual**.

Windows 95/98/Me

Windows should inform you that it doesn't know which configuration to use. Select the option number corresponding to **virtual**.

5.4.4 *Setting Up Your System for Dual Configuration*

Now that you know how to start Windows with a different hardware profile, it's time to set up your system for use under VMware:

1. Boot into your host system and start VMware Workstation.

2. Run the VMware Configuration Wizard to create a new VMware configuration, and when the disk options appear, select **Existing Physical Disk**. (You'll need read-write access to the devices; in particular, on a Linux host system, you must be able to read and write to the device file in /dev. If you don't have read-write access, the wizard complains about it, and you must click **Cancel**, fix the permissions, and rerun the wizard.)

3. Verify that your dual-boot system works properly. If LILO is your boot manager, turn off the **linear** option, if present (see the discussion on page 222 in section 12.2.10 for more information). Also, consider losing any graphic shown by the **message** keyword in your /etc/lilo.conf file.

4. When the partition table appears in the wizard, each partition should be marked **Read Only**. Choose **Read Write** for the guest system's partition, but leave the rest alone (you may want to mark any non-Microsoft partitions with **No Access**).

5. Complete the Configuration Wizard as usual and power on the virtual machine.

6. When the machine boots, go to the Hardware Profiles menu and choose the **virtual** profile, just like you did when you tested the profile earlier.

7. As soon as the guest system boots, install VMware Tools for Windows. Windows may open the **Display** control panel for you, and if the guest is Windows 95, 98, Me, 2000, or XP, you may have to do some of the next step before installing the VMware Tools.

8. Configure and install any other drivers necessary for the guest Windows system under VMware, such as an Ethernet driver. With the exception of sound, Windows 95, 98, 2000, and XP automatically detect VMware's virtual devices.

You're now ready to use the system as either a VMware guest or natively. Just remember that every time that you run Windows as a guest system under VMware, you should use your **virtual** hardware profile. When you switch between real and virtual configurations, the boot loader may open the profile option screen for you because it detects that the hardware has changed.

NOTE *To use the virtual hardware profile as the default, go to the **Hardware Profiles** tab on the **System** control panel again (see Figure 5.4 on page 86), select **virtual**, and then click the up arrow button a few times to get to the top of the list. Unless you change the profile options, your virtual profile should now be the default.*

5.5. Unix/GNU Utilities for Windows

If you're accustomed to a Unix environment, you may find it difficult to work with Windows due to a lack of powerful command-line tools. Even the command-line (DOS) prompt is a far cry from a normal shell. Fortunately, there are ports of many popular Unix utilities to Windows, most of which are based on the Cygwin Tools project (http://cygwin.com).

To install the Cygwin utilities, follow these steps:

1. Grab the setup.exe program on the Cygwin website and run it.

2. A new Cygwin Setup window comes up; click **Next** until the dialog box gives you a few installation options.

3. The easiest way to install the utilities if you have a network connection is to choose **Install from Internet**. Choose that option and click **Next**.

4. After a few more screens, choose **Direct Connection** for a list of mirror sites.

5. Pick a mirror site that is close to you and click **Next** to proceed.

6. A list of packages appears. By default, the setup program selects all packages for download. You can click any of them to skip them, or in some cases, also flip through version numbers. If you know Unix, then most of these packages should look familiar. Four in particular that you should get are fileutils, sh-utils, textutils, and bash. These include most of the familiar programs in /bin on a Unix machine, such as ls, mv, the [test program, and so on. You won't be able to do much of anything without a shell like bash.

7. When you're happy with your choices, click **Next** to begin the download.

8. Wait until everything downloads and installs. (This may take a while, depending on the speed of your connection.)

9. The setup program now gives you the option to add a desktop icon on your screen and a **Cygwin** item on your **Start** menu. Select whatever you prefer.

When you start Cygwin, a `bash` shell comes up in a new window. At first glance, this looks like an MS-DOS prompt. However, Cygwin twists the Windows environment to look like Unix. You type pathnames as you would on a Unix system—that is, you use a forward slash (/) instead of a backslash (\) as a path separator, and the / directory looks kind of like a Unix root. To get to your Windows files, use a command like `cd c:`. This takes you to `/cygdrive/c`. The `/cygdrive` directory maps Windows drive letters to the Cygwin directory space.

Although Cygwin gives you the option of installing `vim`, a `vi` imitation, there are plenty of other versions of `vi` out there, and if you're a diehard `vi` addict, you may have your own preference for this little editor. There are many versions: `elvis`, `stevie`, `vile`, and so on. Most have Windows versions, and some, like `elvis`, are even available for DOS. You may want to check out the `vi` lovers' home page at http://www.thomer.com/thomer/vi/vi.html if you have any particular interest in getting a `vi` clone. (You'll probably find a lot more at this website than you ever wanted to know.)

5.6 DOS and Windows 3.1

VMware runs many versions of DOS and Windows 3.1. These older systems are primitive compared to any modern operating system, and their driver structures are not very uniform. For example, there are several different network driver types, and to use one of the drivers, you need a set of network clients suitable for one specific kind of driver. Windows 3.1 may have additional drivers for some devices, which only adds to the confusion. Furthermore, a number of these drivers don't come with DOS or Windows 3.1; you need to get them from various vendors.

Installing DOS and Windows 3.1 onto a new virtual machine is the same as for a real computer, though you may find the process tedious because it involves floppy disks. You can speed this up a bit under VMware by dumping the floppy disk images to files on your host system and using the **File** type in the Configuration Editor. See sections 11.2 and 11.3 for more information.

NOTE *When you choose DOS or Windows 3.1 as your guest operating system from the Configuration Editor or Configuration Wizard, VMware chooses 16 MB of system memory. Although you might be able to get more to work (with the EMM386 driver), VMware reports that there are occasional problems with EMM386 and that you should comment out references to EMM386 in your CONFIG.SYS file if at all possible.*

There are no VMware Tools for Windows 3.1 or DOS. The generic Windows 3.1 VGA16 graphics driver works fairly well most of the time because the processor speed of any current computer is far greater than that of the machines that Windows 3.1 originally ran on. However, certain operations, such as maximizing windows, may be slow, especially if your host system is Linux and you don't turn on APM support (see the next section for help). Full-screen mode will improve graphics performance slightly.

5.6.1 DOS CPU Idler Utility and APM under Windows 3.1

By default, DOS doesn't idle the processor when it isn't doing anything. This has fairly serious consequences when you run a DOS system as a VMware guest—see section 8.1 for a full explanation. You can get around this in DOS with a program called DOSidle (available at the VMware website). This is a terminate-and-stay-resident (TSR) utility that runs a CPU halt instruction or advanced power management BIOS calls during idle loops. This effectively reduces the CPU usage to zero when DOS isn't doing anything—which is most of the time. To make DOSidle active every time you start your system, put it in your autoexec.bat file.

To achieve the same power savings under Windows 3.x, activate APM support:

1. At the DOS prompt, go to your WINDOWS directory (usually C:\WINDOWS) and run setup.

2. Move the cursor up to the line that starts Computer: and press ENTER.

3. A list of choices appears in a box; move the cursor down to MS-DOS System with APM and press ENTER. You'll probably need your Windows 3.x install disks handy, because Windows will need to copy the drivers.

NOTE *Because DOS doesn't have a real kernel, this utility doesn't work during execution of all programs; it functions only when a program runs a DOS library call.*

5.6.2 IDE Disks

DOS and Windows get their information about VMware's IDE disks through the BIOS. However, the drive letter assignments are a function of the partition tables on the disks. Each DOS (FAT) partition gets its own drive letter, and DOS usually assigns letters as it finds partitions and drives.

When you add a new VMware virtual disk to a DOS/Windows configuration, it has no partition table, and DOS does not recognize it. To set up the disk properly, you must partition it with FDISK. The procedure for doing so is exactly as described earlier in this chapter for Windows 95/98/Me, in section 5.3.3 on page 80.

Once you get the partition table on the disk, determine the drive letter DOS has assigned to the disk (run FDISK again, press 5, and then view the display). Next, format the new drive (for example, with format d:), but be very sure that you choose the correct drive letter or you will lose data. (You can test your choice by trying to access that drive before you format; if you get the "Abort, Retry, Fail" error message, it's likely that you found the right drive.)

NOTE *Don't configure any SCSI disks (explained later) while partitioning new IDE disks. FDISK won't see more than one drive if the VMware virtual SCSI controller is present.*

5.6.3 CD-ROM Drive

Although ATAPI CD-ROM support doesn't come with DOS, plenty of add-in drivers are available, though not all of them work under VMware Workstation. One driver that reportedly performs well is the Mitsumi driver (http://www. mitsumi.com). The driver archive has a name like IDE158.EXE. After unpacking this archive, you can run the setupd command to put the driver in place, or look at the manual installation instructions. The end result in any case is that you'll change your AUTOEXEC.BAT and CONFIG.SYS files. After the driver is installed, you must reboot your system for the changes to take place.

You do not need an additional Windows 3.1 driver for VMware CD-ROM drives.

5.6.4 SCSI Devices

To use SCSI disks and devices under VMware, you'll need the BusLogic Multi-Master drivers from Mylex (http://www.mylex.com). These drivers are for the BT series, and the driver archive should have a name like DOSASPI.EXE.

To add the drivers to your system, add this line to your CONFIG.SYS file:

```
DEVICE=C:\BUSLOGIC\BTDOSM.SYS /D
```

This entry assumes that you unpacked the drivers into C:\BUSLOGIC, and turns the DOS BusLogic SCSI Manager driver on at boot time. It is not strictly necessary for disk support, but some utilities require it, as discussed later.

If you're adding new SCSI virtual disks, use BTFDISK (BTFDISK.EXE) to put a table and partitions on the disks. This program will not work without the BTDOSM.SYS driver, and it operates only on SCSI disks; however, though you should not need the BTMDISK.SYS driver that comes with the package (the VMware BIOS and DOS should be able to figure out the disk assignments). If you put a reference to BTMDISK.SYS in your CONFIG.SYS file, each SCSI disk appears under *two* drive letter assignments (say, D: and E:).

You won't need an additional driver to access SCSI disks with Windows 3.1 under VMware.

5.6.5 Floppy Drives

PC-style floppy drives and their controller interfaces are primitive and don't really give the operating system much information unless specifically called upon. True to form, DOS won't recognize a VMware floppy drive until you enter something like cd a:\ to switch to the first floppy drive.

One odd feature of DOS is that you can multiplex a single floppy drive. If you try to access B: with only one floppy present, DOS prompts you to insert the floppy for that particular drive letter and press ENTER. Afterward, when you access something on A:, DOS prompts you to put a floppy in again. However, because VMware offers two floppy drives and you can map them to files instead of actual devices, you might think to add another floppy to B:. Make sure that you go into the VMware BIOS and add the drive there if you configure another floppy drive. DOS believes the BIOS, and if it still thinks that you only have one floppy drive, any access to B: won't go to the second virtual floppy, but to the multiplexer system, and DOS will ask you to put a floppy disk into the first drive.

All of this talk about floppies under DOS may seem strange, but remember that most DOS software came on floppy disks. If you master how to use a file as VMware's virtual floppy, as well as disconnecting and reconnecting, you can save yourself a lot of time.

5.6.6 Ethernet Interfaces

Because DOS has no single unified network model for Ethernet cards, the driver that you need for your virtual Ethernet card depends on the client that you want to run. The AMD website (http://www.amd.com/) lists a number of DOS drivers for AMD PCNet32 Family cards. In addition to the drivers for IBM NDIS2/3 and other schemes, there's a packet driver that you'll need if you want to use TCP/IP—it doesn't have a label that marks it as a DOS driver. There are also drivers for different versions of Windows for Workgroups 3.x and Windows 3.11. However, none of the driver archives on AMD's site unpack on 16-bit Windows 3.1 or DOS—you have to unpack them from a 32-bit Windows system such as 95 or NT, then transfer them to a DOS system.

As in the rest of this book, our focus is on IP networking. To get networking working in DOS, you need the packet driver, a TCP stack, and some applications. First, create a directory C:\PACKET and put the entire contents of the packet driver (from AMD) there. PCNTPK.COM should be among the files; this is the actual driver. Put this line in your AUTOEXEC.BAT file to activate the driver at boot time:

```
C:\PACKET\PCNTPK INT=0x60
```

INT=0x60 is called a software interrupt. Any value between 0x60 and 0x80 is fine here (you can test this at the C:\> prompt to see if it works if you don't want to modify your startup file right away). Now reboot your computer. When it comes up again, you should get a confirmation of the IRQ, I/O port and Ethernet address (which should start with 00:50:56). To verify that the driver is active, use a command like PKTCHK 0x60—you'll find this program and others along with the packet driver. Note that some of the utilities try to put the interface into promiscuous mode, and if you (as the user running VMware Workstation) don't have permission to do that on your host machine, then VMware won't let you do it on the guest machine.

Now you're ready to deal with the TCP stack and applications. Unfortunately, there are too many stacks and applications to list here. If you're interested in a free-of-charge stack, look for WATTCP. Otherwise, you can purchase them (for example, from IBM or Microsoft).

To install the driver under Windows for Workgroups 3.1, open the **Network Settings** control panel and click the **Adapters** button; a new window appears. Click **Add**. If you don't see the PCnet driver in the list, select **Unlisted**; then enter the path to the drivers (this should be where you put the OEMSETUP.INF and PCNTND.DOS files from the driver archive).

To install the driver under Windows 3.11, follow these steps:

1. Open **Windows Setup** from the Main window to bring up a setup program.
2. Select **Options • Change Network Settings**.
3. Click the **Drivers** button and then **Add Adapter** in the new window that appears.
4. If PCnet is in the list, you might try that; otherwise, choose **Unlisted** and click **OK**.
5. If you chose **Unlisted**, Windows asks where it can find the drivers. Type the path to the PCI drivers, such as a:\pcnet\pci.

5.6.7 Serial and Parallel Ports

In DOS and Windows 3.1, there really isn't much configuration involved on VMware's serial and parallel ports. The serial ports show up as COM1, COM2, COM3, and COM4, and the parallel ports are LPT1 and LPT2. DOS and Windows just expect the ports to be there at the standard hardware assignments, but they don't actually bother much with looking for the hardware until you actually try to use one of the ports.

You can change serial port hardware settings if you wish. For example, in Windows 3.1, the **Ports** control panel offers **Settings** options for a port (use the **Advanced** button to see hardware assignments). However, there's really no need to do any of this unless your installation was copied from a machine that did not have matching hardware.

To see whether VMware's ports are working, change the virtual devices to files in the Configuration Editor. For example, if you change the first parallel port to /tmp/lptest (for a Linux host system), you run a DOS command like copy autoexec.bat lpt1: after you connect the device to see whether DOS is connecting to the VMware device. The command won't run too quickly, but eventually you should get the contents of your DOS guest's autoexec.bat file in /tmp/lptest on your host system.

5.6.8 Mouse

Since VMware's mouse under most configurations is a PS/2 type, you shouldn't have any difficulty getting it to work under Windows 3.1. The Windows 3.1 installation program recognizes VMware's mouse device automatically. If you're using an old configuration that you pulled from an old machine, though, you may need to run the SETUP.EXE program in your WINDOWS directory to configure it correctly, because many older mouse devices connected to the serial port. The proper setting under Mouse: is Microsoft or IBM PS/2. (You will also need to remove any serial port mouse drivers in your CONFIG.SYS file.)

If you really need a mouse driver for DOS, or if you want to use a mouse with three buttons, try a commonly available driver. There's a free-of-charge driver called CuteMouse mentioned in section 8.5.1. Other than games (which may or may not run quickly under VMware), not a lot of programs support the mouse under DOS (elvis, interestingly enough, does).

5.6.9 Sound Card

To get sound to work with DOS or Windows 3.1 on a guest system under VMware, install the Sound Blaster 16 driver from the Support section of the Creative Technology website (http://www.creative.com). You should find this driver as a single executable file called sbbasic.exe.

Copy sbbasic.exe to a temporary directory on your virtual hard drive and, from an MS-DOS prompt, run sbbasic to extract the contents of the driver archive, including the installer program install.exe; then run install. You'll get a few information screens, one of which gives the default pathnames for the installed drivers. The card's path should be SB16, and if you have Windows 3.1, it should show up as WINDOWS. Press ENTER after you finish with this screen.

If you configured and installed the sound card in VMware's Configuration Editor, the installer should automatically detect the card with its base I/O address at 220, the interrupt at 5, and the Low DMA setting at 1. If the sound card was not configured and installed, you probably forgot to add the sound card to your virtual machine's configuration. If so, press F3 to exit, turn off your guest system, configure the sound card, and try again.

The installer now puts a number of files in place, updates your configuration files (such as AUTOEXEC.BAT), and may give you an option to back up some of your older configuration files. At the end of the installation process, you need to reboot your computer.

If you have Windows 3.1, the next time you start it after installing the drivers you should get a status message from the Windows side of the sound card installer and see a window with the Creative Mixer. To test your sound installation, make sure that it's connected under VMware, open the mixer (in SB16\winappl), and turn the master volume (leftmost slider) all the way up. Then open the **Sound** control panel and test some of the sounds. (The installer also puts a new driver on the **Drivers** control panel, **Creative SB16 Wave / Aux / Mixer / MidiPort**, though you can't really do much at this panel other than remove the driver.)

5.6.10 USB Devices

USB support for MS-DOS and Windows 3.1 is sparse. Some device makers provide drivers for their own devices, usually integrated with a host controller driver. However, it's often easier to get the device working on your host operating system and use it through that driver. For example, you can get a removable-media device working from a Linux host system by installing it as a SCSI device and then adding the device as a SCSI disk to your guest system's configuration.

6

LINUX GUEST
OPERATING SYSTEMS

Linux is the most popular flavor of Unix on the x86 architecture. It began life as Linus Torvalds' little kernel, intended only for hackers. He posted to Usenet in 1991 announcing its availability and saying that it was fine to hack on it. Many people did. Aiding development significantly was the GNU project.

All Linux distributions contain the Linux kernel, numerous system and user packages, and an installer. Because Linux uses open source code, allowing anyone to do almost anything they want with it, there many different Linux distributions. The more common distributions include Red Hat, Mandrake, Debian, S.u.S.E., Caldera, Corel, and TurboLinux, though there are many others.

The Linux distributions differ based on their intended audience. For example, Corel, Mandrake, Red Hat, and S.u.S.E are end-user oriented, while TurboLinux and Caldera target the server platform. (Debian is a clean, low-frills system that appeals more to experienced Unix purists.)

6.1 Running Linux as a Guest under VMware

If you're planning to use Linux under VMware, you'll need to know a few Unix basics to get the most out of it. This chapter assumes that you're familiar with the way files and directories look under Linux, and how to navigate the directory structure (using cd, ls, and so on). This chapter also assumes that you know how to use a text editor, preferably vi or emacs. If you have ever had an account on any kind of Unix system, you probably won't have a problem with anything here.

Much of the material we'll discuss here is intended for use at a shell command prompt, accessed either from a virtual terminal in text mode or from a terminal window, if you're running a Linux GUI under the X Window System. (Look for a menu item labeled **Terminal**, **Shell**, **Command Prompt**, **xterm**, or something like this, or an icon that looks like a black-and-white terminal screen). When this chapter says "type this," type at the command prompt in one of these windows or at the console.

NOTE *Because we'll mainly talk about system configuration, you'll need to do most of the tasks in this chapter as the superuser (root).*

6.2 System Requirements

Linux hardware requirements are relatively light. The kernel itself doesn't use much memory, and the rest of the system's demands depend on how many services you run and whether you use the X Window System.

If you have a machine running VMware, and a guest operating system of Windows runs fairly slowly, there's a good chance that Linux as a guest system will run faster, especially if you run it only in text mode. Adding X consumes more resources, particularly memory, and large GUI environments such as GNOME or KDE consume more memory than almost anything else on a typical Linux system.

6.3 Installing Linux under VMware

Because Linux supports every device that VMware emulates, it's not difficult to install a working Linux system under VMware. Still, knowing a few things will speed up the process and make it as painless as possible.

1. First, if you're using a VMware virtual disk, decide which type of disk you want to use. By default, the VMware Configuration Wizard creates a SCSI virtual disk if you choose Linux as the guest operating system. Although SCSI virtual disks offer better performance than their ATA/IDE counterparts, many Linux distributions include the SCSI controller drivers as modules. Therefore, you may need to perform some extra steps at installation and/or boot time if you choose SCSI disks. (If you want to use an IDE disk instead, use the Configuration Editor to add one and remove the SCSI disk.)

2. If your distribution lets you choose between fancy graphical and plain-text installation interfaces, choose the plain-text one. The graphical interface will likely work under VMware, but not only will it be slow to work with, it will also slow down the installation process itself. This delay occurs because the operating system installer runs the VGA16 X server, which is itself slow; and running it under VMware makes it worse. That's not to mention the extra memory that the X server and installation interface hog—memory that would be better used for caching.

To use the plain-text installer under Red Hat, type text at the prompt when you first start from the CD. (Many other distributions, such as Debian, offer only a text-based installation interface.)

3. Install certain optional packages for your Linux guest system, especially perl. Without perl, the VMware Tools installer won't work. If you want to use many of VMware's extra features, you'll also need to install the X Window System (XFree86 on Linux). Finally, it can be very handy to install a working C compiler along with the Linux kernel source code. Linux installers often refer to these as C Development or Kernel Development.

4. Install the guest Linux system as you would on a real machine. You needn't configure the X server right away, and if you have an option to start a graphical display manager (such as GNOME's gdm, KDE's kdm, or xdm) at boot time, keep it off until you have VMware Tools for Linux installed and working properly (see the next section). If you get in a jam, though, and the installation process demands that you install and configure an X server, use the VGA16 server (also known as Generic VGA). If an installer asks you about video memory, reply with 256K, and if it asks you about a monitor, give it any answer.

   If the installer asks whether you want to make an emergency boot floppy, you can use a VMware trick: disconnect the virtual floppy drive, switch the virtual floppy configuration to a file instead of a device, create the file, and then reconnect the floppy. Tell the Linux installer to make the floppy, and after it finishes, disconnect the floppy drive and restore the floppy configuration to its original state. Remember the file name of your virtual floppy file; it's there if you need it. (See section 11.2.3 to learn how to create a virtual floppy file.)

5. Install VMware Tools for Linux (see section 6.5).

6.4 Running Existing Linux Installations under VMware

If you've already installed Linux on your machine, you'll use a raw (physical) disk device in the VMware configuration for the disk on the machine.

When you boot Linux under VMware Workstation, it's likely that many drivers won't work, instead spewing nasty-looking errors. These drivers tend to be noncritical, and your system will boot fine without them. However, there is one service that, if installed, you must turn off before running your guest system under VMware: any display manager that starts the X Window System immediately upon boot. If you use startx or xinit to run an X session, you need not worry, but if GNOME, KDE, or xdm run the X server and pop up a graphical log-in box as soon as the system boots, you have to figure out how to turn off the display manager, or under VMware, the display manager may continuously respawn (making your guest system unusable until you reboot) or possibly crash the system.

Unfortunately, the configuration is different for each Linux distribution.

Red Hat makes `init` run the display manager, so its configuration is in `/etc/inittab`. If you take a look at this file, you'll see some lines like this:

```
# Default runlevel. The runlevels used by RHS are:
#   0 - halt (Do NOT set initdefault to this)
#   1 - Single user mode
#   2 - Multiuser, without NFS (The same as 3, if you do not have networking)
#   3 - Full multiuser mode
#   4 - unused
#   5 - X11
#   6 - reboot (Do NOT set initdefault to this)
#
:id:5:initdefault
```

Here, you can see that the default runlevel is 5, meaning that `init` tries to start some kind of display manager for X (see the very end of the `inittab` file for the specific command). To deactivate the display manager, change the 5 to a 3 in the `:id:` line, so that it reads

```
:id:3:initdefault
```

The next time you boot, you should get a simple log-in prompt in text mode instead of a fancy graphic log-in box. To return things to the way they were, change the 3 back to a 5.

WARNING *Take special care not to butcher the `/etc/inittab` file. If the changes do not appear exactly as shown in the preceding code, your system will malfunction—possibly spectacularly.*

Other Linux distributions start display managers from the `init.d` and `rc*.d` directories, found either in `/etc` or `/etc/rc.d`. Look in the `init.d` directory for a file named `xdm`, `gnome`, `kde`, or something similar. Using

```
egrep 'xdm|kdm|gdm' *
```

may help.

Once you've found the file, edit it by adding the following after its first line:

```
exit 0
```

NOTE *Be sure to document what you did, because you'll likely want to go back and delete that line to re-enable the display once you have the VMware X server working.*

Once you have the system working under VMware, it's time to install the VMware Tools; see the next section.

6.5 VMware Tools for Linux

Install the VMware Tools to get the most out of your Linux guest system. The primary benefits of VMware Tools are optimal graphics performance and full-screen mode; they also enable several input options, and you can install automatic dual configuration files for dual-boot machines.

6.5.1 Installing VMware Tools

To start the VMware Tools installation, do the following:

1. Unmount any CD-ROMs from your Linux guest system and make sure that you have `perl` installed. Then select the **VMware Tools Install** option from the VMware **Settings** menu.

2. Become `root` and mount the CD-ROM image on your (guest) system:

```
mount -r -t iso9660 /dev/cdrom /cdrom
```

If `/dev/cdrom` is not a link to your guest system's CD-ROM device, use `dmesg | grep hd` to find the correct `/dev` entry. Some systems may automatically attach the CD-ROM drive, in which case you may not need to perform this step at all.

3. You should see a compressed archive called `vmware-linux-tools.tar.gz` in `/cdrom`. Extract its contents and unmount the CD-ROM image from your system (if you forget, the Linux kernel will get angry if you later pull a mounted device out from under its nose):

```
cd /var/tmp
tar zxf /cdrom/vmware-linux-tools.tar.gz
umount /cdrom
```

4. You now have a new directory, `/var/tmp/vmware-linux-tools`. `cd` to that directory and run the installer program:

```
cd vmware-tools-linux
./install.pl
```

5. Enter yes when the installer asks if you really want to proceed. After installing all files, the installer starts the host-to-guest system time synchronization daemon, sets up dual configuration, tweaks a few operating system parameters, and restarts the mouse daemon (gpm) if necessary.

6. Run `ps auxww | grep guestd` to see if the VMware guest operating system daemon (`vmware-guestd`) is running. This program provides synchronization services between the guest and host operating systems.

7. Inspect the VMware X server (see the next section).

NOTE *The best mouse driver for VMware Workstation is the PS/2 Intellimouse type; the installer may ask if you want to use inconsistent drivers if* gpm *doesn't support the Intellimouse (*imps2*) driver. Answer* no *to that question unless you really know what you're doing.*

NOTE *If you change your mind and decide not to install VMware Tools, make sure that the virtual CD-ROM drive is unmounted (*cd /; umount /cdrom*) and select* **Cancel VMware Tools Install** *from the* **Settings** *menu.*

6.5.2 XFree86 Server Configuration

The VMware Tools for Linux includes new graphics drivers and a new server for the X Window System. Using it while running the guest Linux system under VMware not only enables you to run X sessions with higher resolutions and more colors (also in full-screen mode), but also greatly improves session performance over that with the VGA16 driver.

Most Linux distributions include XFree86, the free X Window System server. There are two versions of XFree86 in current distributions: 3.*x* and 4.*x*. The Tools installer detects the version installed on your system and installs the proper programs, drivers, and configuration files. (To determine the version you're using, look for a /usr/X11R6/lib/modules directory. If it exists, you have XFree86 4.)

XFree86 Version 3

Graphics drivers in XFree86 3.*x* are compiled directly into the server program. VMware Tools for Linux includes such a server, called XF86_VMware. The configuration file is called XF86Config. The X server normally looks for this file in /usr/X11R6/lib/X11, but this is often a symbolic link to some other place on the system, the location of which depends on your distribution. Red Hat, for example, keeps the real XF86Config file in /etc/X11, and some versions of Debian use /etc. The VMware Tools installer attempts to place a server configuration file for XF86_VMware, named XF86Config.vm, in this directory.

The installer then renames any preexisting XF86Config file to XF86Config.org and creates a symbolic link from XF86Config to XF86Config.vm. The XF86Config* files should now look something like this:

```
lrwxrwxrwx 1 root root    22 Mar 11  2001 XF86Config -> /etc/X11/XF86Config.vm
-rw-r--r-- 1 root root 15456 Mar  7 04:27 XF86Config.org
-rw-r--r-- 1 root root  3801 Mar  8 14:07 XF86Config.vm
```

The installer does the same thing with the symbolic link to the X server, which is simply named X. This can get confusing, because the installer renames a link and then creates two more. This is how /etc/X11/X on a Red Hat system with the XF86_SVGA server looks before the VMware Tools installer runs:

```
lrwxrwxrwx 1 root root    30 Mar  7 04:27 X -> ../../usr/X11R6/bin/XF86_SVGA
```

(Remember that *../../* is just / here.) This it what it looks like afterward:

```
lrwxrwxrwx 1 root root    13 Mar 11  2001 X -> /etc/X11/X.vm
lrwxrwxrwx 1 root root    30 Mar  7 04:27 X.org -> ../../usr/X11R6/bin/XF86_SVGA
lrwxrwxrwx 1 root root    26 Mar  8 14:07 X.vm -> /usr/X11R6/bin/XF86_VMware
```

On other systems (such as Caldera), the X link may be in /usr/X11R6/bin. If the Tools installer figures out the link, it leaves information in /etc/vmware/ tools_log. If it doesn't, you'll need to hunt down these files and create the links yourself.

Still other distributions (like Debian) use a different scheme. Instead of a link called X, they use the Xserver file, also in /etc/X11. The first two lines of this file look something like this:

```
/usr/X11R6/bin/XF86_VGA16
Console
```

The first line tells you which X server to use. To use the X server that comes with VMware Tools, you can simply change the line to /usr/X11R6/ bin/XF86_VMware.

Given what you've seen of the VMware Tools installer so far, you might expect that it would move the original Xserver file to Xserver.org, create a new file called Xserver.vm with the necessary changes for use under VMware, and create a symbolic link from Xserver to Xserver.vm. However, this is not the case.

Instead, the Tools installer looks for the original server executable in the first line of the Xserver file—say XF86_VGA16. Once it finds the server, the installer renames the server *binary* to XF86_VGA16.org and creates two more symbolic links, one called XF86_VGA16.vm pointing to XF86_VMware, and the other called XF86_VGA16 pointing to the first, XF86_VGA16.vm, so that your /usr/X11R6/bin directory now looks like this:

```
lrwxrwxrwx 1 root root        13 Mar 13 03:04 XF86_VGA16 -> XF86_VGA16.vm
-rwxr-xr-x 1 root root   1846152 Nov 20 18:54 XF86_VGA16.org
lrwxrwxrwx 1 root root        11 Mar 13 03:04 XF86_VGA16.vm -> XF86_Vmware
-r-xr-xr-x 1 root root   1868576 Mar 13 03:03 XF86_VMware
```

You may be wondering what the point is of naming files and links with .org and .vm extensions. The ultimate purpose is to enable dual configurations. For example, if you had not originally installed the Linux guest system under VMware, and if you still want to run it on your real hardware, you'll want your Linux configuration files to match the real hardware instead of VMware's virtual hardware so that the Linux system won't blow up in your face. The VMware Tools installer tries to take care of this for you, and we'll get to how it does this in section 6.5.7. But first let's test the XF86_VMware X server and adjust the resolution to something that suits your monitor and taste (see section 6.5.3).

XFree86 Version 4

In XFree86 version 4.*x*, rather than separate binaries for various video card drivers, there is only one X server binary, and the drivers are loaded as shared libraries. For this reason, VMware also has a driver module for XFree86 4 called vmware_drv.o. In addition to the driver included with VMware Tools for Linux, it also comes with XFree86 4.1 and above.

The Tools installer should put the driver module, vmware_drv.o, in your /usr/X11R6/lib/modules directory. However, the name of your configuration file depends on your distribution. Most distributions use /etc/X11/XF86Config-4, but /etc/X11/XF86Config works fine. This can get confusing because if you have XF86Config *and* XF86Config-4, the X server uses XF86Config-4. In any case, the Tools installer will detect which one you need, rename your original file with a .org extension, and install a new one with a .vm extension, as it would for XFree86 3.*x* (see the previous section).

6.5.3   *Testing and Customizing the VMware X Server*

To test the VMware X server, type X and see if the VMware window or screen changes to a 1280x1024 screen that looks like Figure 6.1. If so, and if you can move the mouse pointer, your server works; kill it with CTRL-ALT-BACKSPACE.

If you get a 640x480 screen that also looks like Figure 6.1, you're running XF86_VGA16, which works under VMware, but is very slow (and ugly). In this case (or if you didn't get anything at all), find the links and/or files mentioned in the previous section and fix them.

Figure 6.1: X server with no applications

A resolution of 1280x1024 can be uncomfortable to work with if your monitor is small. To change this setting in XFree86 3.*x*, edit the XF86Config.vm file at the end, where it looks like this:

```
Section "Screen"
    Driver "accel"
    Device "SVGA"
    Monitor "vmware"
    Subsection "Display"
        Modes "1280x1024"
#       Modes "1600x1200" "1280x1024" "1152x864" "1024x768" "800x600"
#       Modes "640x480"
#       Modes "800x600"
#       Modes "1024x768"

..
```

Lines beginning with # are commented out and inactive; as you can see, the mode 1280x1028 is the default active mode since it's the only one without the #. To change modes, put a # in front of the active line to deactivate it, and remove the # in front of the mode you want to use.

The change takes effect when the X server restarts.

For XFree86 4.*x*, you have to change the Screen section in the XF86Config or XF86Config-4 file. Here's an example for a 24-bit, 1024x768 display:

```
Section "Screen"
    Identifier          "Screen 1"
    Device              "VMware SVGA"
    Monitor             "VMware Monitor"

    SubSection "Display"
        Depth           24
        Modes           "1024x768"
    EndSubSection
EndSection
```

Now you're ready to use the X Window System. You can either use startx or xinit to start a session, or you can activate a display manager, such as gdm (GNOME), kdm (KDE), or xdm. (We discussed how to deactivate these systems in section 6.4 earlier in the chapter when we discussed how to make a preexisting Linux installation run under VMware.)

If you have trouble with the XF86_VMware server, it might be because of shared library dependencies. Although it doesn't depend on any XFree86 3.*x* shared libraries and can run without the rest of XFree86 3.*x*, there may be other dependencies; use ldd XF86_VMware to find them. If you can't install the libraries, then you should consider using the VMware SVGA driver for XFree86 4.*x*.

6.5.4   Additional VMware X Server Information

Unlike most display drivers, XFree86 servers and their driver modules are meant to provide almost any resolution and bit depth without complaint. XFree86 lets you get away with almost anything; if you want a resolution of 800x100, that's fine, as long as you can figure out the monitor timings.

The VMware X server takes this one step further; because it runs through a virtual display, you really can define the resolution any way you like.

If you look at the Monitor section in the XF86Config file provided by VMware (and you should), you'll see a number of display sizes that aren't standard (such as 2364x1773). If you want to add a new mode, the ModeLine is simple to "compute" — just add 1 to each consecutive number after the horizontal and vertical pixel figures. However, there is one small constraint: the horizontal resolution must be a multiple of 8 (if it's not, the VMware X server rounds it up to the next multiple of 8).

6.5.5   The VMware Toolbox

To access a few additional VMware features pertaining to the interaction between the host and guest operating systems, you'll need to use the VMware Toolbox. By default, the tools installer puts this in the X binary directory, /usr/X11R6/bin, as a single program named vmware-toolbox.

The Toolbox enables copying and pasting between the guest and host systems. Specifically, the Toolbox grabs and manipulates information about the XA_PRIMARY selection. The vmware-toolbox program must be running for this feature to work on a Linux guest system.

There's also an option here for time synchronization. Time synchronization causes the guest operating system to set its system time to the host system's clock. You'll likely never need to use it, because vmware-guestd already takes care of time synchronization.

6.5.6   The VMware Toolbox and X Startup Files

Because vmware-toolbox also acts as a mediator between VMware and guest operating system input devices (the mouse in particular), you should keep it running whenever you have an X session open on your guest system. In addition to the menu item on the **View** menu, there are two command-line options, --iconify and --minimize, which instruct the VMware Toolbox to start as an icon, to keep it out of your way.

Probably the best startup command is

```
vmware-toolbox --minimize -geometry -0+0 &
```

which runs the Toolbox minimized at the top right of the screen. For simple windowing startup schemes like xinit and xdm, all you have to do is insert that line before your window manager's invocation in your .xinitrc or .xsession file. However, more complicated systems generally require some pointing and clicking. For example, in GNOME (see Figure 6.2), you have to click the little toolbox icon in the panel in the lower part of the screen to bring up the GNOME configuration tool and then click **Startup Programs**, under **Session**, and add the command (just type the line above, without the &, in the text entry box). The result is that the config tool makes some entries in your `.gnome/session-manual` file that you probably wouldn't have liked typing by hand, and the next time you start a GNOME session, you'll see a `vmware-toolbox` icon at the top right of the screen.

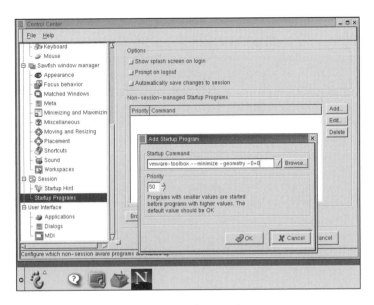

Figure 6.2: VMware Toolbox startup with GNOME

For KDE, it's easiest just to hack up a KDE startup file by hand, as you would a `.xinitrc` file. On Red Hat 7, for instance, the KDE startup sequence is `/usr/sbin/startkde`. If you add the preceding line just before the invocation of `kwm` (near the end of the file), `vmware-toolbox` will start before a KDE session. When you exit the session, KDE complains that VMware Tools for Linux isn't X11 aware. Ignore that message.

NOTE *If, after making these changes, your X session starts the VMware Toolbox but not the window manager (no title bars on your windows, or your session somehow looks incomplete), you probably forgot to add the ampersand (&) to the end of the* vmware-toolbox *command. To get your window manager in your current session, quit the VMware Toolbox and then fix your startup file.*

6.5.7 Other VMware Tools for Linux and Dual Configuration

In addition to the new X server and `vmware-toolbox`, the installer places a number of items elsewhere on the system. To find out what they are, look in the file `/etc/vmware-tools/tools_log`, which the tools installer creates.

In addition to `tools_log`, you'll find some files pertaining to `dualconf`. These allow for seamless *dual configuration* of the Linux guest operating system if it is located on a real disk instead of in a virtual disk file. If you originally installed Linux on a multiboot system without VMware, your distribution likely probed your real hardware and customized the kernel module configuration as well as the XFree86 configuration file.

Even if you don't actually use two different configurations, VMware Tools for Linux still uses the dual-configuration tools to set up certain services for your guest system when it boots.

Because VMware Workstation provides a hardware interface different than your real hardware, your system must figure out whether it's running on your real hardware or as a guest operating system and adjust the configuration files accordingly. The program /etc/vmware-tools/checkvm is the key to this. If run under VMware, it gives an affirmative message, and more important, it sets its exit code to 0. This is not only useful at system boot time, but you can also employ it in your X session startup scripts. We'll go into a little more detail about that in section 6.5.8.

Most Linux systems use the System V init program to boot. In this scheme, a directory called init.d contains a number of system startup scripts, which initialize system services. There are also a number of directories named rc0.d through rc6.d; the number corresponds to a *runlevel*; different runlevels specify normal boot, single-user boot, halt, shutdown, and other statuses. Each rc*n*.d directory contains symbolic links pointing to the scripts in the init.d directory, named S*XYname* or K*XYname*, where *XY* is a number between 00 and 99 (specifying when init runs this link in relation to the other links), and *name* is usually the name of the script in init.d. S means run the script in start mode, and K means to use stop mode.

The location of these directories depends on your Linux distribution. Red Hat puts them in /etc/rc.d; Debian keeps them right in /etc. Other distributions follow one of these conventions, or a mix.

The VMware Tools installer looks for these directories, and if it finds them, it installs a script called dualconf in init.d and attempts links to it in the rc*.d directories. Specifically, it looks for existing links matching S*network, and if it finds them, it adds a new S*XY*dualconf link, where *XY* is the same as it was for the network script. Although this works for some distributions, such as Red Hat, it does not work for others (Debian, for instance), so you'll need to put the links in by hand if the Tools installer can't figure out what to do.

If you look at the dualconf script in the init.d directory, you'll notice that it's very simple: if the system is running under VMware, it executes /etc/vmware-tools/dualconf.vm; otherwise, it runs /etc/vmware-tools/dualconf.org.

These scripts manipulate three symbolic links: to /etc/modules.conf, the XFree86 configuration file (see section 6.5.2), and if you're running XFree86 3.*x* on the guest system, the X server executable (named X; in Red Hat, it's another symbolic link in /etc/X11). The /etc/modules.conf file is a general configuration file for kernel modules and their options. Because most distributions try to use modules for as many drivers as possible, you may very well need a different /etc/modules.conf file for use under VMware (assuming that you installed this system without VMware).

The VMware Tools installer achieves this by renaming your original /etc/modules.conf file to /etc/modules.conf.org, and it installs a new file /etc/modules.conf.vm. The /etc/vmware/dualconf.* scripts simply put the proper link from /etc/modules.conf to one of these two in place so that the module loader will insert the appropriate modules.

As mentioned before, links pertaining to the XFree86 configuration vary among Linux systems; check your distribution's link system against what the Tools installer does.

vmware-guestd

Along with providing the dual-configuration details, the dualconf script starts a program called vmware-guestd. This daemon's job when operating under VMware Workstation is to provide time synchronization between the host and guest operating systems (vmware-guestd provides other features when operating under one of VMware's server products).

Upon system startup, vmware-guestd normally writes its process ID to /var/run/vmware-guestd.pid.

6.5.8   Using checkvm in X Startup Scripts

You may want to make your X startup session look different inside and outside of VMware on a dual configuration machine. The way to do this is with the checkvm program that VMware Tools installs in /etc/vmware. For example, you could write a wrapper for vmware-toolbox to make it start only under VMware:

```
#!/bin/sh
/etc/vmware-tools/checkvm > /dev/null 2>&1

case $? In
   0) vmware-toolbox --minimize -geometry -0+0 &
       ;;
   *)
       ;;
esac
```

6.6   Linux Devices

Linux, like other Unix variants, keeps device files that correspond to the devices on the machine in the /dev directory. You can read from and write to your system's devices using regular system commands such as cat and dd, as well as use output redirection such as the following example, which reads input from a file called hello.au and sends it to the device file /dev/audio. The Linux kernel redirects anything that /dev/audio receives to the sound driver.

```
cat hello.au > /dev/audio
```

You could use this particular example to test VMware's sound. If you get no sound, there is a problem between VMware and the host operating system. However, if an error message such as

```
/dev/audio: Operation not supported by device
```

appears, there is a problem with the Linux guest operating system configuration.

The following subsections give an overview of VMware Workstation's virtual devices under Linux. In addition to looking at the device names, we'll also look at the utilities that use these devices, where appropriate.

6.6.1 /dev/hd*: IDE Disks and ATAPI CD-ROM/DVD Drives

The prefix hd in /dev represents IDE disks under Linux. In VMware, the name assignment follows the basic configuration of most ordinary desktop machines:

/dev/hda Primary master

/dev/hdb Primary slave

/dev/hdc Secondary master

/dev/hdd Secondary slave

To partition a disk under Linux, use the fdisk or cfdisk command as root (that is, fdisk /dev/hdb). To find out which device in /dev corresponds to a partition on a drive, just append the partition number to the end of the drive; for example, /dev/hdb3 is the third partition on the primary slave disk. ATAPI CD-ROM drives do not use partition numbers; simply use the disk device prefix to work with them. Zip disks are partition number 4 by default.

As with many other Unix variants, the file /etc/fstab contains a list of partitions for the system to mount at boot time, and, of course, you can use the mount command to attach a filesystem on a partition to the system manually.

To make an empty partition usable under Linux, you must first place a filesystem on it. (You may want to do this if you run out of space and want to add a new virtual disk under VMware.) To do so, first make sure that you partitioned the disk with fdisk and then identify the partition you want to wipe out. Let's say it's /dev/hdb1. Create the filesystem with

```
mke2fs /dev/hdb1
```

Then pick a place for it to sit on your system, such as /scratch, and add it to /etc/fstab as follows:

```
/dev/hdb1          /scratch        ext2         defaults 0 2
```

Finally, use mount -a to add the new filesystem to your system. It will also show up on the guest system every time it boots, until you comment out or remove the line above from /etc/fstab.

Linux, like other kinds of Unix, assumes that you know exactly what you're doing when you partition disks and create filesystems. It generally won't even ask or warn you when you're about to wipe out something, even if you're about to delete your currently active filesystems. For this reason, be certain of the partitions you're referring to when you work with these tools. Although VMware does have safeguards to protect a guest operating system from corrupting real and virtual disks, these mechanisms can be overridden, and you can undo only up to a certain point.

CD-ROM/DVD drives have no partition table. To attach one to your system, use a command like this:

```
mount -r /dev/hdc /cdrom
```

The -r option tells Linux to mount the device in read-only mode.

6.6.2 /dev/sd*: SCSI Disks

Although SCSI disks use the same device name scheme as IDE disks (/dev/sda, /dev/sdb, and so on), the Linux kernel assigns SCSI disks differently than it does IDE disks. Rather than using fixed device names for specific SCSI targets, Linux dynamically configures SCSI disks in the order in which it finds host controllers and targets. Therefore, if you have SCSI targets 0, 3, and 4 on a single host controller, the kernel assigns the devices as follows:

```
target 0: /dev/sda
target 3: /dev/sdb
target 4: /dev/sdc
```

Once you know the device name of a SCSI disk, you can work with it just as you would an IDE disk. (See the previous section for details.)

6.6.3 /dev/scd*, /dev/sr*: SCSI CD-ROM Drives

The naming scheme for SCSI CD-ROM drives under Linux is similar to that for disks. The first drive is /dev/scd0 or /dev/sr0, the second /dev/scd1 (/dev/sr1), and so on. As with ATAPI CD-ROM drives, there are no partitions; you refer to the entire device when you use a command such as mount.

6.6.4 /dev/sg*: Generic SCSI Devices

The drivers for some devices, such as scanners and CD-R drives, are not in the kernel; instead, a regular user-mode utility handles all the interaction through a generic SCSI device file. For example, cdrecord is a command that burns a CD-R or CD-RW. Generic SCSI devices appear in /dev as sg0, sg1, and so on. Some distributions use the names sga, sgb, and so on instead.

Tape drives show up as /dev/st* and /dev/nst*: for example, /dev/st0 for the first SCSI tape device and /dev/nst0 for its no-rewind alternate.

6.6.5 /dev/ttyS*: Serial Ports

On Linux systems, VMware's four virtual serial ports are /dev/ttyS0 through /dev/ttyS3, which correspond to the standard COM1 to COM4 port assignments on a real machine. The Linux kernel detects all four ports by default, even if they don't have a VMware configuration. This isn't a problem as long as you keep away from devices not present in your virtual machine configuration; otherwise, the kernel may pass along its confusion to any program that attempts to use these devices.

minicom is a popular terminal program that comes with all Linux distributions. Your distribution may create a symbolic link called /dev/modem that points to your modem's serial port device. To set up PPP (to get a dial-up Internet connection), you'll need to set up pppd, though if you're running under VMware, it's generally easier to go through your host operating system to get a network connection.

6.6.6 /dev/fd*: Floppy Drives

The floppy drives available under VMware are under the devices /dev/fd0 and /dev/fd1. In addition to using mount to access an MS-DOS filesystem on a floppy drive, you can use a package called mtools to gain access to a FAT filesystem on a floppy disk. You may very well prefer this approach because floppy disks are extremely unreliable; the Linux kernel doesn't like to mount unreliable media. The package is simple to use; the commands are similar to those for MS-DOS, except they have an m at the beginning. Here are some examples:

```
mcopy a:somefile .
mcopy somefile a:
mformat a:
mdel a:somefile
```

6.6.7 /dev/lp*, /dev/parport*: Parallel Ports

The Linux equivalents of LPT1 and LPT2 are /dev/lp0 and /dev/lp1. Bidirectional ports use /dev/parport*. (Under kernel versions 2.0 and older, what is now /dev/lp0 was called /dev/lp1. It has been quite a while since these versions were current, but you should keep this change in mind when using old Linux distributions with VMware.)

The printing system in Linux is like many other versions of Unix; Berkeley lpd and LPRng are the most popular print spooling systems. Most distributions have tools that can correctly configure a local printer attached to the parallel port.

6.6.8 Ethernet Interfaces

Unlike most Linux devices, the Ethernet interfaces eth0, eth1, and eth2 do not have corresponding device files in /dev. See the log files or use a command such as dmesg to find out which Ethernet interfaces the Linux kernel found. To manually configure the Ethernet interface eth0 and its routing, use the ifconfig and route commands as root, as shown here:

```
ifconfig eth0 10.2.3.121 netmask 255.255.255.0 broadcast 10.2.3.255
route add default gw 10.2.3.1
```

You can also use the `ifconfig` and `route` commands without any arguments to see the current interface and route configuration.

6.6.9 /dev/psaux: PS/2 Mouse

If you choose to leave your virtual mouse available as a PS/2 mouse (one of the easiest types for Linux to use under the X Window System), it shows up at /dev/psaux. As for a modem, your Linux distribution may create a symbolic link from /dev/mouse to the mouse device. The X server and a text-mode mouse management program called gpm are practically the only programs in Linux that need to directly access the mouse device.

6.6.10 /dev/dsp, /dev/audio: Sound Card

The simplest way to use the sound devices under Linux is to dump an audio file to the /dev/audio device, as illustrated at the beginning of this section. If the file is not an audio file, you'll get what is best described as cacophony, and even if the file contains sound, it still may not work because of file format issues. Most programs that use sound employ the /dev/dsp device; the play program will play many audio formats.

Because the sound data runs through VMware Workstation and out through another sound driver, you may want to automatically set the volume of the Linux guest system at its maximum value in the dualconf.vm script mentioned earlier in this chapter. Do so through the mixer device, using command-line utilities to manipulate it. (Red Hat provides one called aumix.) To turn the master, PCM, and synthesizer volumes all the way up with this utility, use this command:

```
aumix -w 100 -s 100 -v 100
```

NOTE *Some distributions save mixer settings at shutdown so they can be recalled again at the next boot. If you're running VMware, you may want to disable this feature (look in the* rc*.d *directories), placing the desired settings in the* dualconf.* *files instead.*

6.6.11 USB Devices

Because there are a variety of different USB devices, the interfaces show up in a variety of places. Here are a few examples:

Mouse Devices: When you plug in a mouse, it shows up in /dev/input/mice. The protocol is PS/2.

Storage Devices: USB fixed- and removable-media devices appear as SCSI disks. When you plug one in, it automatically configures itself (you'll see the details in the output of a command such as dmesg).

Serial Ports: Traditional serial port adapters show up as regular serial ports (`/dev/ttyS*`).

Keyboards: You don't need to do anything special to use a USB keyboard once the driver is installed; it attaches itself to the regular input system.

A number of USB utilities are available for determining the devices on your system. Perhaps the most useful is `lsusb` (though it may not come with your system).

6.7 The Linux Kernel and Device Drivers

We've now talked about device files and how to use them, but haven't mentioned much about the Linux kernel, which lies behind the device files. The kernel is the core of the operating system; in addition to managing processes, memory, and filesystems, it also contains all of the device drivers. You can configure and build by linking the drivers directly to the kernel (thus activating them immediately upon boot), or by creating a kernel module, to be inserted on demand into a running kernel. Most distributions compile critical drivers, such as IDE disk drivers, directly into the kernel and relegate everything, such as drivers for a sound card or filesystem types that aren't used much, to modules.

NOTE *Though it's a fun process, configuring and compiling a kernel along with its modules is beyond the scope of this chapter. If you're interested in this process, two places to look are the Linux Kernel-HOWTO and the kernel chapter of* Linux Problem Solver *(No Starch Press, 2000). Moreover, it's likely that your distribution already installed all of the drivers that VMware needs on your system. They're probably in modules, and they just need you to coax them to do what you want them to do.*

6.7.1 Working with Kernel Modules

Before you get started with kernel modules, you should know which kernel version your system is running. Type `uname -r` to determine this. If your version of Linux is an official release, the version number will be a three-part value, such as 2.4.1. However, many distributions apply a number of patches to their kernels, giving them version numbers such as 2.2.18pre21 and 2.2.18-27.

You'll find the actual kernel module files in the subdirectories under `/lib/modules/version`, where `version` is your kernel version. These files have a `.o` extension, to denote an object file.

Manually inserting a kernel module file into a currently running system is easy. For example, if you want to insert `pcnet32.o`, which contains the Ethernet driver that VMware knows how to talk to, use

```
modprobe pcnet32
```

Because modules may use parts of other kernel modules, `modprobe` looks at the `depmod` module dependency list and inserts any other necessary modules before the one you request.

NOTE *To see the system's active modules, run* `lsmod`.

Normally, you don't need to install kernel modules by hand. Instead, the kernel runs an automatic module loader. When you try to access a device for which the driver isn't present, the loader tries to find a module for it and, if it succeeds, runs `modprobe`.

Because of the wide variety of PC hardware types, the module loader needs some hints about the specific machine that it's running on, which you place in a configuration file called `/etc/modules.conf`. Although Linux distributions vary in how they generate this file, the format is the same.

We've already mentioned that the VMware Tools and `dualconf.*` scripts manipulate `/etc/modules.conf`; to master its use under VMware, there are two keywords you need to know about. The first is `alias`. For example, a line in `/etc/modules.conf` that reads

```
alias eth0 pcnet32
```

instructs the module loader that the device driver known as `eth0` is in a module called `pcnet32` on this system. As mentioned before, this module contains an Ethernet driver that knows how to talk to VMware, so you'll need this line in your `/etc/modules.conf` file if this driver isn't compiled directly into your kernel.

The other important keyword is `options`, which specifies parameters for a particular module. For example, the sound module needs this line in `/etc/modules.conf`:

```
options sb io=0x220 irq=5 dma=1 dma16=5 mpu_io=0x330
```

NOTE *Some distributions frown on modifying* `/etc/modules.conf` *directly, preferring that you go through some other interface. One of them is Debian; the scheme there is based on the* `update-modules` *program, where you add special entries in* `/etc/modutils/arch/i386`. *The* `update-modules` *program takes this information and combines it with other sources to create a new* `/etc/modules.conf` *file.*

6.7.2   Linux Device Drivers for VMware Workstation

This section lists the driver names, modules, and `/etc/modules.conf` lines that Linux can use while running under VMware, as well as where to find the drivers in the kernel configuration (in case you're compiling a custom kernel).

IDE Devices
Module names: `ide`, `ide-disk`, `ide-cd`.
Kernel configuration: Under **Block Devices**.
Notes: Because most real systems boot from an IDE disk, your kernel probably has IDE disk support compiled directly into it. However, the other drivers are likely to be in modules. The kernel autoloader is generally smart enough to figure out when to load them without help from `modules.conf`.

SCSI Support, SCSI Devices
Module names: scsi_mod, sd_mod, sr_mod, sg_mod, BusLogic.
modules.conf:

```
alias block-major-8 BusLogic
options -k BusLogic
```

If SCSI disk support isn't compiled directly into your kernel, use something like this instead:

```
alias block-major-8 myscsi
probeall myscsi BusLogic sd
options -k BusLogic
options -k sd
```

Kernel configuration: Under **SCSI support - SCSI disk support** and in **SCSI low-level drivers, BusLogic SCSI support**. If you want SCSI CD-ROM, generic, and tape support, you'll find drivers under **SCSI support** as well.
Notes: Red Hat 7's kudzu system doesn't get the modules.conf settings quite right. Also, if you remove the SCSI driver's module (after loading it once), it won't function again unless you reboot the machine, so make sure that you turn off autoclean (with options -k). This works under Red Hat 7.

Floppy Drives
Module name: floppy.
Kernel configuration: Under **Block Devices - Normal PC floppy disk support**.
Notes: This driver is unlikely to be configured as a module; it is most likely configured directly in your distribution's kernel.

Ethernet Interfaces
Module name: pcnet32.
modules.conf: Device can be eth0, eth1, and/or eth2:

```
alias eth0 pcnet32
```

Kernel configuration: Under **Network device support - Ethernet (10 or 100Mbit)**.
Notes: Enabling EISA, VLB, PCI, and onboard controllers brings up a number of other options; AMD PCnet32 (VLB and PCI) support is among them.

Serial Ports
Module name: serial.
Kernel configuration: Under **Character devices - Standard/generic (dumb) serial support**.
Notes: These usually work better when compiled directly into the kernel.

Parallel Ports

Module names: `parport_probe`, `parport`, `parport_pc`, `lp` (for printers), others.
modules.conf:

```
alias parport_lowlevel parport_pc
```

Kernel configuration: In three places: (1) under **General Setup - Parallel port support** and **PC-style hardware**, (2) under **Character devices - Parallel printer support**, and (3) various others under **Block devices** and **SCSI support**; in kernel version 2.4.0 and up, location (1) is **Parallel port support** under the main menu instead.
Notes: Because of the large number of dependencies in the modules, kernel configuration for parallel ports is a bit more complicated than for other drivers. Keep in mind that bidirectional devices (generally the block devices, such as Zip drives and similar devices) require bidirectional port support on the host operating system.

Sound

Module names: `soundcore`, `sb`, `uart401`, `soundlow`.
modules.conf:

```
alias char-major-14 sb
options sb io=0x220 irq=5 dma=1 dma16=5 mpu_io=0x330
```

Kernel configuration: Under **Sound**, enable **Sound card support** and **OSS sound modules**. Then choose **Sound Blaster compatibles (SB16/32/64, ESS, Jazz16) support**.
Notes: For various reasons, sound cards have always been the most frustrating to configure under Linux. For virtual machines, the process is remarkably straightforward.

USB Support

Kernel configuration: Under **USB support**, enable one of the **UHCI** drivers and any other devices you like. The **USB device filesystem** is necessary for some USB utility programs such as `lsusb`. You may need to enable experimental kernel options to see all USB device drivers.
Notes: USB support is fairly new in Linux, so implementation details are more prone to change than those for other devices.

Mouse Support

Kernel configuration: For a PS/2-type mouse, under **Character Devices - Mice - PS/2 mouse (aka "auxiliary device") support**. Serial mice are connected to serial ports and use that type of configuration.
Notes: Because the PS/2 mouse device is not available as a module, it's compiled into every distribution's default kernel.

6.8   Linux System Information

The /proc filesystem is a valuable source of information about a currently running Linux system. The items in /proc look like files to normal Linux programs, but the Linux kernel generates the actual content dynamically. To look at something in the filesystem, such as /proc/meminfo, just use cat /proc/meminfo, or if the output is too large, use less instead of cat.

/proc/meminfo: Memory information. The output indicates how much real memory is available to the system, how much is used, and how much of that is shared with more than one process, as well as buffer and cache utilization and swap space statistics.

/proc/cpuinfo: Processor information. Don't believe everything you see here if Linux is running under VMware. While things will look much like they do on your real hardware, VMware interferes with a few of the algorithms used to calculate some entries. One is the CPU MHz value. For example, an AMD K6-3/400 usually comes up around 475 MHz when running under VMware (and that doesn't mean that VMware speeds up the processor). However, if you're curious about the bogomips entry, you can be assured that it is just as worthless on a virtual machine as on a real machine.

/proc/devices, /proc/misc: A list of devices, along with major device numbers. Be careful about this; some devices don't appear because they aren't in use, and others may show up even though they are currently disconnected at the VMware level (remember that VMware fakes disconnected devices until you connect them).

/proc/mounts: List of mounted filesystems. Although the system attempts to keep the information in /etc/mtab, this is the most reliable indicator of the systems' currently attached filesystems. It doesn't show the mount options, though.

/proc/filesystems: Filesystem types known to the current kernel. This information can also be misleading, because most distributions include nonessential filesystems as modules. When the system needs a new filesystem type, the automatic kernel module loader looks for a module with that name and runs modprobe on it. Afterward, the module shows up in /proc/filesystems.

/proc/partitions: Disks and partitions known to the current kernel. With removable media, in some cases the kernel doesn't see a partition list until someone accesses the device after a media change. SCSI disks may act this way as well.

/proc/version: The currently running kernel version.

6.9 Booting Linux: LILO

Linux distributions install a small program called Linux Loader, or LILO, on the boot block of a hard disk. Typically, you'll want this boot block on your first hard disk, /dev/hda. You specify LILO's configuration with the /etc/lilo.conf file. Here is a typical example:

```
boot=/dev/hda
root=/dev/hda1
install=/boot/boot.b
map=/boot/map

image=/boot/vmlinuz
label=Linux
read-only
```

You can see here that the boot block is set to /dev/hda, and the initial root directory is set to /dev/hda1. The other important entry is the Linux kernel, /boot/vmlinuz. This is what LILO loads and runs.

NOTE *Just having a lilo.conf file doesn't make LILO active; you must run the lilo command every time you change the kernel image.*

For whatever reason, you may not have LILO installed on your boot block, or VMware may not be able to boot your kernel because of its BIOS. A machine may be unable to boot a Linux installation on a secondary disk, for example. Many people use floppy disks and other means (such as the LOADLIN program) to get around this. Although a floppy disk may be workable under VMware, LOADLIN may not be, and in any case, floppy disks are slow. Thankfully, VMware gives you two nice ways to cheat.

For the examples here, assume that you installed the Linux guest operating system on the primary slave disk, /dev/hdb, and that some other operating system is installed on the primary master, /dev/hda.

6.9.1 Method 1: New Virtual Disk

If you don't need to access anything on the primary master when running Linux as the guest operating system, you can remove that disk from the configuration and install a small virtual disk as the primary master instead. Partition it, put a filesystem on it (as described in the "Linux Devices" section earlier in this chapter), make that filesystem bootable, and copy everything from /boot (or wherever the LILO's files are) to the new partition. *Make sure that the kernel image is among the files you copy.* Then use umount on the new partition and immediately use mount to mount it again under /boot. Copy your /etc/lilo.conf file to /etc/lilo.conf.vm and make sure that it contains lines like these:

```
boot=/dev/hda
root=/dev/hdb1
```

Make any other necessary alterations; then use

```
lilo -C lilo.conf.vm
```

to install a boot block on the new virtual disk to make it bootable.

6.9.2 Method 2: Fake Floppy Disk

If you're a poor soul booting your Linux system from a floppy disk (for example, on a dual-boot system), or if you're using a floppy for some other reason, you can fake a floppy disk and make booting go faster. Here's how:

1. If you already have a boot floppy, connect your real floppy drive to VMware as a virtual floppy drive and use this under your Linux guest operating system to pull the image into a file called bootdisk.floppy:

```
dd if=/dev/fd0 of=bootdisk.floppy bs=512
```

2. Disconnect the virtual floppy drive under VMware and reconfigure the virtual floppy drive as a file, instead of your real floppy drive.

3. Reconnect the floppy drive to the virtual machine and use

```
dd if=bootdisk.floppy of=/dev/fd0 bs=512
```

to transfer the image to the virtual floppy drive, which is now a file on your real system.

4. Save your VMware configuration, making sure that the floppy drive is connected at boot time, and your system will now boot from the floppy file.

If you have a kernel image, you can use a similar method. Reconfigure your virtual floppy drive as a file under VMware (as described earlier) and connect it. Assuming that the kernel image is called vmlinuz and your root filesystem is at /dev/hdb1, you'd run these commands to copy the kernel image to the new virtual floppy drive:

```
dd if=vmlinuz of=/dev/fd0 bs=512
rdev /dev/fd0 /dev/hdb1
```

As you might surmise, this technique is handy for testing new kernels without altering the boot block. A bonus perk is that the new virtual floppy drive is far faster than a real floppy drive.

7

FREEBSD GUEST SYSTEMS

This chapter is all about FreeBSD: in particular, how to install FreeBSD on a virtual machine, activate the VMware Tools for FreeBSD, manage a virtual machine hardware configuration at boot time, configure the VMware Tools graphics drivers (in the X server), work with VMware Workstation's devices under FreeBSD, and customize a FreeBSD kernel for use with VMware Workstation.

BSD is a family of Unix versions that takes its name from the University of California at Berkeley. (BSD stands for Berkeley Software Distribution.) Here's a brief history. BSD played an important role in operating system and network research in the late 1970s and 1980s, influencing the original AT&T Bell Labs Unix. It became a favorite in academic computing systems and even went on to become the basis for some commercial Unix variants, such as SunOS (until version 5). Unix and BSD have an interesting history; for more information, you may want to read Peter Salus' *A Quarter-Century of Unix* (Addison-Wesley, 1994).

Today, there are several versions of BSD-based Unix available for the PC, the most popular of which is likely FreeBSD. FreeBSD strives for the best device support and performance, but only for a limited number of platforms. Its primary architecture is the x86. VMware, Inc., supports FreeBSD as a guest operating system and provides VMware Tools for FreeBSD. (We'll discuss two other BSD variants that work with VMware Workstation, NetBSD and OpenBSD, in Chapter 8.)

The setup and installation of each BSD system is uniform: that is, unlike Linux, there aren't several FreeBSD distributions (though, of course, the system file configuration and the kernel may change between versions).

The FreeBSD team attempts to provide backward compatibility between versions, particularly with shared link libraries. Also of interest is Linux binary compatibility. User applications including VMware Workstation generally work fine in Linux compatibility mode, but anything that talks to a hardware device (such as an X server) won't.

NOTE *If you've worked with Linux or any other Unix system, you'll have no problem with the material in this chapter. Otherwise, you should read up on some basic Unix tasks, such as navigating filesystems, editing files, and rebooting and shutting down the system.*

7.1 Installing FreeBSD under VMware

Because FreeBSD supports all of VMware's hardware, installation is relatively simple. The VMware Configuration Wizard defaults to an IDE virtual disk to create a new virtual machine, avoiding controller compatibility issues. Furthermore, the FreeBSD installer doesn't try to start a graphics mode for you, so the installation is relatively quick.

Still, there are a number of packages that you should install to get the most out of your system, especially packages related to VMware Tools. When the FreeBSD installer asks you which type of system you want to install, a good option is the **X-Kern-Developer** configuration. This includes the X Window System, the kernel source code, and the C compiler (you'll need a C compiler to configure and compile a BSD kernel; it's usually never a good idea to install a Unix system without a C compiler).

As for disk partitioning, you may want to skip forward in this chapter to the "BSD Devices" section for a look at how FreeBSD lays out its filesystems on disks. If you're using a virtual disk, the defaults should be fine; let the installer determine the layout for you.

In addition, look around for perl; you'll want that for the VMware Tools installer.

7.2 Using an Existing FreeBSD Installation under VMware

If you want to boot FreeBSD from an installation already present on your system, you must turn off any automatic startup of xdm until you install the VMware Tools. However, if your system finishes booting in text mode and you use startx or xinit to begin an X session, you don't need to do anything.

If you see a log-in box when you start, turn it off by first looking in the /etc/ttys file for a line like this:

```
ttyv8    "/usr/X11R6/bin/xdm -nodaemon"  xterm  on  secure
```

Then change on to off:

```
ttyv8    "/usr/X11R6/bin/xdm -nodaemon"  xterm  off secure
```

Next, save the file and reboot your system. You should get a plain-text console log-in when the system comes up again. If you don't, xdm may start in your system from one of the /etc/rc* boot files. To track it down, run

```
grep xdm /etc/*
```

NOTE *If you have a SCSI-only system, make sure that your kernel supports the BusLogic SCSI controller that VMware provides. Look ahead in this chapter at section 7.5 if you need SCSI support now.*

7.3 VMware Tools for FreeBSD

VMware Tools for FreeBSD include the same components as the other VMware Tools packages: an improved graphics driver, a Toolbox program for interacting with the host operating system, and dual configuration utilities. To install the tools, follow these steps:

1. Select **VMware Tools Install** from VMware Workstation's **Settings** menu.
2. Attach the CD-ROM to your system:

```
mount /cdrom
```

3. Extract the archive and unmount the CD-ROM image:

```
cd /tmp
zcat /cdrom/vmware-freebsd-tools.tar.gz | tar xvf -
umount /cdrom
```

4. Change to the install directory and run the installer:

```
cd vmware-tools-freebsd
./install.pl
```

5. The installer asks where your X server is, where the link to the server binary is, and where the configuration file is. The default locations start with /usr/X11R6, the standard for FreeBSD systems. If you're running XFree86 4.1 or later, answer /tmp so that the Tools installer won't overwrite your current X server. If you don't have the X Window System installed on the FreeBSD guest, any answer is fine.
6. Before changing your system configuration, the installer tells you what files it will change. After you've read the list, press ENTER.

7. Test the installation: Run the X server with the command X. If VMware Workstation switches to a high-resolution graphics mode, your server works (press CTRL-ALT-BACKSPACE to kill the server). If the installation doesn't work, you need to tweak your X server a little; see the next two sections.

7.3.1 The VMware X Server

To enable the optimized graphics drivers on FreeBSD, the VMware Tools installer does the following in /usr/X11R6/bin:

- Installs XF86_VMware, the VMware X server.
- Renames X as X.org.
- Links X.vm to XF86_VMware (a symbolic link).
- Links X to X.vm (a symbolic link).

In FreeBSD, the X server configuration file for XFree86 3.*x* is /etc/XF86Config. The VMware Tools installer supplies a new XF86Config.vm file, renames your original configuration file as XF86Config.org, and links XF86Config to XF86Config.vm.

The biggest issue is that you must change the resolution in the XF86Config.vm file to suit your monitor. The procedure is identical to the procedure for a Linux guest system, described in section 6.5.3; in the Screen section, comment out the current Modes setting and uncomment the one you want to use.

7.3.2 XFree86 Version 4

If you want to use XFree86 4.*x* with a FreeBSD guest operating system, use XFree86 4.1 or later. These versions include the VMware SVGA driver module. Configuration is the same as that for XFree86 4 in Linux, described on page 102, except for the mouse configuration, which should look like this:

```
Option   "Protocol"   "Auto"
Option   "Device"   "/dev/psm0"
```

Or if you enable moused (see section 7.9.9), it should look like this:

```
Option   "Protocol"   "Auto"
Option   "Device"   "/dev/sysmouse"
```

7.3.3 The VMware Toolbox

The companion to the VMware X server is the Toolbox (vmware-toolbox), a graphic interface to some of VMware's features. The Tools installer places vmware-toolbox in /usr/X11R6/bin if that directory exists. You can't run the Toolbox outside the X Window System.

The Toolbox generally works as described in section 4.11.1. The **Devices** tab lets you connect and disconnect devices; you can also shrink a virtual disk, and do a few other things.

NOTE *As with the Linux Toolbox described in section 6.5.6, you must run* vmware-toolbox *in your FreeBSD guest system to take advantage of certain virtual machine features, such as copying and pasting between guest and host systems and automatic release of the input focus when the mouse pointer leaves the virtual machine. Therefore, place the proper Toolbox command in your* .xinitrc *or* .xsession *file that runs every time you start a session.*

7.3.4 Single and Dual Configuration

As discussed in earlier sections, when the VMware Tools installer runs, it renames a few of your original configuration files with a .org extension and creates new ones with a .vm suffix. These correspond to the original and virtual machine configurations. If you used a raw disk to run a previously installed FreeBSD installation under VMware Workstation, you have a dual configuration: one for your real hardware, and the other for VMware's virtual hardware. The VMware Tools for FreeBSD support automatic dual configuration at boot time.

Even if you don't have a dual configuration, you still need to know about the .vm files, because they are the active set on your system.

FreeBSD uses much simpler boot scripts than the System V init scripts found on other versions of Unix, such as Solaris and Linux distributions. These include a master script, /etc/rc, which may call other /etc/rc.* scripts (note that these are scripts, *not* directories on FreeBSD), and two master configuration files for the rc* scripts, /etc/defaults/rc.conf (BSD-wide defaults) and /etc/rc.conf (for customizations on your local machine).

The VMware Tools installer moves /etc/rc.conf to /etc/rc.conf.org and creates a new /etc/rc.conf.vm file based on the original; then it makes a symbolic link from the rc.conf.vm file to rc.conf:

```
lrwxr-xr-x  1 root  wheel   15 Mar 21 15:06 /etc/rc.conf -> /etc/rc.conf.vm
-rw-r--r--  1 root  wheel  516 Mar 20 02:09 /etc/rc.conf.org
-rw-r--r--  1 root  wheel  515 Mar 20 02:31 /etc/rc.conf.vm
```

The first difference between the .vm files and the .org files is that the installer sets

```
moused_enable="NO"
```

to ensure that moused won't interfere with the X server when you start it (this isn't strictly necessary; see section 7.4.9 to see how to get moused and the X server to cooperate).

If you enabled host-only networking for your virtual machine, here is another handy configuration option to turn off the mailer daemon and make booting a bit quicker:

```
sendmail_enable="NO"
```

If you have a dual configuration, you will need to change the Ethernet configuration in the rc.conf.vm file. For example, if your real hardware is a DEC Tulip-based card using the de0 interface, you should have a line like this:

```
ifconfig_de0="10.34.21.144 netmask 255.255.255.0"
```

Under VMware, FreeBSD won't see that de0 interface, because it knows about another kind of driver with a different name, lnc. Therefore, change the line to something like

```
ifconfig_lnc0="172.16.144.100 netmask 255.255.255.0"
```

or

```
ifconfig_lnc0="DHCP"
```

NOTE *Your particular changes will depend on how you configured VMware networking, which we'll discuss in more detail in Chapter 9.*

The Boot Process

To run the .vm or .org files at boot time, the VMware Tools installer tries to add a few lines to /etc/rc. They look something like this:

```
### <InstalledByVMware> ### Do not edit this tag!
# ...
ldconfig -elf /usr/lib /usr/lib/compat
/etc/vmware-tools/dualconf.sh start
### </InstalledByVMware> ### Do not edit this tag!
```

The `/etc/vmware-tools/dualconf.sh` script uses a program called `checkvm` to see whether the operating system is running inside of VMware. If it is, `checkvm` enables the scripts and configuration files that end with `.vm`. Otherwise, it activates the `.org` scripts and files. The `checkvm` program works like its Linux counterpart, described in section 6.5.7.

NOTE *Take a close look at* `/etc/rc`. *If the script says* `$install_dir/dualconf.sh` *instead of* `/etc/vmware-tools/dualconf.sh`, *change it to the latter. (The script is incorrect because of a bug in some versions of the Tools installer.)*

In addition to making sure that the dual configuration scripts are set up correctly, you must make sure that your kernel supports both your real hardware and VMware's hardware, usually by compiling all of the drivers that you need into the kernel. Although this may not be possible with certain combinations of drivers (such as those for sound cards), for important devices such as disks, you should be able to do so without a problem.

7.4   BSD Devices

Like the kernels for Linux and other kinds of Unix systems, BSD kernels use special device files (found in the `/dev` directory) to talk to the rest of the operating system. Here's how they operate and how to work with them.

7.4.1   ATA/IDE Disks

To work comfortably with disks under FreeBSD, you must first understand FreeBSD's device assignments and partitioning scheme. At the most basic level, FreeBSD uses `/dev/ad*` to represent ATA/IDE drives:

`/dev/ad0`	Primary master
`/dev/ad1`	Primary slave
`/dev/ad2`	Secondary master
`/dev/ad3`	Secondary slave

FreeBSD's partition scheme is not as simple as that of Linux and other Unix systems. In a BSD *disk label*, traditional systems append letters (a to h) to the disk device to denote partitions on a disk; for example, `/dev/xy0a` would be the first partition of a disk for an old interface on a certain BSD-based system. However, FreeBSD is more complicated because it must integrate with other PC operating systems.

If you want to share a disk between different operating systems—FreeBSD and Windows, for instance—you cannot do so if you place the BSD disk label directly on the main disk device. The label completely replaces the regular PC partition map, but Windows and other operating systems must read this map to make sense of the disk. To get around this problem, FreeBSD supports the usual PC disk maps, referring to the PC partitions as *slices*. In our example of `/dev/ad0`, slices `/dev/ad0s1` through `/dev/ad0s4` refer to PC-style partitions 1 through 4.

FreeBSD treats a slice as it would a disk device and places the disk label *inside* the slice. BSD further cuts the slice into BSD-style partitions; because it uses the disk label scheme mentioned earlier, a letter in the range a through h appears after the slice device to denote the actual partitions (for example, /dev/ad0s1a). Figure 7.1 illustrates this.

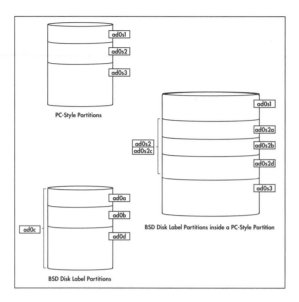

Figure 7.1: Three partitioning schemes

Letter Assignments and Modes

BSD partition letters have (more or less) followed a particular convention throughout the years. For example, a means a mount point of /, b is for swap, and g says that the partition's mount point is probably /usr. However, these letter assignments are only guidelines.

Even though this is convention, there is, however, one rule that you must follow when working with a disk: when you put a new disk label on a slice or disk, you must not alter or delete partition c. This partition is sometimes called the *overlap*; it spans the entire slice or disk. Many programs rely on it to determine device geometry.

In addition to the different partitions, BSD offers two disk device modes: *raw* and *cooked*. Disk and filesystem utilities generally work with raw devices, but normal disk operation is with the cooked devices. So far, we've mentioned only the cooked device names, but each disk, slice, and partition has both a raw and cooked device associated with it in /dev. The raw devices start with the letter r (for example, the raw device for /dev/ad0s1a is /dev/rad0s1a). In FreeBSD, though, most of this rarely matters; you can normally get away with using the cooked device name because the disk utilities can distinguish between the two and automatically adapt.

Adding a Disk

To add a disk to FreeBSD, you must first determine the kind of partitioning scheme you want to use, run any necessary disk formatting programs, and determine what the disk devices are so that you can create filesystems and attach them to your system.

For the reasons mentioned earlier, you should probably use Fdisk to create PC-style partitions (slices) on your new disk even if you're planning to use the whole disk for BSD (if you're adding a new virtual disk to VMware, this is likely the case). The easiest way to do this is to run /stand/sysinstall, select **Configure**, and then select **Fdisk**. When sysinstall asks you about the beginning and size of a PC partition, it expects an answer in sectors, which are typically 512 bytes long, also called blocks.

You should try to place a FreeBSD slice on cylinder boundaries. Fdisk displays a line like this at the top of its screen:

```
DISK Geometry:  216 cyls/15 heads/63 sectors = 204120 sectors (99MB)
```

This means that there are 216 cylinders on the disk, 15 disk heads, 63 sectors per track, and 204,120 sectors on the whole disk. To get the number of sectors per cylinder, divide the total number of sectors on the disk by the number of cylinders on the disk (in this case, the result is 945).

NOTE *If you opt to use another operating system's disk partitioning utility, remember that the ID for a FreeBSD slice is decimal 165. There's also another way to create PC-style partitions under FreeBSD: with the fdisk program. It's not an exceedingly friendly program, but it works. If you want to use it, you should carefully read its manual page.*

A Practice Disk

VMware gives you a chance to practice formatting disks with virtual disks, so create a new virtual disk with the Configuration Editor. You can make it any size you like; for the rest of this section, we'll assume that it's a 100-MB virtual disk with 215 cylinders, 63 sectors per track, 15 tracks per cylinder (945 sectors per cylinder), and 204,120 sectors on the disk. Follow this procedure for the practice disk:

1. With the VMware Configuration Editor, create a new virtual disk at your primary slave (/dev/ad1).

2. Run /stand/sysinstall for Fdisk and dedicate the whole disk to FreeBSD slice 1, /dev/ad1s1.

3. Label the slice with BSD partitions. There are two ways. One procedure is interactive; you can use /stand/sysinstall, choosing the **Configure - Label** option. However, the disklabel program might be a better choice. In this example, running

```
disklabel /dev/ad1s1 > ad1s1_geom
```

places the disk label in a file called ad1s1_geom. You can edit that file, making any desired changes. You'll find disk geometry information at the start of the file, and this information at the end:

```
8 partitions:
#        size    offset    fstype    [fsize bsize bps/cpg]
  c:    204057        0    unused        0     0          # (Cyl.    0 - 215*)
```

Notice that the c partition represents the whole slice: it's that important overlap partition that we mentioned before. Create two new partitions: first a, taking 95 of the 215 cylinders (95 x 945 = 89775 sectors), and then b, taking 40,000 sectors, by inserting these lines before the c entry in the ad1s1_geom file:

```
a:    89775        0    unused        0     0
b:    40000    89775    unused        0     0
```

Then write the label back to the disk with

```
disklabel -R /dev/ad1s1 ad1s1_geom
```

If you read the label back, you'll notice that there's now an asterisk (*) next to the b entry but not the a entry. That's because b doesn't end on a cylinder boundary. You'll see the significance of this in a second.

4. If necessary, create the device files in /dev (FreeBSD often doesn't create them by default):

```
(cd /dev; ./MAKEDEV ad1s1a)
```

5. Put filesystems on the new partitions with newfs:

```
newfs /dev/ad1s1a
newfs /dev/ad1s1b
```

Notice that the output of the second newfs command warns you about unallocated sectors in the last cylinder; that's because BSD filesystems like to be on cylinder boundaries, and that's why we've been noting this.

6. Attach one of the new filesystems to the system at /mnt:

```
mount /dev/ad1s1a /mnt
```

Because this was only a practice example, you can now shut down your machine and remove the drive from your configuration. However, if you were adding a disk in earnest, you would make a permanent mount point for the filesystem other than /mnt and add an entry to /etc/fstab so that you don't have to manually attach the partition every time the system boots.

7.4.2 ATAPI CD-ROM Drive

FreeBSD uses the devices /dev/acd* for ATAPI CD-ROM drives. It makes its assignments the same way that Linux assigns SCSI drives: in the order that the kernel finds the drives. The first one found gets acd0, the second gets acd1, the third gets acd2, and the fourth gets acd3. To mount an ISO9660 CD-ROM drive in acd0 at /mnt, use this command:

```
mount -t cd9660 /dev/acd0c /mnt
```

7.4.3 SCSI Devices

Under FreeBSD, SCSI disk devices are the /dev/da* files. As in the ATAPI CD-ROM assignment scheme, as well as Linux's SCSI disk assignments, the first SCSI target found is /dev/da0, the next is /dev/da1, and so on. Partitioning, layout, and filesystem creation are the same as for IDE disks.

SCSI CD-ROM drives are at /dev/cd* (*not* /dev/scd*). Because you refer to an entire CD-ROM drive at once, you use the overlap partition—for example, /dev/cd0c—but you may need to look at the a partition if there happens to be a BSD filesystem on the CD-ROM drive.

Several other SCSI device drivers are available in /dev. Among them are /dev/[n]sa* for SCSI tapes and /dev/ch* for media changers. The best way to find a driver on a system is to run man -k scsi to get an overview of available drivers.

7.4.4 Floppy Drives

FreeBSD floppy drives are at /dev/fd0 and /dev/fd1. In addition to a command like mount /dev/fd0c /mnt, you can use mtools, described in section 6.6.6.

7.4.5 Ethernet Interfaces

As in Linux systems, there are no files in /dev for Ethernet cards in BSD. BSD recognizes VMware's virtual Ethernet cards as lnc0 through lnc2 (named for AMD Lance/PCnet). You can configure the interface and routing manually with ifconfig and route:

```
ifconfig lnc0 172.16.144.100 netmask 255.255.255.0
route add default 172.16.144.1
```

Because each Ethernet driver has its own interface name, if you want to create a dual configuration, you may need to swap the interface name when the machine boots, as described in section 7.3.4.

7.4.6   Serial Ports

There are two main sets of serial port devices under FreeBSD: one for dialing in, and one for dialing out. Dial-in ports are /dev/ttyd*—under VMware, they're /dev/ttyd0 through /dev/ttyd3 for COM1 through COM4. The corresponding dial-out ports are /dev/cua0 through /dev/cua3. A rule of thumb is that if a program such as pppd, cu, tip, minicom needs to use a serial port to reach a remote system or device, it uses the cua* device, but it uses ttyd* for any attached terminal or modem where users may log in and run a shell. Normally, you need to configure only one system daemon for the ttyd* ports: getty. The configuration file that normally turns that on is /etc/ttys.

Under the default kernel configuration, FreeBSD won't recognize the third and fourth serial ports (COM3 and COM4). You can reconfigure and recompile a new kernel, but it won't help you recognize more than two serial ports. VMware Workstation uses shared IRQs in its virtual serial ports; FreeBSD doesn't support shared IRQs on standard PC serial ports.

7.4.7   Parallel Ports

The unidirectional parallel ports on FreeBSD are /dev/lpt*. The line printer, lpd, is the most likely to use these ports. The bidirectional ports are /dev/ppi*.

7.4.8   USB Devices

FreeBSD uses a daemon called usbd to manage USB devices. This program primarily handles device attachment and removal. To activate it at boot time, put

```
usbd_enable="YES"
```

in your /etc/rc.conf (or /etc/rc.conf.vm) file. The usbd configuration file is /etc/usbd.conf. You shouldn't need to change this for a basic setup, but if you have some special commands that you need to run when you plug in a USB device, you can specify them here.

To show all USB devices attached to the system, use the command usbdevs. The -v option specifies verbose mode and can display interesting data on the current devices.

As in other operating systems, individual USB devices work through other device interfaces in FreeBSD. For example, mass storage devices show up as SCSI disks, and mouse devices work through the MouseSystems protocol. The best way to check the device drivers on your system is to use man -k usb to get an index of all USB-related pages. If you see an entry of interest, use man to examine the page: for example, use man uscanner to look at the scanner support.

HINT *For USB mouse devices, keep the /etc/usb.conf file as is and configure your XF86Config file's mouse pointer section for the* moused *virtualized mode. See the next section for details.*

7.4.9 PS/2 Mouse Port

You'll find the mouse at /dev/psm0 on FreeBSD. As in any Unix system on an x86 architecture, the XFree86 server is nearly always the only program that actually uses the mouse. FreeBSD also has an equivalent of Linux's gpm daemon called moused. When run automatically from the console, the /etc/rc.i386 script runs moused. You can activate it at boot time with the moused_port parameter in /etc/defaults/rc.conf.

The moused program can block the mouse port, causing VMware's X server to abort. For this reason, when you install the VMware Tools for FreeBSD, the installer attempts to turn moused off in the /etc/rc.conf.vm script when booting under VMware.

However, you can use moused in a virtualized mode, which is similar to the repeater mode in Linux's gpm. To do this, put this in your /etc/rc.conf file:

```
moused_enable="YES"
moused_type="ps/2"
moused_port="/dev/psm0"
```

Now change the mouse device in your XF86Config file to the system (repeated) mouse, /dev/sysmouse, and set its protocol to Auto.

7.4.10 Sound

FreeBSD supports sound when running under VMware Workstation, but to use a sound card, you must create the sound devices and recompile the kernel. We'll get to the kernel later in this chapter. The devices are /dev/audio, /dev/dsp, and /dev/mixer. Create them in /dev with

```
(cd /dev; ./MAKEDEV snd0)
```

The devices work like their counterparts in other Unix flavors; a command such as

```
cat blab.au > /dev/audio
```

dumps an audio sample to the sound card, but because the driver may not be able to figure out the sample's parameters, it's best to use a utility like play. There's a mixer as well. Keep in mind that you'll normally want the volume level at the maximum setting for a VMware guest operating system, leaving the real volume setting controlled by the host. Make sure that you installed the mixer program, and use

```
mixer vol 100 pcm 100 synth 100
```

to set the FreeBSD mixer volumes to their highest values. Running mixer without any arguments displays a list of the current volumes. You'll probably want to include the preceding line in your /etc/rc.dualconf.vm script to set those volumes when running FreeBSD under VMware.

7.5 Customizing a FreeBSD Kernel for VMware

Adding new device drivers for BSD involves creating a new kernel configuration, setting up a build directory, and then compiling and linking the new kernel. If you plan to use sound when running under VMware, you should create a new kernel; the generic kernel doesn't include sound support. Furthermore, the generic kernel contains many drivers that you don't need. If you remove them, the kernel uses less memory (and boots faster).

Creating a kernel is a fairly straightforward process. Suppose that you want to build a new kernel with the label VMWARE. Here's how:

1. Change to the kernel configuration directory and create a new configuration file from the GENERIC file:

    ```
    cd /sys/i386/conf
    cp GENERIC VMWARE
    ```

2. Edit the new VMWARE file. You'll find numerous devices listed here, possibly with parameters if the driver can't automatically probe for a device. For now, just add the driver for the sound card by appending these two lines to the end of the file:

    ```
    device    sbc0 at isa? port 0x220 irq 5 drq 1 flags 0x15
    device    pcm
    ```

3. Set up the build directory and change to it with

    ```
    config VMWARE
    cd ../../VMWARE
    ```

    Note that the build directory is /sys/compile/VMWARE.

4. The config command reminded you to issue a make depend command, so run this. The purpose of this command is to check the source code to see if it's all there, and to see if you configured drivers with prerequisite drivers. For example, the de0 driver for a DEC Tulip-based Ethernet card requires miibus support.

5. Run make to compile your new kernel. This may take a while, especially if you configured a large number of drivers.

6. The build creates a new kernel called kernel in the directory where you ran make, and you can now install it. Do this to make a backup of your old kernel and put the new one in place:

    ```
    mv /kernel /kernel.0
    cp kernel /kernel
    ```

7. Reboot your system to see if the new kernel works.

7.5.1 Help! My New Kernel Didn't Work!

If you have problems with your new kernel, you can go back to the old kernel by interrupting the boot process. When FreeBSD's boot manager starts, it displays these lines:

```
F1:    FreeBSD
Default: F1
```

(FreeBSD may be at somewhere other than F1 on your system.) Press F1 and then immediately press ESC. You'll get a prompt similar to this:

```
>> FreeBSD/i386 BOOT
Default: 0:ad(0,a)/boot/loader
boot:
```

Now you can type boot /kernel.0 to load your backup kernel. The keyboard may seem sluggish and unresponsive when you enter commands at the boot: prompt; this is normal.

7.5.2 FreeBSD Kernel Configuration Parameters

There's a list of all configurable kernel parameters in /sys/i386/conf/LINT. This section summarizes important parameters you'll need for a VMware Workstation kernel.

Disk and CD-ROM Drives

You'll need the following in your kernel configuration for the ATA disk and ATAPI CD-ROM drivers:

```
device      ata0     at isa? port IO_WD1 irq 14
device      ata1     at isa? port IO_WD2 irq 15
device      ata
device      atadisk                   # ATA disk drives
device      atapicd                   # ATAPI CDROM drives
```

Almost every FreeBSD kernel has this support built in. The only exception is a system with no ATA devices (only SCSI disks, unless you're particularly determined to run an entire system off a floppy disk, NFS, or some other nondisk).

In addition, you'll want the following options for filesystem support:

options	FFS	#Berkeley Fast Filesystem
options	FFS_ROOT	#FFS usable as root device [keep this!]
options	NFS	#Network Filesystem
options	NFS_ROOT	#NFS usable as root device, NFS required
options	MSDOSFS	#MSDOS Filesystem
options	CD9660	#ISO9660 Filesystem
options	CD9660_ROOT	#CD-ROM usable as root, CD9660 required
options	PROCFS	#Process filesystem
options	COMPAT_43	#Compatible with BSD 4.3 [KEEP THIS!]

The generic kernel defines all of these. In addition, there are several others in the LINT file that you may take interest in, such as NTFS, CODA, and EXT2FS.

For the VMware SCSI controller and disk support, you'll need the following:

device	bt0	at isa?	# BusLogic SCSI host controller
device	scbus		# SCSI bus (required)
device	da		# Direct Access (disks)

There's a SCSI delay option that waits for SCSI devices to finish their initial configuration before beginning the SCSI probe. The default delay is 15,000 ms, but you can set a much lower value for use under VMware so that your system boots a little faster. Take care with dual configuration systems; you may need to set this value higher with real SCSI hardware.

options	SCSI_DELAY=1000

Ethernet Interfaces

You can configure VMware's Ethernet interfaces with just one line:

device	lnc0	at isa? port 0x280 irq 10 drq 0

If you have more than one interface, don't worry that this line says lnc0. The driver's probe also finds lnc1 and lnc2 under this setup. Don't worry about the port and IRQ values, either.

You'll also need these for proper networking support:

pseudo-device	loop	# Network loopback
pseudo-device	ether	# Ethernet support

Serial Ports

FreeBSD doesn't support IRQ sharing, so it's useful only for configuring two serial ports:

device	sio0	at isa? port IO_COM1 flags 0x10 irq 4
device	sio1	at isa? port IO_COM2 irq 3

Parallel Ports

You'll find FreeBSD's all in one place:

```
device         ppc0    at isa? irq 7
device         ppbus            # Parallel port bus (required)
device         lpt              # Printer
device         plip             # TCP/IP over parallel
device         ppi              # Parallel port interface device
```

USB Devices

The following are necessary for basic USB support (controller, keyboard, mouse, and storage devices):

```
device         uhci
device         usb
device         ugen
device         uhid
device         ukbd
device         umass            # (Requires scbus, da)
device         ums
```

There are several other parameters; check the LINT configuration file for all of them.

Floppy Disk, Keyboard, Mouse, and Sound Devices

Here are some miscellaneous drivers for use under VMware, including the sound driver, mentioned earlier:

```
# Floppy controller and drives
device         fdc0    at isa? port IO_FD1 irq 6 drq 2
device         fd0     at fdc0 drive 0
device         fd1     at fdc0 drive 1
# Keyboard and PS/2-type mouse
device         atkbdc0 at isa? port IO_KBD
device         atkbd0  at atkbdc? irq 1 flags 0x1
device         psm0    at atkbdc? irq 12
# Sound Support
device         sbc0 at isa? port 0x220 irq 5 drq 1 flags 0x15
device         pcm
```

7.6   The FreeBSD Boot Manager

For the most part, you probably won't need to change the FreeBSD boot loader. Unlike Linux Loader (LILO), it can actually look inside the BSD filesystem and load a kernel based on just a file name, without having to make a map of the loadable blocks.

The FreeBSD loader uses a language called Forth to do much of its work. You'll find the configuration in the /boot directory. For the most part, you'll typically want to make only cosmetic changes. Look in /boot/defaults/loader.conf for the default configuration. If you want to change anything, put the update in /boot/loader.conf.

7.7   FreeBSD System Statistics

When running FreeBSD under VMware Workstation, you may be interested in how well your guest system manages its resources. An invaluable tool for finding out is the vmstat command. Its output, with no arguments, looks like this:

procs			memory		page							disks		faults			cpu		
r	b	w	avm	fre	flt	re	pi	po	fr	sr	ad0	da0	in	sy	cs	us	sy	id
1	0	0	15896	4512	36	1	1	0	32	7	0	0	206	210	23	3	4	93

One thing of particular interest is the figure under memory and fre; this is the number of remaining free memory pages. Pages are 1024 bytes, so in this example, there are roughly 4.5 MB free on the system. Active pages show up under avm; if a process did something in the past 20 seconds, it is considered active, and its pages go toward the avm total.

The procs statistics pertain to system load. The number under r shows how many processes are ready to go, b signifies blocked processes (those waiting for disk access, for example), and w indicates processes that would be ready to run but are swapped out of real memory. If you have a lot of processes under r, then either you need a faster CPU or you're running some long-term jobs. If anything appears under w, your system is slow because you need more memory.

The rest of the information has to do with kernel performance; page faults and replacements, disk statistics, and CPU usage. If you've ever taken a course on operating systems, this may be of some interest to you, and you should read the vmstat manual page. Running vmstat with a number *n* as an argument keeps vmstat running, printing an update every *n* seconds.

The /proc filesystem on FreeBSD doesn't offer the same kernel-level information that Linux does (the Linux /proc is somewhat "impure" because it has so much extra information in addition to the process statistics). You can get at most of the kernel parameters in FreeBSD through special programs that talk to devices in /dev; an example of this is the mixer utility for a sound card's mixer.

8

OTHER GUEST OPERATING SYSTEMS

The previous three chapters discussed operating systems that are advertised to work under VMware. However, there are many more operating systems for PCs than these, and you might wonder what their status is under VMware Workstation.

The bad news is that you can't run every last PC operating system under VMware Workstation. The biggest technical problem is that the *x*86 architecture (also called IA-32) is not *strictly virtualizable*, meaning that some machine code instructions do different things in protected mode than they do in regular user mode.

Since *all* operating system code running under a virtual machine executes in user mode, this inconsistency can be a big problem for kernel code. However, there are workarounds if you know what the operating system kernel is going to do. The VMware team focused on getting the major operating systems to work based on the behavior of these systems' kernels.

Another problem VMware has to tackle when working with various operating systems is that Workstation's devices have many different kinds of interface modes and commands, some of which are quite esoteric. While considerable effort has gone into making everything work, some of the more peculiar things invariably slip through the cracks, and worse still, some operating systems actually use these strange modes.

The good news is that you can, in fact, get several other operating systems to work under VMware Workstation, or to work at least partially, even if you don't have the source code. However, you need to keep one thing in mind:

VMware, Inc. supports Windows, Linux, and FreeBSD as guest operating systems. Anything else is unsupported: It is considered either experimental or simply unknown. That includes not only everything in this chapter, but beta release operating systems as well. Don't bug VMware's technical support staff with questions about an unsupported guest operating system, even if it burns down your house. (That said, if you're really into experimentation, go to http://www.freeos.com/ for a rundown of systems you can get for a PC for free.)

This chapter covers several very different systems: NetBSD, OpenBSD, Solaris, Novell Netware, FreeDOS, and Oberon. All run to some degree under VMware Workstation but may have their own little quirks.

8.1 CPU Idle and VMware Workstation

As mentioned in Chapter 5, it's important for a guest operating system to call a CPU idle instruction (like HLT) when the kernel isn't doing anything. The same holds true for Solaris and FreeDOS, as discussed in this chapter. In most cases, you can get an add-on utility or operating system upgrade to call the HLT instruction.

If an operating system doesn't call such idle or halt instructions on your processor, the kernel runs a simple processing loop when there is nothing else to do (called *busy-waiting*—the silicon version of twiddling its thumbs). Busy-waiting causes problems under VMware, because the constantly active processor means that VMware asks for use of the processor on the host system all the time.

While under a Windows host, you probably won't be able to tell that the system is busy (unless you look at a performance meter or happen to notice that other applications run a bit more sluggishly than usual), with a Linux host you can tell immediately by running uptime or top. When you do, you'll see that the load average goes to 1 or more, and top always shows VMware at the top of the list, taking up nearly 100 percent in the %CPU column. That's a problem. And busy-waiting further degrades actual performance under a Linux host as a result of the kernel's scheduler.

Under normal circumstances, the kernel gives a process a fair slice of CPU time. It permits the process to run for a while—until the process's time slice is up, or the process needs to access some I/O subsystem.

The kernel will not allow a process to monopolize the CPU. Once a process has used the CPU for a fair amount of time, the kernel preempts it and gives everything else on the system a chance to run before letting the CPU-intensive process run again. The kernel doesn't care or even notice that the process is busy-waiting; it simply knows that this process wants to use the CPU all of the time, and that it's fine to put it on the back burner if necessary. Furthermore, if the process busy-waits most of the time, it's likely that any real computation will come between chunks of busy-waiting. The kernel will inevitably interrupt the process during this time, killing its cache and invoking more cost when its turn comes around again. And you may waste even more CPU while waiting for things to come back into cache.

The bottom line is that VMware acts just like any other process in this regard, except that when it is told to run halt or idle instructions, it lets go of the processor and thus has a much better shot at getting it back when it actually needs to do any real computation.

Even if you don't really notice a slowdown under your host system, there are also serious consequences with regards to power—namely, your processor is always running at full tilt, using much more power and generating more heat than it should. If you decide to run a nonidling guest system under VMware Workstation on a notebook, your batteries will drain quickly.

8.2 NetBSD and OpenBSD

There are two popular BSD Unix variants for the PC in addition to FreeBSD (Chapter 7). They are NetBSD and OpenBSD. Both work as guest operating systems under VMware Workstation. Although VMware, Inc. does not officially support them, the NetBSD and OpenBSD communities do their part to keep their kernels compatible with VMware Workstation.

The NetBSD team tries to make this operating system run on as many architectures as possible. As a result, it enjoys a diverse user base, with support for many machines that most people have never even heard of. It's very much a hacker's operating system, though it's still rather flexible (with a fairly clean installation), and it works under VMware. NetBSD's website is http://www.netbsd.org.

OpenBSD is a NetBSD split-off. It doesn't include quite as much support for exotic platforms as NetBSD, but instead strives to squash as many bugs as possible, especially those related to security, and the OpenBSD team actively adds security features to the system. As a result, OpenBSD is very popular with security-minded people. You'll find OpenBSD on the net at http://www.openbsd.org.

Because VMware does not officially support NetBSD and OpenBSD, there are no VMware Tools for these guest systems. However, if you want graphics, the VMware graphics driver in XFree86 4.1 and above works. Configuration is the same as for FreeBSD and Linux (see section 6.5.2), except for the configuration of the mouse driver. We'll get to the mouse in a bit.

NetBSD 1.5.2 and OpenBSD 2.9 were the specific BSD versions used in this section's preparation.

8.2.1 Installing NetBSD

If you're installing NetBSD, select **FreeBSD** as the guest operating system in VMware's Configuration Editor or Configuration Wizard while you're setting up the virtual machine inside VMware. The NetBSD installer should mostly run fine under VMware, but it may not get the disk geometry right, particularly the number of cylinders. It may guess correctly when the installer asks you to enter the geometry by hand, though. Since this is a concern, check the geometry in the VMware BIOS in the **Main** section by moving the cursor to the disk and pressing ENTER. (Write down the disk information before running the installer.)

If you want to boot an existing NetBSD installation, your concerns are the same as those for FreeBSD (that is, you want to disable any X Window System display manager). Your system starts xdm from /etc/rc.d/xdm. To disable it, place

```
xdm=NO
```

in your /etc/rc.conf file.

To get rid of any other running daemons, look in /etc/defaults/rc.conf, but don't change that file. If you find it, disable it in /etc/rc.conf.

8.2.2   Installing OpenBSD

There's nothing particularly special about the OpenBSD installation under VMware Workstation. Keep the following in mind:

- Choose **FreeBSD** as your guest operating system (among other things, this gives you an IDE virtual disk).

- When you set up a new virtual disk, the easiest way to make OpenBSD happy is to give the OpenBSD installer use of the whole disk and accept the default partitioning scheme. If you really want to create your own scheme, make certain that your partitions are at an offset above 63. You can damage the disk's MBR if you don't do this, and you'll have to reinstall the operating system until you get it right.

- You shouldn't have to worry about disabling xdm, unless you're using a preexisting installation.

- The main system configuration file is /etc/rc.conf.

IMPORTANT   *Don't try to install OpenBSD 2.8 under VMware Workstation. The Ethernet driver may cause VMware to abort. Try version 2.9 or later.*

8.2.3   NetBSD and OpenBSD Devices

Because NetBSD and OpenBSD have the same origin, their device files and interfaces are very similar. The only halfway tricky part is figuring out where your system put them. The fastest way to get started is to run the dmesg (or dmesg | less) command to see the system's startup messages.

If you're having trouble getting a device to work, an excellent place to look for help is the online manual. BSD devices have excellent documentation; each manual page normally lists the device name, the kernel configuration, and other relevant manual pages (in the SEE ALSO section). The other manual pages are important. For example, if you want to find information about the sound driver in OpenBSD, you may notice that dmesg says something about sb0. The man sb page yields the device information and directs you to the audio manual page. At the bottom of this document are references to mixerctl and audioctl, the two commands you need to know about to play a sound. Furthermore, man audioctl provides an example of how to play a sound.

Disks

Disk devices in NetBSD and OpenBSD differ from FreeBSD both in name and partition assignment. The ATA/IDE devices are /dev/wd*. NetBSD and OpenBSD also allow you to use a PC partitioning scheme with their own fdisk program; the NetBSD system ID is 169 (hex A9), and the OpenBSD ID is 166 (hex A6). As with FreeBSD, you normally place the BSD disk label inside a NetBSD or OpenBSD partition. However, there is no extra level of device names; for example, there's no /dev/wd0s1.

NetBSD maps the partitions from disklabel right to the device name, so that if you're working with wd0, you need to use only /dev/wd0a. Furthermore, in NetBSD, /dev/wd0c normally represents only the BSD part of the disk; you'll find the entire disk at /dev/wd0d. In addition, the kernel remaps anything on the PC-style partition table that doesn't have a BSD system ID. If you have a FAT partition on wd0, NetBSD may decide to map it to /dev/wd0e, and OpenBSD may place it at /dev/wd0i. The easiest way to figure out what the kernel and disklabel did (or are going to do) is to run disklabel on the disk and look at the last few lines, as shown in this example, which has two 99-cylinder partitions (this example is from NetBSD; OpenBSD is similar):

#	size	offset	fstype	[fsize	bsize	cpg]			
c:	94500	94500	unused	0	0		#	(Cyl.	100 - 199)
d:	204120	0	unused	0	0		#	(Cyl.	0 - 215)
e:	94500	0	MSDOS				#	(Cyl.	0 - 99)
f:	94500	94500	unused	0	0		#	(Cyl.	100 - 199)

PS/2 Mouse Port

In NetBSD and OpenBSD, the kernel normally puts another protocol level (wsmouse) on top of the actual mouse protocol to provide a uniform interface over all supported hardware (on all architectures, not just the PC). The result is that the original mouse driver is never assigned to a device in /dev, but goes through the /dev/wsmouse* ports instead. XFree86 supports the wsmouse protocol. If you don't want this, then you'll need to remove the wsmouse driver in the kernel configuration and recompile.

USB Devices

The USB support in NetBSD and OpenBSD is extremely similar to the FreeBSD support outlined in section 7.4.8 because much of the kernel source code is the same. (This is common in the BSD community; for example, support for a device could start out in NetBSD, and then someone from the FreeBSD team might pick it up, modify it to work with another kernel, add some more features, and so on.) Because there are so many kinds of USB devices, the easiest way to learn about a particular device under any BSD system is to look at the manual pages: Run man -k usb and search the results for something suitable.

Sound

In NetBSD, this sequence of commands sets a few mixer settings to their maximum values and then plays a sound file (the file here is klaatu5.wav):

```
mixerctl -w inputs.dac=248 outputs.master=248
audioplay klaatu5.wav
```

If you're planning to spend any time on this, you should read NetBSD's manual pages for mixerctl and audioplay.

OpenBSD is similar, but there is no audioplay command. Instead, you first make an adjustment to the current driver settings with the audioctl command and then work with /dev/audio directly. For more information, look at the audioctl manual page.

Miscellaneous NetBSD Devices

Device Type	Device Names	Notes
ATAPI CD-ROM	/dev/cd*	e.g. /dev/cd0a
Floppy drives	/dev/fd*, /dev/rfd*	
Ethernet interfaces	le0-le2	No device files in /dev
Serial ports (dial-out)	/dev/dty0*	Only the first two ports function
Serial ports (dial-up)	/dev/tty0*	Only the first two ports function
Parallel ports	/dev/lpt*	Unidirectional only

Miscellaneous OpenBSD Devices

Device Type	Device Names	Notes
ATAPI CD-ROM	/dev/cd*	ATAPI-to-SCSI emulation
Floppy drives	/dev/fd*, /dev/rfd*	
Ethernet interfaces	le1-le3	No device files in /dev
Serial ports (dial-out)	/dev/cua0*	Only the first two ports function
Serial ports (dial-up)	/dev/tty0*	Only the first two ports function
Parallel ports	/dev/lpa*	Unidirectional polling interface

8.2.4   NetBSD Kernels

NetBSD's kernel parameters are completely different from those of FreeBSD. Before you start, you'll need to install the kernel source code, which you'll find at ftp://ftp.netbsd.org in/pub/NetBSD/NetBSD-*version*/source/sets/syssrc.tgz.

The build process is virtually the same as for any other BSD system:

1. Unpack the source code `tarball` in the `/` directory.

2. The configuration directory is `/sys/arch/i386/conf`; change to this location and examine the contents. You'll find a number of kernel configuration files in addition to `GENERIC`. One of particular interest may be (I'm not making this up) `ZYGORTHIAN-SPACE-RAIDERS`, which turns on every single supported device driver and option. The `GENERIC` kernel is quite large—you'll probably want to pare it somewhat.

3. Copy the `GENERIC` file to a new file called `VMWARE` and cut it down to size as you please. For example, you can get rid of anything that has to do with PCMCIA. Notice that there are several different bus types (`pci`, `eisa`, `isapnp`, and so on), and that the same device may appear under different buses.

4. Run `config VMWARE`. If you eliminated a bus but left in a device that uses that bus, `config` catches it.

5. Check the dependencies:

```
cd ../VMWARE
make depend
```

6. If there are no dependency problems, run `make` to compile the kernel. This can take a while.

7. Your new kernel is in a file called `netbsd`. Install it with

```
mv /netbsd /netbsd.0
cp netbsd /
```

8. Reboot to test your new kernel.

If something doesn't work right and you need to go back to an old kernel, you can get a boot prompt if you press ESC during the wait when the

```
>> NetBSD/i386 BIOS Boot
```

prompt appears. You'll get a simple > prompt. Just enter `boot wd0a:netbsd.0` if you want to boot the backup kernel (assuming that your root is on `wd0a`).

8.2.5 OpenBSD Kernels

The OpenBSD kernel configuration is almost identical to the NetBSD process, except for the following:

- You get the source code via CVS from openbsd.org.
- The compile directory is `../compile/CONFNAME`, where `CONFNAME` is your configuration file name.
- The kernel's name is `bsd`, not `netbsd`.
- The boot loader is different.

For more details, look at the OpenBSD FAQ at http://www.openbsd.org/; there's a whole section on compiling kernels.

8.3 Novell Netware

Though primarily a network software server package, Novell Netware Server comes with its own set of device drivers (for network interface cards, in particular). These special drivers work under VMware Workstation, though VMware's support for Netware Server is experimental at this writing. (Netware was originally DOS based, but it moves farther from DOS with each release.) We'll discuss Netware Server 4 and 5 in this section.

8.3.1 Configuring Your Virtual Machine and Installing Netware

It's fairly simple to install either version of Netware on a virtual machine because the CD installation process works. To do so, first *completely* configure your virtual machine, including all serial and parallel ports. For Server 4, use 48 MB for the guest system memory size. In Server 5, the required amount is 128 MB, though you may be able to get away with 64 MB. Use a virtual disk with a 2-GB capacity for both versions.

For Netware Server in particular, it's likely that you will also want your virtual machine to talk to something on your real network. Therefore, you'll want to use VMware's bridged networking instead of the host-only or NAT networks (unless, of course, you're testing the server with clients on other VMware guest systems).

Create a Partition

Netware requires a small DOS partition to boot. Server version 5 comes with DOS 7, so all you need to do is boot your virtual machine from the CD. For Server 4, you need to create the partition yourself. (See section 5.3.3 for details; do not use FreeDOS.)

This boot partition should be about 50 to 60 MB in size; leave the rest of the disk blank. The important part of installing DOS for a Netware 4 installation is that you need the CD-ROM driver so that you can run the installer on the Server 4 installation CD.

HINT *Make a copy of your virtual disk as soon as you install the DOS partition so that if you mess up the Netware installation, you'll have a backup. You can use a program such as FIPS on the copy to resize the DOS partition later if you need to use the DOS partition for something else.*

Install the Software

Now you need to install the software and make a few customizations for VMware. In particular, you need to install a CPU idle program such as DOSIDLE, described in section 5.6.1, or your virtual machine will drain any CPU time that your host system allows, impairing performance on the host and the guest. You can get these from the VMware website; to locate them, use the search function on nw4-idle.nlm or nw5-idle.nlm.

Server 5

As described earlier, first boot your virtual machine from the CD-ROM.

There's a slight problem with the graphical console; it won't see the mouse unless you happen to move it during the console startup. For now, just use the keyboard to install the system; you'll disable the graphics console in a bit.

When the installer asks you about the network card, pick the AMD PCnet PCI card; then complete your installation. When you've finished installing the server, go to the console and do the following:

1. Copy the `nw5-idle.nlm` CPU idle module from the VMware website to the `C:\NWSERVER` directory.

2. Edit your `AUTOEXEC.NCF` file with a command like `edit sys:\system\ autoexec.ncf`. First, delete `startx.ncf` to disable the graphical console (and get around the mouse problem). Then add this to the *bottom* to enable the CPU idle module you installed in step 1:

```
LOAD C:\NWSERVER\NW5-IDLE
```

3. Reboot the virtual machine to enable these changes.

Server 4

Once you get your DOS partition set up with CD-ROM support (as discussed earlier), insert the Netware 4 installation CD in your drive, make sure that the drive is connected to your virtual machine, use the `cd` command to go to the drive, and run `install` to start the installer.

Install Netware exactly as you normally would, except for the network card. When you get to that part, bypass the driver installation with F10. When you finish, put the finishing touches on as follows:

1. Go to the server console and copy the `nw4-idle.nlm` module from the VMware website to `C:\NWSERVER`.

2. While still at the server console, use

```
edit sys:\system\autoexec.ncf
```

to edit the server startup file. Go to the end and add the two lines shown here for the VMware network virtual card. The first line loads the PCnet driver, and the second binds the IPX protocol stack to the driver:

```
LOAD PCNTNW PCI SLOT=2 FRAME=type
BIND IPX TO PCNTNW NET=address
```

Here, *type* is your frame type (`Ethernet_802.2`, `Ethernet_802.3`, `Ethernet_II`, or whatever), and *address* is your network address number.

NOTE *If you use AMD's driver from the company's website, the driver name is CPCNTNW instead of PCNTNW.*

3. While still in the editor, add

```
LOAD C:\NWSERVER\NW4-IDLE
```

to the very bottom of the file to enable the CPU idler.

4. Reboot your system to make the changes take effect.

8.3.2 Miscellaneous Notes

Since VMware supports multiple network cards, you can load the network driver for multiple cards and specify different frame types for different cards with the SLOT parameter described earlier in the Server 4 section (the same is true for Server 5).

The Ethernet card slots should start at 2. When you use the BIND command, you can specify which frame type goes with which IPX network by using PCNTNW_82, PCNTNW_83, PCNTNW_II, or PCNTNW_SP instead of PCNTNW.

NOTE *If your host system is Linux, you may want to check out its IPX networking capabilities. A good place to start is the IPX-HOWTO. You can make your Linux machine route IPX packets, share files, act as a print server or client, and even tunnel IPX over IP. It's also possible to make Linux guest systems talk IPX, though this is not quite as useful on a host system.*

8.4 Solaris

The Solaris Intel Platform Edition is a port of Sun Microsystems' popular SunOS 5.*x* series operating system to the IA-32 architecture. Its behavior is nearly identical to that of Solaris on the SPARC architecture, and it works as a guest under VMware Workstation for Linux.

NOTE *Solaris's version numbering can be confusing. Solaris 2.x is identical to SunOS 5.x. However, somewhere along the line, Sun decided to drop the first digit and the dot, so Solaris 2.8 is the same as Solaris 8. Solaris 2.x is a System V Release 4–based Unix system, and Solaris 2.8 is free for up to 99 computers with under 8 processors.*

One unfortunate aspect of Solaris under VMware Workstation is that it lacks support for the *x*86 HLT instruction (discussed earlier). When the Solaris kernel runs its idle loop, it busy-waits, not unlike DOS when it has nothing to do, as described in section 8.1. As discussed previously, busy-waiting translates into wasted real CPU time for the VMware process, and as a result, your host system runs more slowly than it should.

In fact, this deficiency means that you can't effectively run Solaris 8 under VMware all the time, sitting in the background, nor can you run it as a server without penalty. However, Solaris under VMware is great for testing package portability, running a Solaris-only program now and then, and looking up Solaris system characteristics.

8.4.1 Installing Solaris

It's not terribly hard to install Solaris 8 under VMware Workstation, but there are a few gotchas. To install, boot from the installation CD and not the floppy drive. (In fact, you should disconnect your virtual floppy device when installing and booting; there's an unimplemented passthrough function that will pop up and cause VMware to abort otherwise.)

- Be sure to configure at least 64 MB of memory on your virtual machine; the Solaris installer will abort if your machine has less (and you will have wasted plenty of time getting up to that point; the Solaris installer is *not* fast).

- When you get to the part of the installation process that mentions kdmconfig, press F4 to bypass the windowing system configuration. (You don't want to deal with the X Window System, at least not yet, and especially not under the slow VGA16 driver and virtual hardware.) The installer will put you in command-line mode. (This isn't speedy by any stretch of the imagination, so you may want to take an extended break while the installer transfers the files to disk.)

- When you first boot, Solaris asks you again about the windowing system, and again you should bypass it. If you run kdmconfig, you can also bypass and suppress the message. When some ugly-looking error messages about the windowing system spill out all over your log-in prompt, ignore them.

- Once installation is complete, log in as root and run catman -w to create the whatis file so that you can run man -k *keyword* to search for manual pages. Then visit http://sunfreeware.com/ to get some free software, notably the gcc C compiler.

8.4.2 Solaris Devices

As for any Unix system, you'll find Solaris devices in /dev. However, most of the device file entries for hardware devices are dynamic, and most of the items in /dev are actually links to special files in the /devices directory. You'll need to make your system create these files at boot time after you add new hardware (a process called reconfiguring the devices).

Reconfiguring Devices

There are two basic ways to initiate device reconfiguration. One way is to enter b -r when you get the boot prompt (this prompt tells you to enter b to boot or i to run an interpreter). The other way is to boot your system normally and then create a trigger file and reboot when your system is up, with these commands:

```
touch /reconfigure
reboot
```

When the reconfiguration occurs in the boot sequence, these lines appear, telling you that the system is creating device file entries:

```
Configuring /dev and /devices
Configuring the /dev directory (compatibility devices)
```

WARNING *Never power off, reset, or interrupt the system during this configuration process; you could lose an important device file such as a disk and be unable to boot again.*

8.4.3 Booting Solaris

Solaris Intel Platform Edition boots through a two-step process. It first loads a (DOS) configuration assistant from a DOS partition.

If you enter the assistant in interactive mode (as you would when first installing), you can boot from an alternative device and probe for new or added hardware. You can also scan for specific hardware, but be careful: If you miss a device in the scan, the Solaris kernel won't find it. (This can be a big problem even for a small device such as the keyboard.)

NOTE *When running under VMware Workstation, you shouldn't need to deal with the configuration assistant much; the kernel should automatically detect most new devices during a reconfigure boot.*

8.4.4 Devices Relevant to VMware Workstation

The following is a guide to the devices relevant to VMware Workstation.

NOTE *For a complete list of devices, see the* Solaris 7 *or* 8 (Intel Platform Edition) Device Configuration Guide, *in the online AnswerBook2. (Sun documentation is at http://docs.sun.com/ and a few mirror sites.)*

IDE Disks

There are two directories in /dev: /dev/dsk for regular devices and /dev/rdsk for raw devices (raw disk devices provide direct access to the disk).

The first VMware IDE device shows up at /dev/dsk/c0d0 and, as with the BSD systems, it's sliced. For example, on the first disk, the /dev/dsk/c0d0s*n* partitions are the Unix partitions on the Solaris slice; the /dev/dsk/c0d0p*n* partitions are the PC-style partitions. Each file in /dev/dsk has a raw disk in /dev/rdsk with the same name. Here is a full list of possible name assignments under VMware Workstation:

c0d0   Primary Master
c0d1   Primary Slave
c1d0   Secondary Master
c1d1   Secondary Slave

To partition a disk and put a filesystem on it, you must work with the raw devices. For example, to work with the slave drive on the primary interface, you'd use /dev/rdsk/c0d1p0, not /dev/dsk/c0d1p0.

To partition a disk, use the format command on the Solaris slice, such as

```
format /dev/rdsk/c0d1p0
```

Here, format is an interactive program. If the disk is blank, with no PC-style partition table (as a new VMware virtual disk would be), you'll have to run fdisk to put one in place. The format program runs fdisk for you if it can't find a PC partition table on the disk. When you have a PC partition table on the disk, run the partition command inside format to put partitions on the disks. Make sure to label the disk before you quit.

Once you're done with format, you must put a filesystem on the partition. Use newfs /dev/rdsk/*devname*, where *devname* is a disk device.

Solaris uses /etc/vfstab (not /etc/fstab) as a list of filesystems to mount at boot time. If you're used to other kinds of Unix, take care when adding an entry that you specify the device name correctly in the first *two* fields in this file.

NOTE *As for SCSI disks, VMware Workstation doesn't yet support the BusLogic 24-bit command set, and unfortunately, Solaris uses these commands. Therefore, SCSI disks won't work on a Solaris virtual machine.*

CD-ROM Drives

VMware's ATAPI CD-ROM drives show up in /dev/dsk alongside the hard disk devices, but with an extra component: a target (for example, t0). If you're used to working with SCSI drives under Solaris, you'll recognize the names.

Normally, the daemon vold attaches the CD-ROM to the system, in a directory under /cdrom. However, if you need to know the device name for some reason (for example, if you want to use dd to copy the content from it), use the first partition. For example, /dev/dsk/c1t0d0p0 works for a CD-ROM located at the master of the secondary interface.

NOTE *VMware may flag a few nonfatal unimplemented commands for the CD-ROM drive when you try to access the drive normally. Just click **OK** when the message comes up; this won't crash your virtual machine.*

Ethernet

VMware's virtual AMD PCnet interfaces show up as pcn0, pcn1, and pcn2. The ifconfig -a command that you'd use for any other Unix system works for determining the IP configuration.

Unfortunately, the virtual Ethernet interface's performance isn't terribly good, in part because the kernel doesn't idle the CPU properly (to give the host system a fair chance to send its data), and also because certain Solaris Intel Edition drivers aren't well optimized.

Serial Ports

As with BSD, there are different devices for call-in/direct and dial-out serial ports. The direct connections, also used for getty connections, are /dev/ttya and /dev/ttyb. These devices also show up as /dev/term/a and /dev/term/b.

For dialing out, /dev/cua0 and /dev/cua1 are available, with /dev/cua/a and /dev/cua/b as synonyms. Solaris does not support more than two 16550A serial ports.

Parallel Ports

One unidirectional parallel port is available at /dev/lp0 on Solaris running on IA-32.

Floppy Drives

Currently, floppy drives don't work with Solaris under VMware Workstation. Don't try to mount a device like /dev/fd0c because the Solaris kernel uses an unimplemented feature of the floppy drive, and you'll make VMware panic and die.

Sound

The first thing you need to do for sound under VMware is to get Solaris to find the sound card if you didn't configure it at installation time. Here's how:

1. Shut down the virtual machine.

2. If you haven't already done so, install the virtual sound card with the VMware Configuration Editor.

3. Power on the virtual machine. When you get the message "Press ESCape to interrupt autoboot within *n* seconds," press ESC to bring up the Solaris *x*86 configuration assistant.

4. Run a full scan in the assistant with F2. It should report that it found a Sound Blaster device on the ISA bus.

5. Continue through the assistant, booting off the disk. When you get all the way through and to the boot prompt, use b -r to reconfigure the devices.

6. Boot; you should now have a /dev/audio device.

NOTE *Though you can dump audio (.au) files right to the audio device with a command such as* cat, *you should probably use a utility such as* audioplay, *which knows the appropriate* ioctl() *calls for the device. In particular, if you use* audioplay -v 100 file, *the system plays* file *at full volume, which is what you want for VMware.*

8.4.5 Graphics Mode under Solaris

Though both the XFree86 and Sun VGA16 X Window System servers work, they are as slow as any other VGA16 graphics mode under VMware. However, the VMware driver included with XFree86 4.1 and later versions works fine. (The XF86Config file is identical to the Linux version described in section 6.5.3, except possibly for the Mouse section.)

There isn't much you can do about graphics speed under Solaris. Since the Solaris network driver doesn't perform well, you can't even skirt the issue by sending an X Window System client from the guest to the host.

8.4.6   Solaris 2.7

You'll find that Solaris 2.7 acts much like Solaris 8 (2.8). The biggest problem is the installation, because many versions don't let you boot from the CD-ROM; you must boot from the floppy drive. However, when the Solaris kernel tries to access the floppy drive, it can cause VMware to panic.

Luckily, though, you can still install the operating system because the boot floppy doesn't run the kernel. When the installation asks you which type of installation you want to perform, use that time to disconnect the floppy drive, and everything will run smoothly.

NOTE   *As with Solaris 8, make sure that you bypass the* kdmconfig *stuff for the windowing system, as this will make the installation miserably slow, if it works at all.*

8.5   FreeDOS

One operating system project floating around on the Internet is a completely free implementation of DOS called FreeDOS. FreeDOS works as a guest under VMware with little difficulty, though it does have a few bugs. (You'll find FreeDOS at http://www.freedos.org/.)

Since FreeDOS runs most DOS programs, it's great to have around if you have an old program that you need to use every now and then. FreeDOS offers more than the usual DOS commands, including several Unix-like utilities which, though they behave differently from the comparable DOS utilities, have better online usage hints.

FreeDOS has a number of other uses, too. For instance, its installation floppy contains versions of FDISK and FORMAT if you need to partition a disk and put a DOS filesystem on it. You may also find FreeDOS much more comfortable to use than DOS—its command-line interface offers several amenities, such as file name completion and better editing features. And the FreeDOS FDISK utility installs a simple boot manager that ought to look familiar if you've ever worked with FreeBSD. If you're not familiar with it, it shows all partitions on the disks that it can find with a function key label next to each partition. Press that function key to boot from that partition. The active partition is the default (see section 2.4).

NOTE   *Like DOS, FreeDOS doesn't call the HLT instruction when it isn't doing anything. The same DOSIDLE program that was covered in section 5.6.1 works fine under FreeDOS, so if you're planning to spend any extended amount of time with FreeDOS, you should install the idler.*

8.5.1 FreeDOS Devices

In general, device drivers under FreeDOS try to act like the DOS drivers, but not all are implemented. As the saying goes, your mileage may vary. The hard disk and floppy drives work fine, though the floppy driver isn't terribly fast. (One very significant feature of the drivers is that they are free—most even use the GPL.)

Mouse Driver

FreeDOS comes with a mouse driver called CuteMouse. This very small (3.5k) driver supports many devices and protocols, and anything using the standard DOS mouse interface should work with it. You'll normally find it in the CTMOUSE directory after a FreeDOS installation.

The easiest way to test the FreeDOS mouse driver is to start the driver by running CTMOUSE.EXE; if it's working properly, you should see the message "Installed at PS/2 port." Next, start the EDIT program; if you can move the cursor around with the mouse, things are probably working fine. If so, go ahead and add this to your AUTOEXEC.BAT:

```
C:\CTMOUSE\CTMOUSE.EXE
```

CD-ROM Driver

One somewhat tricky device is the CD-ROM driver.

DOS CD-ROM drivers look for a CD-ROM redirector program called MSCDEX.EXE to bind a driver-defined name and address to a drive letter. However, FreeDOS is a little vague with respect to this. The official story is that you should use a program called FDCDEX.EXE, but not all FreeDOS distributions come with this (the version on the CD doesn't, either). (FDCDEX.EXE is actually the SHSUCDX.EXE redirector, to which you'll find links from the FreeDOS web pages.)

Complicating matters further is that most CD-ROM driver installation programs look for a program called MSCDEX.EXE, and some won't even install if the program doesn't exist (the Mitsumi driver is one such driver). To fix this problem, copy the FreeDOS redirector to MSCDEX.EXE (or use the Microsoft version if you happen to own it).

8.5.2 FreeDOS Installation Hints

Here's one of the easiest ways to install FreeDOS on a virtual disk under VMware Workstation on a Linux host system:

NOTE *If Windows is your host or you'd prefer not to do this anyway, you'll need to make a lot of floppy disk images, one for each .zip file in the distribution.*

1. Configure the floppy image (the .bin file) as your first floppy drive and then power on the virtual machine.

2. When the system boots, use fdisk to partition your virtual disk and use format c: /s to put a filesystem and boot files on the hard drive.

3. Power off the virtual machine and return to your host. Use `vmware-mount.pl` (described in section 11.5) to attach the virtual disk to your host system, create a directory there called `i`, `cd`, and unzip all of the distribution files there.

4. Boot from the floppy image again (if you haven't already) and run `install`. If you were able to put the unpacked distribution files in the `i` directory, enter `c:\i` when the installer asks you for the source.

5. Reboot the virtual machine after first making sure that you disconnect the floppy drive or revert it to a real device so that you don't boot from the wrong device. You should now have a fairly bare (but working) FreeDOS system.

6. You won't have a `CONFIG.SYS` or `AUTOEXEC.BAT` file, so create an `AUTOEXEC.BAT` file with

---

```
PATH=C:\BIN
```

Otherwise, only the usual `COMMAND.COM` commands like `dir` will work unless you actually use `cd` to go to the `BIN` directory; you won't be able to find any system executables. (You can use the `edit` program to create the file; try `c:\bin\ edit autoexec.bat` as soon as the system boots.)

8.6 Oberon

So far, we've talked about systems that are based on traditional ideas or on some variations on older ideas. If you want to try something that's a little different, there's Oberon, a research operating system from ETH Zürich.

Oberon is more than an operating system; it also includes a user environment and programming language. It has two modes of operation. One is a hosted mode, where you run the system under another operating system, such as Linux. You can certainly do this in a guest system running under VMware. The other mode is a native mode, where Oberon takes over the entire hardware. This native mode also works under VMware Workstation.

One thing to remember about research operating systems is that they don't need to follow any rules set forth by any previous system. That includes the user interface, and Oberon's is probably unlike anything you've ever seen. You could describe it as a hyperlinked command-based system, where you construct and customize commands within each "document." Therefore, the documentation for a program can double as the program's user interface.

8.6.1 Oberon Installation Hints

Part of the fun of Oberon is figuring out how the installation process works. This will prove invaluable later, because the installer gets you started with the Oberon user interface right away. However, there are some things you should know about it before you dive right in.

First, you must partition your disk before you boot from the installation floppy. To prepare your hard disk, use whatever boot floppy you can find (Free-DOS works fine); then create two partitions: one large partition for Oberon and one fairly small piece about 50 MB or so. Make both DOS partitions, and put a FAT filesystem on the small one. Now, using either a guest system or something like vmware-mount.pl, copy all of the .Arc files from the Oberon distribution to the smaller filesystem. (You'll use this later to install the extra optional packages on your Oberon system.)

Now you're ready to boot the Oberon installation floppy (the image should be named Oberon0.Dsk or something similar). It contains the Oberon kernel, windowing environment, several drivers, and the installer programs. Don't bother making a boot floppy from the image; just connect your virtual floppy drive to the image itself. The installer system boots and runs almost instantaneously under this configuration; if it seems like you have to wait a while, you may be having some trouble.

At this point, carefully read and follow the on-screen instructions because the installation interface is embedded within them. During the installation, you'll see an option for putting the Oberon filesystem in a big file on a DOS partition or setting up the filesystem on a real partition. Choose the latter, since you're running under VMware and it doesn't really matter if you make a mistake on a virtual disk. Put the filesystem on the larger disk partition you made. (Don't worry if you mess up something—you can always boot from the image again to reinstall or reconfigure the system.)

In the final installation stage, you'll have a few things to configure. The first part is the video driver configuration. In newer versions, a VMware driver will show up in this list. Otherwise, you'll have to stick with VGA16. In the second part, you need to decide how to boot the system. For a VMware virtual disk, make it boot directly from the disk.

You should now be ready to reboot the system. Under some versions of VMware Workstation, the System.Reboot command may make VMware abort, so you might just want to click VMware's Reset button.

After you boot the system from the disk for the first time, you should install the optional packages. As with the installer, a script/document helps you do this. If you put an extra DOS partition on your disk, then all you need to do is copy the files from there. They'll be in the c: drive, though you'll likely need to change the path after the c: in the installer script. Further on down in the script is a pointer to the machine configuration.

Like any well-behaved system, Oberon calls the *x*86 HLT instruction when it isn't doing anything, so it's fine to leave the system running as a VMware Workstation even if you aren't using it.

9

HOST AND GUEST SYSTEM
NETWORK CONFIGURATION

Networking is an important component of VMware's host-guest operating system interaction. Although you can perform a simple file transfer with other virtual devices, such as the virtual CD-ROM and floppy drives, these are generally inconvenient to work with. VMware's networking allows you to do anything you can do between two hosts on a normal network, such as share entire filesystems between host and guest, set up web servers on guest systems, use proxy servers, and send X Window System clients between the host and guest.

This chapter explains how to get VMware's base networking up and running between your host and guest systems. (We'll cover actual network services and applications in the next chapter.)

9.1 VMware's Networking Options

As mentioned in earlier chapters, VMware has three types of network interface card configuration: bridged, host-only, and NAT networking.

A *bridged network* interface puts your virtual machine's network interface on the same level as your host's network interface. Think of it as connecting the network card in your virtual machine to your host machine's network.

Host-only networking creates an entire virtual Ethernet local area network inside the host machine; it does not depend on any external network interfaces.

NAT networking is identical to host-only networking, except that VMware uses network address translation (NAT) to enable communication between guest systems and the rest of the Internet. The link to the outside world is different than in bridged networking; the link is not direct and works only over IP (Internet) networks.

You can configure a virtual machine with any combination of host-only, bridged, and NAT networking.

9.1.1   Network Basics

There are two basic layers to worry about when you configure your network: the link layer and the protocol layer.

The lowest level is a link layer, comprising the actual physical connection and the basic protocol that all interfaces on this kind of connection communicate with. In VMware Workstation, you have an Ethernet link that is relatively easy to set up. The VMware Workstation installer configures everything you need initially on the host system side. All you have to do is install the network drivers, as discussed in the previous four chapters.

Sitting on top of the link level is a lower protocol layer. It specifies how to send data from one host (possibly through several network links) to another host. Higher-level communication schemes build on top of this piece. For example, the current Internet uses the Internet Protocol (IP)[1] as its lower protocol layer. (If you're interested in the full picture, the World Wide Web has two higher-level protocols on top of IP: TCP is the next up, and HTTP is at the very top level.)

9.1.2   IP

This chapter focuses on IP. Nearly everything here relates to IP configuration in some way. Each host on the Internet has an *IP address*—four numbers connected by dots, like this: 10.45.23.124. The numbers range from 1 to 254 (the middle two can also be 0).

The most important thing to know about IP networks is that they are divided into *subnets*. A subnet is a partition of the Internet address space. Normally, this is a simple block of addresses—10.34.23.1 to 10.34.23.254, for example. A *subnet mask* (or *netmask*) blocks off the parts of an Internet address common to its subnet. In the previous example, any IP address of the form 10.34.23.*x* has a 255.255.255.0 netmask. (Each number in an IP address is 8 bits wide; a bit in the mask blocks off a bit in the address.)

When working with VMware's host-only and NAT networks, you'll work primarily with subnets with a mask of 255.255.255.0 (sometimes called *class C subnets*).

To learn more about IP networking, read Andrew Tanenbaum's *Computer Networks* (Prentice-Hall, 1996); for the ultimate programming reference, look at W. Richard Stevens' *Unix Network Programming, Volume 1* (Prentice-Hall, 1998). In addition, your author's *Linux Problem Solver* (No Starch Press, 2000) provides hands-on systems administration information for Linux kernel version 2.2.

---

[1]When we say *IP*, we mean IPv4 (IP version 4), the basis for the current Internet.

There are several other kinds of lower-level protocol types for Ethernet interfaces in addition to IP, such as Novell's IPX and Apple's EtherTalk Phase 2. VMware Workstation supports these as well as anything else that runs on top of Ethernet.

Some operating systems refer to IP in one lump along with TCP/IP (TCP stands for transmission control protocol). Although TCP is the most common protocol paired with IP, IP is also paired with the user datagram protocol (UDP) and the Internet control message protocol (ICMP), among other protocols.

9.2 Bridged Networking

The easiest way to connect a virtual machine to your local area network and the rest of the Internet is with a bridged network interface. Think of this approach as putting an Ethernet card into your virtual machine and plugging it into your local network. Use bridged networking when:

- Your virtual machines need access to the Internet.
- Your local area network is Ethernet.
- Your local area network has plenty of free addresses.
- Connection tracking shortcomings in NAT make it unusable for your applications. See section 9.7 for more details.

Figure 9.1 shows a host machine and three virtual machines with bridged networking. (Note that there is a layer of virtualization between the guest systems and the real network interface, but the connection is essentially direct.)

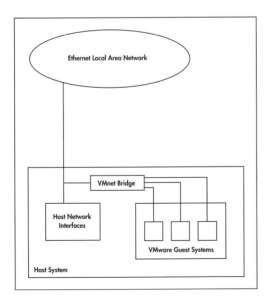

Figure 9.1: Bridged network interface

Setting up a bridged interface on your virtual machine is just like setting up a network interface on any other machine on your real local area network (see section 9.5 for information on each guest operating system). However, bear in mind that each bridged network interface *must* have its own unique network address (an IP address for most networks). You cannot use the same address as your host machine or any other machine on the network, and you should never pick an address at random if you don't know what to choose. (In some cases, you can safely get an address with the DHCP protocol, but if you don't know for sure, ask your network administrator.)

You can't use bridged networking if your host machine's network interface isn't Ethernet (if your sole network connection is a PPP dial-up connection, or if your local network is not Ethernet based—FDDI, for example).

If you can't come up with a network address, can't use bridged networking, or don't want to use a bridged network, your alternative is NAT networking (see section 9.7).

9.3 Host-Only Networking

In contrast to bridged networking, host-only networking exists only within VMware Workstation and the host operating system. The entire network infrastructure (interface cards, hubs, and so on) is entirely virtual and invisible to everything outside your host and guest systems.

With host-only networking, each guest operating system has a network interface as usual. In addition, the host system has a connection to the guest systems' network. These provisions allow communication not only between the host and guest systems, but also between any concurrent guest systems. Figure 9.2 shows a host-only network. The dashed lines indicate that the external network is optional.

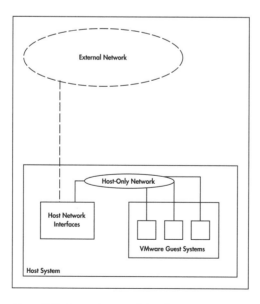

Figure 9.2: Host-only network interface

As the name implies, VMware's default host-only network setup options are geared to services on the host machine only, such as file sharing and printing.

For example, VMware Workstation for Linux comes with a version of an SMB server called SAMBA that allows a Windows guest system to access a filesystem on the Linux host over a host-only network. (NT, 2000, and XP already come with SMB servers, so VMware Workstation for those platforms need not include them.)

9.3.1   Host-Only IP Configuration (Host Operating System)

You can view the host-only interface like a real interface. For example, if you run ifconfig on a Linux host system, part of the output looks like this:

```
vmnet1    Link encap:Ethernet  HWaddr 00:50:56:01:00:00
          inet addr:172.16.144.1  Bcast:172.16.144.255  Mask:255.255.255.0
          UP BROADCAST RUNNING MULTICAST  MTU:1500  Metric:1
          RX packets:3715 errors:0 dropped:0 overruns:0 frame:0
          TX packets:9958 errors:0 dropped:0 overruns:0 carrier:0
          Collisions:0
```

(The output is similar for ipconfig on a Windows host machine.)

Notice in the preceding output that the last number of the IP address (172.16.144.1) is 1. Although you can set this last number to any number you like, it's a good idea to make the host machine number 1 so that you always know where to find it on the network. (The side benefit is that this address won't conflict with the VMware host-only pool of DHCP addresses described in section 9.4.)

When using host-only networking, you'll employ, on a *private subnet*, Internet addresses that do not conflict with those of any other hosts on the Internet—that is, you can use a private subnet for anything you want. An Internet standards document, RFC 1918, defines these addresses as follows:

Network	Netmask
10.0.0.0	255.0.0.0
192.168.0.0	255.255.0.0
172.16.0.0	255.255.0.0

VMware uses pieces of the latter two networks listed in the table for its host-only configuration.

9.3.2   Viewing and Changing Your Host-Only Network Settings

Because private subnets are extremely useful for setting up internal networks, you may already have one in your organization. Therefore, you should be careful that you don't accidentally set up VMware's host-only network so that it conflicts with another network already in use. The VMware installers try to do this for you with a simple ping probe over the subnets.

Though the VMware installer configures host-only networking for you, you may want to set it up by hand (or simply view the current settings). To change or view the settings under each host system, do the following:

Windows NT

Go to the **Network** control panel and click the **Protocols** tab to bring up the **TCP/IP Protocol** properties. Under **Adapter**, select the **VMware Virtual Ethernet Adapter (VMnet*n*)** and pick your new network.

Windows 2000/XP

On Windows 2000 and XP, you'll find a **VMnet** interface inside the **Network** (and **Dial-up**) **Connections** control panel folder. To view its settings, click the icon; then (when the status window appears) click the **Properties** button to bring up the **Internet Protocol (TCP/IP)** properties.

Linux

The easiest way to view the host-only network under a Linux host system is to look at the /etc/vmware/locations file for lines like the last two:

```
answer VNET_1_HOSTONLY yes
answer VNET_1_HOSTONLY_HOSTADDR 192.168.87.1
answer VNET_1_HOSTONLY_NETMASK 255.255.255.0
```

To change this setting, run vmware-config.pl. When this program asks you about networking, use the network editor to alter interface 1.

Although you can change these addresses in /etc/vmware/locations directly, adding host-only network devices is not so easy. (To learn how to do that, see section 9.9.3, which discusses custom network interfaces, later in this chapter.)

NOTE *If you change your host-only network IP configuration and subnet by hand, you'll need to update your VMware DHCP server configuration to reflect the change (as discussed in the following section). If you feel comfortable editing these files, there's nothing wrong with doing it this way; just remember to restart your VMware services after you're done.*

9.4   VMware Host-Only and NAT DHCP Server

One of the most popular ways to configure a networking interface is with the Dynamic Host Configuration Protocol (DHCP). A DHCP server holds network configuration data, so rather than manually setting the IP address, subnet mask, and other information on an operating system, you ask the system to look on the network for a DHCP server. The DHCP server responds with the necessary configuration data. DHCP is the most convenient way to configure guest operating system networking under VMware Workstation's host-only networking, and VMware comes with a DHCP server.

You can tell a DHCP server to hand out information in two ways. One way is to assign IP addresses based on the Ethernet address (which ensures that a client gets the same IP address every time it boots). The other way is to use a pool of IP addresses. The DHCP server draws from this pool to hand out a *lease* on a certain address, saying that it is valid until a certain time. (The client may renew the lease if it needs it for longer.)

VMware's DHCP server is based on the ISC DHCP server, a free package from the Internet Software Consortium (http://www.isc.org/). The difference between the consortium's stock DHCP server and VMware's variant is primarily in that VMware's version does not require any special kernel support for network packet filtering, because it knows how to talk directly to the VMware host-only network interface. You configure the VMware version just as you would the ISC software. Here are the configuration file, lease file, and executable names for Windows and Linux host systems:

File	Windows NT/2000/XP	Linux
Config	\WINNT\system32\vmnetdhcp.conf	/etc/vmware/vmnet1/dhcp/dhcpd.conf
Leases	\WINNT\system32\vmnetdhcp.leases	/etc/vmware/vmnet1/dhcp/dhcpd.leases
Executable	\WINNT\system32\VMNetDHCP.exe	*bindir*/vmnet-dhcpd

In the preceding file listing, *bindir* is the binary directory that you gave to the installation script in Chapter 3. Note the location of the configuration file; it's a text file that you can edit with any text editor. Also, in some host operating system versions, you may have to replace WINNT with WINDOWS.

9.4.1 Creating and Customizing DHCP Configuration Files

Whenever you add a host-only or NAT network interface to a host operating system, the system generates a new DHCP server configuration file (vmnet-dhcp.conf for Windows, dhcpd.conf for Linux). Even though you don't have to write the file by hand, you may want to add some customizations.

The DHCP configuration file has a set of global parameters and sections. The global parameters appear at the beginning of the file. They control general server behavior and look like this:

```
allow unknown-clients;
default-lease-time 1800;        # 30 minutes
max-lease-time 7200;            # 2 hours
```

The sections that follow depend on your host-only network settings. For example, say that your host-only network interface is at 172.16.144.1 on your host system. Your DHCP configuration file should have this section, which tells the DHCP server how to hand out IP addresses:

```
subnet 172.16.144.0 netmask 255.255.255.0 {
    range 172.16.144.128 172.16.144.254;
    option broadcast-address 172.16.144.255;
    option domain-name-servers 172.16.144.1;
    option domain-name "localdomain";
}
```

In the output shown here, subnet and netmask denote the network on which the section parameters are valid, and the range parameter specifies a pool of IP addresses to hand out to any client that asks for one. (You can have more than one range line if you want more than one range of addresses.) And by default, VMware's setup program always reserves IP addresses ending with 128 to 254 for the DHCP pool.

NOTE *You can tell the DHCP server to give the same address to a virtual machine whenever that machine requests an address. You need to fix the MAC address of the virtual machine's Ethernet interface to achieve this; section 9.10 describes how.*

9.5 Guest Operating System Networking Configuration

Each guest operating system has its own interface for networking settings; the following sections provide an overview of each major one. To configure your network interface properly and get it talking to the host system and/or the rest of the world, you'll need to know the essentials for an IP connection, such as how to enter an IP address or choose DHCP configuration.

NOTE *If you choose to configure your guest operating system's network interface manually on a host-only network, pick an IP address where the last number is between 3 and 127, because VMware's default DHCP server configuration (described in the previous section) reserves the numbers 128 through 254. Unless you build a custom network, the subnet mask for a host-only network is always 255.255.255.0.*

To view (and set) your network connections on guest operating systems, use ifconfig (Unix) or ipconfig (Windows) from the command line. When you view your settings, turn on the verbose options (so that you'll get more information), using ifconfig -a and ipconfig /all. (Some versions of Unix require you to use -a to view any configuration whatsoever.)

Test the connection with a ping command on both your host and guest. From the guest, ping your host system with a command like ping 172.16.144.1. Then do the same thing from your host system to the guest.

All modern operating systems can deal with more than one Ethernet interface; VMware offers up to three for its guest systems.

9.5.1   Windows 95, 98, and Me

To configure your network interface under Windows 95/98/Me, do the following:

1. Open the **Network** control panel and click the **Configuration** tab.
2. You should see a **TCP/IP • AMD PCNET Family Ethernet Adapter (PCI-ISA)** component. Double-click it, and the TCP/IP Properties window should appear.
3. On the **IP Address** tab, choose **DHCP** with **Obtain an IP address automatically**, or enter an IP address.
4. If you choose manual configuration and have a bridged or NAT network, add your default gateway on the **Gateway** tab.

9.5.2   Windows NT

To configure your network interface under Windows NT, do the following:

1. On the **Network** control panel, click the **Protocols** tab to bring up the TCP/IP Protocol Properties window.
2. Select the **IP Address** tab; pick the interface you want to configure under **Adapter** and then set the appropriate options for DHCP or static addresses.

9.5.3   Windows 2000/XP

To configure your network interface under Windows 2000 or XP, do the following:

1. Open the **Network and Dial-up Connections** (2000) or **Network Connections** (XP) folder on the control panel.
2. Double-click the **Local Area Connection** corresponding to the VMware network interface that you want to change to get a status window.
3. Configure the interface by clicking **Properties**.
4. For the TCP/IP settings, display the Internet Protocol (TCP/IP) Properties window (a new window). The selections for obtaining addresses automatically here specify DHCP configuration.

9.5.4   Linux

Each Linux distribution has its own way of configuring an Ethernet interface. Still, it's always possible to set up the interface manually with the `ifconfig` command.
  For example, this sets the guest system's IP address to 172.16.144.99:

```
ifconfig eth0 172.16.144.99 netmask 255.255.255.0 up
```

As mentioned in Chapter 6, `eth0` is the first Ethernet interface on the system.

To add a default route for this example, you can use the route command:

```
route add default gw 172.16.144.1
```

As far as the various Linux distributions go, every configuration tool ultimately creates or modifies some file on your system. (For example, when you configure an interface in Red Hat 7 [Config - Networking - Client tasks - Basic host information in the linuxconf program], you change a /etc/sysconfig/network-scripts/ifcfg-ethn file.)

If your network has a static (non-DHCP) configuration, you'll find that each distribution ultimately runs ifconfig in some network startup script at boot time. For example, Debian's /etc/init.d/networking script performs this function.

DHCP is another story. Most Linux distributions use the ISC dhclient program to get a DHCP connection at boot time if the Ethernet interface is set to an automatic configuration. Red Hat, however, uses a program called pump for DHCP client configuration.

By default, dhclient tries to configure all network interfaces, but you can single out an interface by supplying an argument. For instance, dhclient eth0 configures the DHCP server for the first Ethernet interface.

9.5.5 FreeBSD

As with Linux, you can manually specify the IP settings for VMware's lnc interfaces with the ifconfig command. You can either set the options manually in /etc/rc.conf or use the /stand/sysinstall command. For the sysinstall utility, go through the menus as follows: **Configure • Networking • Interfaces** (press space on this option instead of ENTER); then specify **lnc***n*, where *n* is the number of the interface you want to configure.

You can also change the settings in /etc/rc.conf. If you're configuring interface lnc0, use something like

```
ifconfig_lnc0="172.16.144.103 netmask 255.255.255.0"
```

for a fixed configuration. To use DHCP, use the following instead:

```
ifconfig_lnc0="DHCP"
```

9.5.6 NetBSD

In NetBSD, put your parameters for your interfaces in /etc/ifconfig.le*n*. For example, /etc/ifconfig.le0 could look like this:

```
172.16.144.98 netmask 255.255.255.0
```

To use DHCP with NetBSD, don't create this file; instead, edit /etc/rc.conf and add

```
dhclient=YES
```

To run DHCP on only one specific interface (say le0), use

```
dhclient_flags="le0"
```

You can manually set the default gateway for any BSD system as follows:

```
route add default 172.16.144.1
```

Checking the routing table is the same as in Linux; use netstat -nr.

9.6   Hostname Lookup

When you set IP networking in a guest operating system, one of the most important configuration steps is setting up hostname resolution of some sort. Without it, your host and guest systems won't be able to convert names to IP addresses for the VMware network, and the problems you may encounter will range from minor annoyances (typing in IP addresses instead of names) to major breakdowns, because some services refuse to function if they can't resolve hostnames.

Setting up hostnames on a virtual machine with bridged networking is no different than doing so for any other node on your local area network because the machine can talk directly to a DNS server. However, a host-only network without extra provisions (such as NAT) cannot do this, so you have to provide some extra hints to both the host and guest operating systems.

9.6.1   Creating a Hosts File

The easiest way to add hostname mappings is to create a hosts file. Though the file format is the same across all types of host and guest systems, the location is not. Here are the locations:

Unix	/etc/hosts
Windows NT/2000/XP	\WINNT\system32\drivers\etc\HOSTS
Windows 95/98/Me	\WINDOWS\HOSTS.SAM
Windows 3.x	Varies; it's easiest to do a search

(For some Windows NT–based installations, you may need WINDOWS instead of WINNT.) The hosts file is a plain-text file, so you can use any text editor to change it. To get hostname resolution working for a host-only network, do the following:

1. Change the `hosts` file on your host system. The easiest way to understand the process is to look at an example. Say that your host system, `blubber`, has a real connection at 10.2.2.1. It has a host-only networking interface at 172.16.144.1 and a FreeBSD guest called `flog` at 172.16.144.20. In such a case, the file on your host system should include lines like these:

```
10.2.2.1          blubber

# These are for VMware host-only or NAT network
172.16.144.1      vm-host   # vmnet1 host-only/NAT interface
172.16.144.20     flog      # FreeBSD guest operating system
```

NOTE *The* `vm-host` *name should not be the domain name of your host system, because this will cause problems with internal services.*

2. Create the `hosts` file on your guest system(s). Continuing with the example, this would be the `hosts` file for the system named `flog` (172.16.144.20):

```
172.16.144.1      blubber   # host system
172.16.144.20     flog
```

3. Test everything. Boot your guest system; then bring up a shell or command prompt on your host system and use `ping` to see if the hostname resolves properly and the host-only network is functional. For the example, you'd type `ping flog`, and if you get a response, everything is working on the host end. (To ping the guest from the host system, you'd use `ping blubber`.)

NOTE *If you need more flexibility and convenience for hostname resolution, you should set up a Domain Name Service (DNS) server like BIND. This is a fairly complex process, and we won't cover it in any detail in this book. If you're unfamiliar with using DNS or BIND, consider picking up a reference book on the topic, such as* DNS and BIND *by P. Albitz and C. Liu (O'Reilly and Associates, 2001).*

9.7 NAT Networking

VMware Workstation 3.0 and above offer an additional network interface type for virtual machines with NAT networking. Under VMware Workstation, these are host-only networks with an additional feature that allows guest operating systems to talk to the outside world. Therefore, it is an alternative to bridged networking.

NAT stands for network address translation. Under this scheme, the guest operating system does not have a true Internet connection, but talks to a special router. When the guest system makes a connection to the outside world, the following occurs:

1. The connection goes through the router.

2. Rather than sending the connection directly to its destination, the router tracks the connection by recording the source port and destination port. The router records this information in a translation table.

3. The router opens its own connection to the outside world to the destination port.

4. When traffic from the source machine goes to the outside world, the router looks it up in the translation table and funnels it out through the connection it made in step 3. Similarly, the router sends any traffic from the other end of the connection in step 3 to the original host in its translation table.

Figure 9.3 shows a logical diagram of a VMware NAT configuration. There is an extra node on the internal network for the address translator; notice how it connects to the outside world. If you've worked with NAT before, you might think it a little odd that the host system connection does not handle the address translation. The VMware approach is different because it requires no additional support from the host operating system.

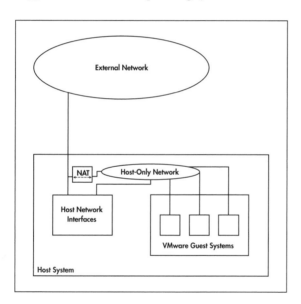

Figure 9.3: VMware Workstation NAT networking

There are several advantages to using NAT over bridged networking:

- You don't need to get another IP address for your guest system.
- NAT works on all kinds of network interfaces; bridged networking works only with Ethernet.
- Because NAT is a special kind of firewall, your guest operating systems are much less vulnerable to external attack.

- NAT works over suspends on notebooks. When using NAT, you can suspend a virtual machine on a notebook, shut down the notebook, and move it to a different network, and when you resume the virtual machine, the NAT setup allows networking to continue functioning.

NOTE *NAT doesn't work with all IP-based protocols without help, because it allows the opening only of an initial connection from a client behind the NAT router to a server on the Internet (it does not work in the other direction). One classic example of a problematic protocol is FTP, where the server wants to connect back to the client. Most implementations (Linux in particular) have extra plug-in modules to enable certain protocols. However, the vast majority of network protocols in use today work fine with NAT.*

9.7.1 Configuring VMware NAT Networks

VMware NAT networks are based on host-only networks, so configuration is nearly identical to host-only networks. If you let VMware configure the host interface for you at installation time (or with vmware-config.pl on a Linux host system) and tell the guest systems to configure themselves with DHCP, everything works smoothly.

However, there are several opportunities for customization. Most settings are in the NAT configuration file. This is C:\WINNT\system32\vmnetnat.conf for a Windows host system and /etc/vmware/vmnet8/nat/nat.conf for a Linux host. The file is divided into sections, denoted with [*section*], where *section* is the name of the section. Here is an overview of the parameters in each section:

[host]
Parameters here relate to VMware Workstation and the host operating system.

- ip: The IP address of the NAT router on the internal VMware (host-only) network.
- hostMac: The hardware (Ethernet) address of the NAT router; not necessary on Linux host systems.
- device: The VMnet device to use on the host system. Examples: VMnet8 on a Windows host, /dev/vmnet8 on a Linux host.
- activeFTP: Setting this to 1 enables PORT and EPRT commands for FTP. You need this if you want FTP to work on guest operating systems.
- allowAnyOUI: OUI stands for organizationally unique identifier; it is the string of the first three bytes of an Ethernet MAC address. You can change the MAC address of your virtual machine's Ethernet cards to anything you like (see section 9.10), but if you change the OUI, NAT will not work unless you turn on this option.

[udp]

This section tweaks user datagram protocol (UDP) settings. UDP is a data protocol, like TCP.

- timeout: Amount of time, in seconds, to wait for a response before assuming that a remote host has dropped a UDP packet. (Servers are allowed to drop UDP packets.)

[incomingtcp]

NAT in VMware Workstation has an incoming port feature that allows you to connect to ports on a guest operating system on a NAT network through a port on the host operating system. The NAT system listens on a port on the host system and sends any connections directly to guest systems, tracking the connections as it goes.

For example, let's say you want to be able to access a web server on a guest system. If the web server on that guest system on a NAT network with IP address 172.16.144.98 listens on its port 80, then you can tell VMware Workstation to make the server available at port 8080 on the host machine with this line:

```
8080 = 172.16.144.98:80
```

Now, if your host system were called host.example.com, you'd use this URL to access the web server on the guest system:

```
http://host.example.com:8080/
```

NOTE *Use this feature with caution. Not only does it open your guest systems to possible network security problems, but you can also introduce conflicts between servers on your host and guest systems. In the example here, the host port is different than the guest port. If your host system were already running a web server on its port 80, the NAT mechanism wouldn't be able to listen on port 80 because some other service is already doing that.*

[dns] (Windows Host Only)

VMware Workstation's NAT implementation forwards Domain Name Service (DNS) requests to look up remote hostnames. In a Windows host system, you can specify a nameserver and tell the DNS forwarding system how to look for names.

- autodetect: Set this parameter to 1 if you want to get nameserver information automatically from the host system. This doesn't work on a Windows NT host system.
- nameserver1, nameserver2, nameserver3: The IP addresses of your first, second, and third nameservers. You can comment these out (with #) if you have autodetect on. You may have one, two, or three of these parameters.

- policy: The order of queries for DNS forward requests. The order option tells the forwarder to check the first nameserver, then the second, and then the third, in that order. The rotate option instructs the forwarder to ask a different server each time. Finally, the burst option tells the forwarder to blast off queries to all servers at once and use the first reply that comes in. Unless you really know what you're doing, it's a good idea to leave this parameter set to order because you can invite nonuniform replies to DNS requests otherwise.
- timeout: How long to wait until trying a DNS query again.
- retries: The number of times to try again before the DNS query fails.

9.7.2 NAT Configuration for Guest Systems

Once you've configured NAT on your host system, you must tell your guest systems that the host system is the default gateway. If you configure a guest system's network with DHCP, you don't need to do anything, because VMware's network configuration programs add router and nameserver information to the DHCP configuration file, described in section 9.41.

However, if you decide to configure IP settings manually on your guest system, you must supply the router and nameserver information yourself. This is the IP address of the NAT system on your host system. The easiest way to get this information is to look in your NAT configuration file for the ip parameter in the [host] section. The IP address there will work both as a default router (gateway) and DNS server. Normally, it's "node 2" of your network—for example, if your NAT network is 172.16.144.0/255.255.255.0, the NAT system usually sits at 172.16.144.2.

Testing Guest Systems

After you get your NAT network up and running, shut down all of your virtual machines. The next time a guest system gets its IP configuration with DHCP, it should have the default gateway. (Use netstat -nr [Unix] or ipconfig [Windows] to find out.) Then use ping to probe a machine on your local area network or the rest of the Internet.

9.7.3 Other NAT Alternatives (for Advanced Users)

If you need more flexibility than VMware Workstation's NAT offers, you are always free to use a VMware host-only network to do the job. You may find that other NAT implementations have features that you need; Linux, in particular, comes with drivers capable of tracking a number of protocols (and you can always write more if you need to).

For example, this sequence of commands sets up NAT on a host-only network:

```
echo 1 > /proc/sys/net/ipv4/ip_forward
iptables -P FORWARD DROP
iptables -t nat -A POSTROUTING -o eth0 -j MASQUERADE
iptables -A FORWARD -i vmnet1 -j ACCEPT
iptables -A FORWARD -m state --state ESTABLISHED,RELATED -j ACCEPT
```

Notice that the third line specifies the interface connected to the outside world (eth0 in this case), and the fourth line turns forwarding access on for the vmnet1 interface (the default host-only network interface).

If you choose to configure NAT this way, you must modify your host-only DHCP configuration file to provide a default gateway and nameserver to your guest operating systems.

9.8 VMnet Devices

To coordinate the virtual network interfaces on the host operating system, VMware Workstation configures several special VMnet devices, numbered starting at 0. Normally, VMware assigns device 0 to the bridged network, device 1 to the host-only network interface, and device 8 to the NAT network. When you use the Configuration Editor to set up a guest system, these device numbers correspond to the bridged, host-only, and NAT network connections. (We'll discuss the other devices, reserved for custom networks, in section 9.9.)

The next two subsections tell you how to view the active interfaces for the two host systems.

9.8.1   Linux Host

To see the current VMnet device assignments on a Linux host system where there are several /dev/vmnet*n* special devices, enter

```
ps auxww | grep dev/vmnet
```

On a normal system, you should get output with vmnet-bridge and vmnet-netifup processes running on their respective /dev/vmnet devices.

9.8.2   Windows Host

It's not too hard to find the configuration on a Windows host, but you have to look in two different places. You've already seen how to view the host-only and NAT networks in section 9.32, "Host-Only IP Configuration (Host Operating System)"]. For bridged networks, open the **Services** control panel (on Windows NT systems, it's in the regular control panel folder; on Windows 2000/XP systems, it's in **Administrative Tools** on the control panel). You should see a line that says **VMnet Bridge (for VMnet0)**. If there are other bridged networks, they appear here.

9.9 Custom Networks

As mentioned earlier, any interfaces other than VMnet0, VMnet1, and VMnet8 are yours to configure in any way you please and allow you to set up additional bridged or host-only networks for your virtual machines.

There are two primary reasons for setting up custom networking. The first is that you may have more than one Ethernet card in your host machine and want to allow your virtual machines bridged access to these additional cards.

The other reason is that you may want to use different host-only network subnets—for testing router or firewall options or if you have servers listening on multiple subnets. Or you may simply want to isolate a particular virtual machine, due to its use of an obnoxious network protocol or something else that you don't want all of your virtual machines to see.

To set up a virtual machine with a custom interface in VMware Workstation for Windows, select the **Custom** option in the Configuration Editor; then select the VMnet interface that you want. In Workstation for Linux, choose **Custom** and type the interface device name (such as /dev/vmnet2 or /dev/vmnet3) in the **VMnet** entry box.

The procedure for configuring the interface on your host system differs depending on the operating system and the type of interface. The next sections discuss each case.

9.9.1   Windows 2000/XP Host: Bridged Network

Use the Configuration Editor to install a bridged network on a Windows 2000 or XP host operating system:

1. Open a virtual machine in a powered-down state.
2. Double-click the virtual machine's network adapter to start the Configuration Editor on the virtual network card.
3. Click the **Settings** button. A new window (VMware Virtual Network Configuration) appears.
4. Click the **Bridge Mapping** tab. The screen shown in Figure 9.4 appears.

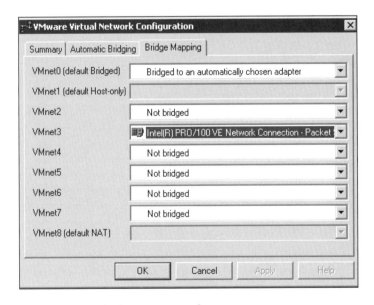

Figure 9.4: VMnet bridge mapping configuration

5. Select a VMnet interface (VMnet0, or VMnet2 through VMnet7) and choose the bridge that you want to associate with the interface from the pull-down menu to the right of the interface name.

6. Click **OK**.

To remove a bridged adapter, go through the preceding process and choose **Not bridged** from the pull-down menu mentioned in step 5.

The **Automatic Bridging** tab in the network configuration window gives you finer control over the interface mapping. If you want to force VMware not to automatically choose a network adapter for the VMnet0 bridge, add the bridge to the **Excluded adapters** box.

9.9.2   Windows NT Host: Bridged Network

Under Windows NT, you must use the command prompt to set up a new bridged network. Run **Start • Programs • Command Prompt**, use cd to go to the \Program Files\VMware\VMware Workstation\Programs directory, and run the VMware network initializer:

```
vnetconfig -s -ib VMnetn
```

Here, VMnet*n* is the VMnet interface you want to install (you can use VMnet2 through VMnet7). If you have more than one network interface, vnet-config asks you which network interface you want to use; choose one. If you open **Services** on the control panel, you should now see a bridged network for that VMnet interface. Finally, reboot your host machine to start the new service.

To remove a bridged interface, use this command:

```
vnetconfig -ub VMnetn
```

9.9.3   Linux Host: All Network Types

The easiest way to configure custom vmnet network adapters in VMware Work-station 3 on a Linux host is with the vmware-config.pl command, explained in section 3.6. Run the command, answer the questions as you normally would, and when you get to the networking configuration, do this:

1. Answer editor to the question about whether to use the wizard or the editor.

2. Select a vmnet interface number. It can be 0 through 99, but the best numbers for custom interfaces are 2 through 7, and 9. These do not conflict with reserved interfaces. Also, if you want to use a number higher than 9, you need to create the device in /dev (for example, mknod /dev/vmnet15 c 119 15 for vmnet15).

3. Enter bridged, hostonly, or nat to select the type of network.

4. For bridged networks, the Configuration Editor asks you which Ethernet interface you want to use. Otherwise, it asks for the subnet details of the host-only or NAT network.

5. When you leave vmware-config.pl, the VMware services restart just before the program exits.

These configuration details go into /etc/vmware/locations. The VMware system startup scripts parse this file. Use

```
grep VNET_N /etc/vmware/locations
```

to see what vmware-config.pl did, where N is the vmnet number that you chose for the new interface in step 2. If you configured a host-only or NAT network, the output should include something like this:

```
answer VNET_4_HOSTONLY_HOSTADDR 172.16.144.1
answer VNET_4_HOSTONLY_NETMASK 255.255.255.0
```

If you were using NAT networking on that interface, NAT would show up in the output instead of HOSTONLY. Also for host-only and NAT networks, vmware-config.pl creates new configuration files in a /etc/vmware/vmnetN directory (again, where N is the number you chose in step 2).

For bridged networks, the output of the grep command looks like this:

```
answer VNET_4_INTERFACE eth0
```

NOTE *If you get a lot of output from your grep command, remember that only the last entries are the active ones.*

To remove an interface, go through the process just described, but answer none when prompted for an interface type in step 3.

9.9.4 Windows Host: Host-Only Network

Adding a new custom host-only network on a Windows host system is just like adding any new hardware. The process differs slightly between host operating system versions. It's possible to add new interfaces by going through a series of hardware wizards and such, but it's far quicker to use the command prompt.

Windows NT

For Windows NT, the procedure is as follows:

1. Bring up the command prompt (**Start • Programs • Command Prompt**).

2. Type

```
vnetconfig -ih VMnetN
```

where N is the interface number that you want to use (it can normally be between 2 and 7).

3. Wait until all of the WinSock stuff completes; then reboot your host machine. Your host operating system may now refuse to boot, crashing with a horrible-looking error (Windows does that). If this happens, press the spacebar in the boot process when the screen says "Press spacebar NOW to..." and the hardware profile selection screen will appear. At this screen, press L (for the Last Known Good profile) and then ENTER, and your system should boot.

4. Bring up the command prompt again and type `ipconfig /all` to see the IP configuration.

5. Have a look at the changes to `C:\WINNT\system32\vmnetdhcp.conf`.

To remove a network adapter, use `vnetconfig -uh VMnetN` (and reboot your computer, possibly making it crash again when it boots).

Windows 2000/XP

As with a Windows NT system, you go to the command prompt to set up a new host-only or NAT interface:

1. Bring up the command prompt (**Start • Programs • Accessories • Command Prompt**).

2. Type `cd c:\program files\vmware\vmware workstation\programs`.

3. Pick a virtual interface number *N* between 2 and 7 that's not in use and type

---
```
vmware_netinstall -h *VMnetN
```
---

4. When the annoying Microsoft digital signature dialog box appears, ignore it and click the **Yes/Continue** button.

5. Reboot your host system to allow the DHCP server to restart and then give the new virtual adapter a hostname.

6. Bring up the command prompt again and type `ipconfig /all` to inspect the IP configuration. Also, read the changes to `C:\WINDOWS\system32\vmnetdhcp.conf`.

To remove an adapter, enter the following:

```
vmware_netinstall –r *VMnetN
```

9.10 Ethernet MAC Addresses

Every Ethernet network interface card has a unique identifier called a media access control (MAC) address. It is not the same as an IP address; it consists of six 8-bit numbers in hexadecimal format, separated by colons (for example, 00:40:05:A0:7F:96). VMware Workstation assigns a virtual machine's MAC address(es) dynamically at boot time. However, you may want to change this to a fixed address of your own choice.

To set a MAC address on a virtual machine's first virtual Ethernet interface, edit its configuration file (.cfg for a Linux host, .vmx for a Windows host), and add this line:

```
ethernet0.address = 00:50:56:ab:cd:ef
```

You can set *cd* and *ef* to anything between 00 and FF, but *ab* can go up to 3F only. This is important, because VMware starts its dynamic assignment at 00:50:56:40:*xx*:*xx*. If you choose a number above 3F for the fourth number, you risk a conflict with other active virtual machines.

The 00:50:56 designation is VMware's organizationally unique identifier (OUI). You can change this in the Ethernet address if you like, but if you do so, you may have trouble with services like NAT (see section 9.7). Therefore, it's best not to alter it if you have a choice.

If you set a fixed MAC address for a virtual machine, you can tell VMware's DHCP server to hand out the same IP address and other configuration to the virtual machine every time it boots. For example, say you set the guest system's address to 00:50:56:05:05:05. To set its IP address to 172.16.144.101, add these lines to the end of your VMnet DHCP configuration file (see section 9.4 for information on the VMware DHCP server):

```
host my-vmware-guest {
    hardware ethernet 00:50:56:05:05:05;
    fixed-address 172.16.144.101;
}
```

It's important that *my-vmware-guest* be unique in this file; to set up another mapping with another host section, use a different name for the section (which need not correspond to a real hostname).

If you want to get rid of the explicit IP address in the DHCP configuration file, first put a host-to-IP address mapping in DNS or your hosts file (see section 9.6). For example, say you put myguest in hosts as 172.16.144.101. Then use this in your configuration file instead:

```
host my-vmware-guest {
    hardware ethernet 00:50:56:05:05:05;
    fixed-address myguest;
}
```

The advantage of using this form is that if you decide to change the IP address of the guest, you have to do it in one place only, and you won't need to alter the DHCP configuration file again.

9.11   Using the VMnet Sniffer

VMware Workstation comes with a handy command-line packet sniffer for its virtual network interfaces, which you can use to debug your network connections. On a Windows host system, it's vnetsniffer; you'll find it along with vnet-config in C:\Program Files\VMware\VMware Workstation\Programs. On a Linux host, it's a program called vmnet-sniffer in your VMware binary directory.

To run the sniffer on your host-only network, run one of the following:

Windows host   vnetsniffer VMnet1

Linux host   vmnet-sniffer /dev/vmnet1

Here is the output for a Red Hat guest system power-on with the system getting its address over DHCP. Notice the MAC addresses.

```
IP src 172.16.144.1    dst 172.16.144.255  UDP
IP src 172.16.144.1    dst 172.16.144.255  UDP
IP src 0.0.0.0         dst 255.255.255.255 UDP
IP src 172.16.144.254  dst 172.16.144.130
  ICMP ping request - len=28 type=8
  00:50:56:00:00:00 08 00 43 c4 d4 08 00 00 38 80 05 08 e8 08 07 08 b4 db ff bf 7e
86 05 08 74 67 07 08
```

Here is an address resolution protocol (ARP) request, along with its reply:

```
ARP sender 00:50:56:d4:9c:db 172.16.144.130
  target 00:00:00:00:00:00 172.16.144.1    ARP request
ARP sender 00:50:56:01:00:00 172.16.144.1
  target 00:50:56:d4:9c:db 172.16.144.130  ARP reply
```

NOTE   *On a Linux host, anyone can run the* vmnet-sniffer *program, but only those users with read access to a* /dev/vmnet* *device can use the program on that device. If you have remote users but still want the local user to have access to the sniffer, you may want to change the ownership and permissions of the* /dev/vmnet* *devices upon console log-in to control access to the sniffer.*

You can also run the vnetstats program on a Windows host to get utilization statistics on a VMnet interface. Run this program without any arguments for a quick overview of the options; then use vnetstats VMnet1 to get information on your host-only connection. The program reports the number of packets transmitted, received, dropped, and so on. (VMware Workstation for Linux doesn't come with this utility because you can run ifconfig -a or look at /proc/net/dev for *all* network interfaces, not just those specific to VMware.)

10

NETWORK SERVICES

Now that your VMware network is up and running, it's time to look at some of the services you can run over the network. We'll emphasize file sharing between the host and guest operating systems in this chapter. However, we'll also touch on other neat stuff such as how to send X Window System clients from the guest to the host, and the use of web proxy servers.

This chapter focuses on the things you can do with host-only and NAT networks because these types of network are unique to VMware. (Bridged networking is no different than for any other network client; therefore, you may find only the sections dealing with client configuration useful for this type of networking.)

Remember that you're not limited to the services mentioned in this chapter, since you can do anything on a VMware host-only or NAT network that you can on a real network.

The material in this chapter is divided into categories of network services. The topics are network file sharing with SMB shares, network printing, remote log-in access to a guest system, and proxy servers (an alternative to NAT for broader network access for guest systems on a host-only network). Because the procedures vary for the different host and guest systems, we'll split the material first by host system (which is normally the server) and then by the type of guest.

Because there are several kinds of host and guest systems, you'll probably need to read only pieces of this chapter. Go ahead and mix and match as you see fit. For example, if you're running VMware Workstation for Windows, read the Windows host sections and then look for the guest sections that fit your situation. But there is one exception: The SAMBA printing server for a Linux host uses the same utilities as the SAMBA file sharing server on a Linux host, so you need to read section 10.1 before section 10.5.1 to learn about the configuration file and daemon processes.

NOTE *The order of presentation for host systems is a little different than in other chapters. Because the trickiest system to configure is a Linux host that wants to talk to a Windows guest, the Linux host sections are first, but the order goes in reverse for the guest systems. In general, the configuration of all services depends on the host operating system (unless you're configuring a server on a guest for use by the host and other guests; in this case, most Unix servers work the same).*

10.1 SMB Fileserver (Linux Host)

This section tells you how to give access to files on a Linux host operating system to Windows guest systems on a VMware host-only or NAT network. The material here goes with section 10.3, which explains how to access files with the Windows guest system. If you have a Windows host system, skip ahead to section 10.2.

VMware Workstation for Linux comes with SAMBA, a server that allows Windows machines to access Linux filesystems using the SMB/CIFS protocol. Aside from a small extension to allow multiple servers on the same host, there's nothing particularly special about VMware's version. One of the most important things to know is that the vmware-config.pl script can automatically create a configuration file for host-only or NAT networks and add users to the SAMBA password file. This feature can save you a lot of time: Since SAMBA has several million configuration parameters, it can take a while to get down to the right subset.

The easiest way to create a SAMBA configuration file and start the server is to run vmware-config.pl and answer y to the question about whether to automatically configure your system to allow your virtual machines to access the Linux host's filesystem. By answering yes, you create a /etc/vmware/vmnet1/smb directory containing the configuration files (for NAT networking, the directory is /etc/vmware/vmnet8/smb).

The vmware-config.pl script also asks whether to add any users. If you do, the username you provide must be one that already exists on your host system. For each new user, VMware creates a new entry with a new password in the SAMBA password file. This is *not* the same as your /etc/passwd file. The usernames identify valid users on your system, but the passwords are completely independent. See section 10.1.1 for more information on the password file. If you aren't interested in SAMBA server details, skip to section 10.3 to attach the newly shared filesystem to your Windows guest system.

10.1.1   The SAMBA Server Side

The SAMBA server side consists of two daemons: smbd, which handles the actual work of serving data, and nmbd, a NetBIOS-over-IP nameserver. In VMware, they're called vmware-smbd and vmware-nmbd; you'll find them in the same place as the rest of the VMware binaries. The main SAMBA configuration file for both daemons, found in /etc/vmware/vmnet1/smb or /etc/vmware/vmnet8/smb, is smb.conf.

The configuration file has several sections. This first contains a set of global parameters denoted with [global] (the brackets [] denote a section in the configuration file). The vmware-config.pl script determines the socket address, interfaces, and bind interfaces only settings.

The socket address parameter identifies the IP address of the host machine's network interface—in the case here, VMware's host-only or NAT interface. The interfaces parameter marks out a subnet for the servers to monitor. The last parameter says that the servers should respond only to instructions coming from requests listed by the interfaces parameter. This interfaces parameter is important because it blocks any access from outside networks. Here is an example:

```
socket address = 172.16.144.1
interfaces = 172.16.144.0/255.255.255.0
```

Aside from [global], all other sections of the smb.conf file correspond to network shares. There are two sections with special meanings: [homes] and [printers], for sharing a dynamic number of home directories and printers. Refer to page 183 for [homes] and page 187 for [printers].

SAMBA User Management

For Windows guest operating systems to communicate with the SAMBA server, they must log in with a username and password. Two lines in the server's smb.conf [global] section control how users send passwords to the server. By default, they are

```
security = user
  encrypt passwords = yes
```

The security parameter sets the type of access control. The user setting is the only setting that makes much sense with the VMware version of SAMBA. The user specification instructs SAMBA to match usernames that Windows clients send with the ones in the host machine's /etc/passwd file.

Now that the server knows about usernames, it needs to know how to verify the passwords that Windows clients send. The encrypt passwords parameter controls the way that the host asks the guest to send a password.

Because Windows passwords have a different encryption scheme than Unix passwords, you can't use the same password transmission scheme between Unix and Windows. Therefore, when you set encrypt passwords to yes, SAMBA uses an auxiliary password file.

This file, /etc/vmware/vmnet1/smb/private/smbpasswd holds not just encrypted passwords, but also some other assorted information for smbd. This file looks slightly like the /etc/passwd file on your Linux host; it also works in conjunction with the regular system password file. The following sections describe some common administrative commands.

Adding and Deleting Users

To allow a user to log in from a Windows guest system and give them write access to their home directory from that guest system, you must give them an entry in the SMB password file. To add the user *username* with the password *passwd*, use the command

```
vmware-smbpasswd vmnet1 -a username passwd
```

If *username* isn't in your /etc/passwd file or map, you'll get an error: *username* must be a valid user on your host system.

To remove a SAMBA user, edit the smbpasswd file, and delete the line corresponding to the user.

Changing a Password

To change the user's password in the SMB password file, run

```
vmware-smbpasswd vmnet1 username passwd
```

You can remove the password entirely with the -n option, but be sure that no other machine on your network has access to the SMB server. Remember that the VMware host system can talk to its own host-only interface, so if you have other users on your host machine, you might want to either remove access to the host in your configuration or forget about removing passwords altogether.

Disabling and Enabling Users

To disable a user, run

```
vmware-smbpasswd vmnet1 -d username
```

To reenable access, use -e instead of -d.

Sharing SMB Password Files

If you set up more than one host-only or NAT network and also have more than one vmware-smbd running (which means you'll have more than one smb.conf file), you can use the same SMB password file for all of the vmware-smbd processes. Find the line in each of your smb.conf files that reads something like this:

```
smb passwd file = /etc/vmware/vmnet1/smb/private/smbpasswd
```

To share one smbpasswd file, set this line in all of your smb.conf files to the same thing.

SAMBA Filesharing Management

Two sections in a VMware-configured smb.conf file control filesystem access to clients: namely, [homes] and [HostFS]. The [homes] section controls access to home directories and looks like this:

```
[homes]
  comment = Home directories
  browseable = no
  writable = yes
```

This special section maps usernames to home directories upon log-in. When a user logs in, smbd looks up that username in the system /etc/passwd file, finds the user's home directory, and offers the directory to the client as a share. The last setting (writable) in the lines above allows you to turn off write permission if you don't particularly trust your guest system.

The [HostFS] section gives your guest system access to the rest of your host's filesystem. By default, it looks like this:

```
[HostFS]
  comment = VMware host filesystem
  path = /
  public = no
  writeable = yes
  printable = no
```

There are a few things to note here. The first is that the path parameter specifies where in the host filesystem to begin; in this case, it's /, meaning all files and directories on the host. You can make the parameter more restrictive (for example, /data/blah), or if you want to add more sections with more specific path components, just copy the section with a new path parameter and change HostFS to a new name of your choice.

(Do you see the disparity between the `writeable` keyword here and `writable` in the [`homes`] section? As far as `smbd` is concerned, they're synonymous.)

More on SAMBA

Though this chapter covers many issues relevant to VMware's Linux SMB server, it really only scratches the surface of what SAMBA can do. In particular, you can do a lot with the `smbclient` program in the regular distribution if you have a Windows host and a Unix guest system. SAMBA can act as a WINS server (if, for example, you want to connect the guests in a host-only network over NAT to a bigger network); it also has several network browsing capabilities, can communicate over SSL, and has extensive access restriction configuration options. To learn more about SAMBA, visit http://www.samba.org/ and look at the documentation and pointers there.

10.2 SMB Fileserver (Windows Host)

If your host operating system is Windows, then you already have an SMB server on your filesystem, making it simple to give access to a guest operating system.

To make a directory available over the network in Windows NT, 2000, or XP, do the following:

1. Find its folder icon in the **My Computer** (file browser) hierarchy.
2. Right-click that icon and select **Properties** from the menu.
3. A new window appears. Click the **Sharing** tab.
4. Select **Shared As** or **Share this folder** and give the share a name.
5. (Optional) Restrict the permissions with the **Permissions** button.
6. Click **OK**.

The share should now appear on the network.

NOTE *You must run the Server service for file sharing to work.*

10.3 SMB File Sharing Client (Windows Guest)

Once you tell your host operating system to export files and directories over a VMware network, you need to tell your guest operating system where to find them. There are two basic ways to get at SMB shares from Windows. One is with the **Network Neighborhood** browser, and the other is to map the remote filesystem to a drive letter on your system.

10.3.1 Using Network Neighborhood

To use the Network Neighborhood on a Windows guest to access files on the host, follow these steps:

1. Double-click the **Network Neighborhood** icon on the main Windows screen (on a Windows 2000/XP system, choose **My Network Places • Computers Near Me**). A window should appear with a list of network machines, one of which should be your host system.

2. Double-click the host system. If you kept the default VMware security settings, what you see next will depend on your version of Windows:

Windows NT/2000/XP A log-in and password dialog box appears. Enter a username and password.

Windows 95/98/Me You must be logged in as a valid user on the host to go further. If you aren't, create a new user with Users on the control panel. Windows automatically sends the password to the server; if you have everything set up, you won't need to enter a username or password in this step.

3. You'll get a list of shares that you should be able to browse.

Once you enter the username and password, you won't need to do it again until you log out or reboot the guest system. However, the server may decide to disconnect after a certain amount of time, and you'll get an error message saying that the server service hasn't started. If this happens, just try again; it should work the second time.

NOTE *Remember that if you're using SAMBA to export shares on a Linux host machine, the password is the special one mentioned in section 10.1, not necessarily your regular Linux password.*

10.3.2 Mapping a Network Share Folder to a Drive Letter

Mapping a network share folder to a drive letter to obtain remote filesystem access gives your Windows guest system more direct access to a network share. You can access the files directly from the command prompt and other programs, and you can also tell the Windows guest system to attach the network share at every boot. Consequently, if you frequently use your host system's files on your guest, it's worth using this method.

1. Open the list of shares in the **Network Neighborhood** browser as described in the preceding section.

2. Right-click the folder you want to attach and, from the pop-up menu, select **Map Network Drive**.

3. Select the letter you want to use from the **Drive** pull-down menu.

4. To have this drive appear as this letter each time you log in, check **Reconnect at Logon**.

5. Click **OK**. The drive should now appear in the **My Computer** browser.

SHORTCUT *If you know the server and share name, you can bypass browsing by right-clicking the* **Network Neighborhood** *icon and selecting* **Map Network Drive** *from the menu there.*

To detach the drive from your system, right-click its icon in the **My Computer** browser and select **Disconnect** from the menu that appears. (This also removes any connect-at-logon settings specified in step 4.)

10.3.3 Attaching a Share Directly

You can attach a share directly to your system on Windows 98, NT, Me, and 2000 with a DOS-style command such as this:

```
net use N: \\VMHOST\HOSTFS /user:bigcheese
```

In this example, the host machine is VMHOST, the remote share name is HOSTFS, and the user is bigcheese. Upon success, this command makes the share available at N:. To detach this drive from your system, run the following:

```
net use N: /delete
```

10.4 The SAMBA File Sharing Client (Linux Guest)

If you have a Linux guest operating system, you still can access Windows SMB shares. There are two ways: by using an FTP-like interface (useful for connection debugging and sporadic file access) and by attaching the share directly to your directory tree like any other filesystem. If you work with files from a Windows system constantly, you should choose the latter option.

Both methods require the use of SAMBA on your Linux guest system, the same package that you'd use for a server. (Remember that SMB is the protocol and SAMBA is a specific package that can speak this protocol.)

NOTE *This is not the same version of SAMBA that comes with VMware Workstation for Linux. If your Linux guest system's distribution didn't come with SAMBA, you must install it yourself (get it at http://www.samba.org/).*

10.4.1 Testing SAMBA and Accessing Shares

Before attempting to use SAMBA to share your files, test it with the smbclient client:

```
smbclient -L server
```

Here, *server* is the machine with the SMB server—for a Linux guest operating system on a Windows host, this is the Windows host machine. The output of this command is a list of the available shares on *server*.

To do anything useful with smbclient, you will likely need a username and password. The default is your log-in name, but you can change the default with the -U option (as shown here). Here's an example without a password:

```
smbclient '\\VMHOST\DATA' -U user
```

The server here is *VMHOST* (as defined in your /etc/hosts or SAMBA lmhosts file), the share is *DATA*, and the username is *user*. This command starts the smbclient interactive mode. Its interface is much like FTP's, and you can run commands such as cd, ls, put, and get.

The smbclient program asks for a password if you don't supply one on the command line with the -P option.

Once you have the smbclient interactive mode working, try attaching the share directly to a Linux system with SAMBA's smbmount program:

```
smbmount '\\SERVER\SHARE' -c 'mount /mount' -U username -P passwd
```

If you're happy with this, you can add it to your system startup scripts.

10.5 Network Printing

Printing is one of the more esoteric networking tasks. Although it's not difficult to share printers between two similar operating systems (say, Linux and FreeBSD, or Windows NT and 98), the task becomes much more frustrating when two fundamentally different operating systems come into play. Because VMware is built for running different systems simultaneously, we'll take a look at how to translate from one printing system to another.

As for file sharing, SAMBA is a key part of the solution. Because Windows systems don't particularly like to speak foreign protocols, the burden of translation falls mainly on a Unix system's shoulders, through SAMBA.

You'll first see how to make a Linux host system's printers available to Windows guests. Following this is a brief example of how to do this on a Windows host. Finally, you'll see how to use these shares on a Unix guest system through its SAMBA installation.

NOTE *As with SMB file sharing on Unix guests, you'll need to retrieve and install SAMBA if your system doesn't come with it; VMware Workstation doesn't include it.*

10.5.1 Configuring SAMBA Printer Sharing (Linux Host)

This section tells you how to share your printers from a Linux host operating system for use by Windows guest systems. When you configure SAMBA with vmware-config.pl as described in section 10.1, the resulting configuration already includes support for printer sharing. Specifically, the [printers] section of your smb.conf file looks like this:

```
[printers]
```

```
comment = All printers
path = /var/lpd
browseable = no
guest ok = no
writable = no
printable = yes
```

Because printer configurations vary wildly over Linux installations, you may need to change a few things in the section of the smb.conf file shown in the preceding lines. The first thing you may need to change is the path parameter, which specifies where to put intermediate (spool) files before smbd sends them to the printer spooling system.

Since Unix printing programs need write access to this spool directory, most printing systems keep this directory world-writable, so that all processes can access it. However, /var/lpd may not even exist on your system, much less be writable. Thus, consider changing /var/lpd to /tmp if the former doesn't work.

Settings for a Particular Printer

You may want to change the options for a particular printer to get finer control. You can specify settings for a single printer in the smb.conf file as shown here:

```
[someprinter]
comment = one particular printer
printer name = someprinter
path=/var/spool/lpd/someprinter
guest ok = yes
browseable = yes
printable = yes
printer driver = HP LaserJet 4M
```

The parameter here that distinguishes the share as a printer and not a shared directory is printable. All printer share entries in smb.conf must set this option to yes. Set the parameters guest ok and browseable to anything you like. Note, too, that this example includes the optional printer driver parameter: If a Windows guest can match this string with a printer driver that it knows about, it automatically selects that driver when you set up the network printer.

Printing Subsystems

There are several printing subsystems for Linux. Three are in common use: Berkeley LPD, LPRng, and PLP. For printing to work properly from Windows guest operating systems, you must tell SAMBA which one to use. The printing parameter in your smb.conf file selects the print system. This example specifies the LPRng system:

```
printing = LPRNG
```

For PLP, use PLP instead of LPRNG. Berkeley LPD is the default.

Log-in and Password Requirements

The VMware `smb.conf` file also specifies that only users with a log-in and password can print, by setting `guest ok` to no. This can get tiresome if you print a lot, so you can change this setting with

```
guest ok = true
guest only = true
```

Windows Guest Printer Driver

On your Windows guest systems, you should set your printer driver to a laser printer that supports PostScript, no matter what printer is actually connected to your host system. The HP LaserJet 5M (PS) and Apple LaserWriter IINTX are two drivers that work.

The reason for this is that Linux print servers expect to see PostScript input, because most Unix programs produce PostScript output. Even if your printer doesn't understand PostScript, your print system likely processes PostScript input as something that your printer can understand.

10.6 Windows Host Printer Sharing

If your host operating system is Windows, you can give network printer access through SMB shares. This service is included in all Windows-NT based systems.

To share a printer under Windows NT, 2000, and XP, follow these steps:

1. Open the **Printers** folder from the **Settings** submenu.

2. Right-click the printer you want to share and select **Properties** from the menu. The printer properties window appears.

3. Click the **Sharing** tab and select the **Shared** option.

4. To restrict access to the printer, use the **Security** tab.

5. Click **OK**.

You must have an active Server service on your Windows host for printer sharing to function.

10.7 Unix Guest Printing

The next few sections describe how to print from a Unix guest operating system (Linux, FreeBSD, NetBSD, or OpenBSD) over a VMware network. Here are a few basic points about Unix printing:

- Unix print clients send PostScript output. If a connected printer does not understand PostScript, a Unix printing subsystem translates it from PostScript to whatever that printer understands.

- The Unix printing system daemon is called `lpd`. However, there are three `lpd` varieties: Berkeley LPD, LPRng, and PLP. Examples in this book are compatible with all three.

- The main print configuration file on Unix systems is `/etc/printcap`.
- Consistency is not a strong point of Unix printing.

10.7.1 Printing from a Unix Guest to a Unix Host

It's fairly easy to get a Unix guest system to send print jobs to a Unix host:

1. Set up your guest system's `/etc/printcap` file. This example assumes a host-only or NAT network with the host at 172.16.144.1. The printer name on the host is `myprinter`.

```
lp|host|hostprinter:Host System Printer:\
    :lp=:sd=/var/spool/lpd/host:\
    :mx#0:rm=172.16.144.1:rp=myprinter:
```

2. Create a spool directory called `/var/spool/lpd/host` on the guest and make sure that the print daemon (normally running as user `daemon`) can write to this directory.

3. Add the guest system's hostname or IP address to the host system's `/etc/hosts.lpd` file.

10.7.2 Printing from a Unix Guest to a Windows Host

Unfortunately, printing to a Windows host from a Unix guest tends to be difficult. You must overcome two obstacles: you need to send the print job through SMB, and possibly process PostScript files in the target printer's language. If you can connect to your host system's printer directly through a parallel port and configure it as a local printer, you should probably choose that route, because things are going to get ugly otherwise.

Sending the job is the easy part. To do so, you'll need SAMBA and its `smbclient` program, described in section 10.4. To send the job, use a command like this:

```
smbclient '\\SERVER\PRINTER' passwd -U user -N -P < file
```

Here, *SERVER* is the server (in this case, the Windows host), *PRINTER* is the name of the printer, *user* and *passwd* are your username and password on *SERVER*, and *file* is the file you want to print.

If the printer on your host operating system can understand PostScript, this is all you need to know. The easiest thing to do is create a shell script that runs a command like the one just shown and then use that to print.

NOTE *If your host system printer does not support PostScript, you can still test sending jobs to the host system over the VMware network. On the host system, print a document to a file instead of the printer. Then send the file to your guest system and test sending that file from the guest to the host with `smbclient`.*

Tackling Print Drivers

If your host system's printer does not support PostScript, then if you want to print over the network from a Unix guest system to a Windows host, you will need to configure the correct print driver. The driver *rasterizes* the PostScript information, meaning that it runs the PostScript code in a print job and produces a bitmap image as the output suitable for sending to your printer.

Ghostscript is the standard Unix program for rasterizing PostScript input for another type of printer to understand. Ghostscript is a program that comes with virtually all Linux distributions; its executable is gs.

All you need to do is insert a gs command in a pipeline before running smb-client. The tricky part is getting the correct arguments for your printer. A full guide to Ghostscript is beyond the scope of this book, but here are a few hints. You need to take the PostScript file from standard input and send the rasterized result to standard output. There are two main driver styles. The traditional approach looks like this:

```
gs -q -dBATCH -dNOPAUSE -dSAFER -sOutputFile=- \
   -r600x600 -sDEVICE=lj5mono file | smbclient args
```

This command produces output for the HP LaserJet 5. Here, file is the PostScript file you want to print, and args are the smbclient arguments from the previous section. Because this is a balky command, you should put it in a script if you need to use it—for example, like this:

```
#!/bin/sh
if [ "x$1" != x ]; then
  FILE=$1
else
  FILE=-
fi
gs -q -dBATCH -dNOPAUSE -dSAFER -sOutputFile=- \
   -r600x600 -sDEVICE=lj5mono $FILE | smbclient args
```

There is a relatively new Ghostscript driver called uniprint that supports many kinds of printers. Here's a command that rasterizes PostScript files for the Epson Stylus Color 600:

```
gs @stc600p.upp -q -dBATCH -dNOPAUSE -dSAFER -sOutputFile=- file
```

If you don't know what driver to use, first check the .upp files in your Ghostscript library directory to see if any fit your printer. If none look right, use gs -help to display a list of all drivers, or consult the Ghostscript website and documentation at http://www.ghostscript.com/.

10.8 SSH Remote Shell Access for Unix Guest Systems

Unix systems make it easy for you to log-in from a remote location and do many of the things that you normally do at the console. You can take advantage of this under VMware Workstation: You can log-in from your host system to a Unix guest system. This approach means that you can avoid switching between your host system and VMware window/full-screen mode all the time; all you need to do is switch windows. Furthermore, if you use Secure Shell (SSH), you can send graphics clients though the connection.

There are several SSH packages. The one we'll refer to in this book is OpenSSH, an implementation from the OpenBSD people. It supports the SSH version 1 and 2 protocols, and you can get it from http://www.openssh.com/.

10.8.1 Installing and Configuring the SSH Server Software

Binaries for the SSH server software are available for Red Hat Linux systems at the OpenSSH website, but for most other implementations, you'll need to get the source code and build it from there if it doesn't already come with your guest system. To compile OpenSSH, you need OpenSSL, an implementation of the Secure Socket Layer (SSL) protocol.

After you have OpenSSH installed, verify the configuration file and host key locations:

1. Find the etc directory of your OpenSSH installation prefix (the default is /usr/local/etc). You should see two configuration files: ssh_config and sshd_config. (You need to change these files if you want to use X client forwarding; we'll get to that shortly.)

2. In this same etc directory, look for the host key files. All key files begin with a ssh_host_ prefix. There should be three sets. If the key file name contains rsa or dsa, it is for the SSH version 2 protocol. The other key files are for SSH version 1. Anything with a .pub suffix is a public key. However, anything without a suffix is a private key. Don't let anyone see those.

3. If you're missing these key files, create them manually (be sure to put them in the same directory as the one that contains the sshd_config file). Use the following for the version 1 key pair:

```
ssh-keygen -t rsa1 -N "" -f ssh_host_key
```

Use this for the version 2 files:

```
ssh-keygen -t rsa -N "" -f ssh_host_rsa_key
ssh-keygen -t dsa -N "" -f ssh_host_dsa_key
```

You should now be able to start the SSH server on the guest operating system.

10.8.2   Starting the SSH Server

To enable remote access with SSH, you need to start sshd on the guest system you want to access. You should be able to find the server in one of the guest system's sbin directories: either /usr/sbin or /usr/local/sbin.

To make sshd start at boot time, you can add a script to your normal startup script sets. On most Linux distributions, this is the init.d system script; on BSD systems, you use the /etc/rc* scripts. See Chapters 6, 7, and 8 for more information on these boot scripts.

You can also start sshd through the inetd superserver with the -i option. This is normally not a good idea because sshd performs some numeric computations each time it starts, and since inetd invokes a brand-new process for each connection, you can end up waiting a while for every connection to initialize.

10.8.3   SSH, Host-Only Networks, and Hostname Resolution

SSH clients and servers are very strict about hostname resolution. In particular, they perform checks on the forward and reverse records and may bypass any records in /etc/hosts, going directly to a DNS server regardless of your /etc/nsswitch.conf file. This can be a problem if you're using a host-only network without any extra configuration, because the DHCP server gives the host machine's IP address as a DNS server by default. Unless you actually have a nameserver running on the host, when the SSH server on a guest system sends a request to the host, it never gets a response, and any incoming SSH connections hang.

To get around this on a guest system, change the DNS server configuration on the guest system and/or the host's DHCP configuration file (see section 9.4) to a real nameserver or an IP address on a network that a guest on the host-only network can't reach. The latter approach works because the guest has no idea where to send its packets and generates a "network unreachable" error message immediately. One other way around the problem is to use IP numbers instead of names, but this can be very inconvenient.

10.8.4   SSH Clients

Now that you have a server running on your guest operating system, you need a way to connect from your host operating system to your guest operating system.

The best way for most applications is also with OpenSSH. Because the client and server packages come together, the installation procedure for a Linux host operating system is the same as for a guest operating system, as described in the previous sections, except that you don't need to worry about starting the sshd server.

For Windows host operating systems, get OpenSSH for Cygwin. See section 5.5 for more information on how to install Cygwin; even though Chapter 5 focuses on Windows as a guest system, this section is the same for host and guest systems.

To log in from your host operating system to your guest system, run this at a command prompt:

```
ssh user@guest_system
```

Here, *user* is your username on the guest system, and *guest_system* is the name or IP address of your guest operating system. The ssh program then asks for your password on the guest system.

You can copy files to and from the guest operating system with another OpenSSH program called scp (which stands for secure copy). For example, to copy *file* from *guest_system* to the current directory (.) on the host system, enter the following:

```
scp user@guest_system:file .
```

And to do it the other way around, enter

```
scp file user@guest_system:
```

OpenSSH also includes a handy utility called sftp, which looks and feels like a Unix FTP client.

Other Windows SSH Clients

Even though OpenSSH for Cygwin is just like the Unix version, you may want a client with a more Windows-like look and feel. There are several other commercial and open source SSH clients available for Windows systems. We'll concentrate on the open source clients in this section; you can find some of the commercial SSH clients at http://www.ssh.com/.

There is an extension for Teraterm that supports SSH protocol version 1. You can get the extension from http://www.zip.com.au/~roca/ttssh.html (if this link is dead, try typing teraterm ssh at http://google.com/). You'll find a link to download a version of Teraterm there as well. The terminal client acts like a regular stand-alone Windows application and has many customizations for appearance. When you connect to the remote server, make sure that you select **SSH** as a protocol. There are two drawbacks to Teraterm SSH. One is that the installation process has two stages: You first must install Teraterm, and then you must install the extension. There can also be some confusion because there are two clients after the installation: one for the regular version, and one for the SSH extension. The other limitation is that Teraterm doesn't support SSH protocol version 2, though for OpenSSH on a VMware guest operating system, this isn't much of an issue.

Another popular SSH client for Windows is PuTTY. Like OpenSSH for Unix, this is a command-line utility, but it doesn't require Cygwin. It supports SSH protocol versions 1 and 2 and can perform X11 forwarding. PuTTY is fairly small and comes with handy file transfer utilities such as pscp and psftp. You can get PuTTY from the U.S. mirror at http://putty.bhni.net/, or as with Teraterm SSH, if you can't find it there, try typing putty ssh at http://google.com/. (If you're not used to doing this for software packages, you probably soon will be, because noncommercial software packages tend to drift from one site to another until they get their own domains.)

10.8.5 X Client Forwarding with SSH

As mentioned before, you can send X Window System clients from the guest operating system to the host. To do so, you set up a new X11 server display and port on the remote machine, with all traffic going through the encrypted SSH channel and then being forwarded to the X11 server port on the originating machine. The connection authorization happens through xauth; ssh generates a cookie value for the display and sends it to the remote machine.

Though some SSH implementations automatically set up forwarding, OpenSSH does not. Therefore, you need to make some alterations to your ssh_config and sshd_config files. To set up forwarding from a Linux host to a Unix guest system, do the following:

1. Look in your guest system's sshd_config file for these two lines:

```
X11Forwarding no
X11DisplayOffset 10
```

Change the no to yes. The other line should be okay (unless, for some reason, you happen to have more than 10 X displays running on that machine).

2. Shut down the guest system's sshd file and start it again, so that it rereads the configuration file.

3. Edit your host system's ssh_config file. Look for these lines:

```
# Host *
#    ForwardAgent no
#    ForwardX11 yes
```

Remove the comment characters in front of the Host and ForwardX11 lines. If you want to allow forwarding for your guest systems only, change the * to your host-only network's subnet.

4. Test your forwarding installation. Send ssh to your guest system from your host, and when you get a shell, type a command such as xterm. If you get a new window, the installation works.

Occasionally the forwarding mechanism doesn't work with preexisting installations of SSH due to changes in the library and protocol. In this case, upgrading everything to a fresh version of OpenSSH should fix things.

What About Windows Host Systems?

You can also forward X client connections through SSH from Unix to a Windows system. Teraterm SSH supports this, as does OpenSSH. To forward connections, you need an X server on your Windows host system. One popular option is the Cygwin port of XFree86 (see section 5.5 for more information on Cygwin). A popular commercial package is Exceed, from Hummingbird Communications (http://www.hummingbird.com).

10.9   Using a Proxy Server

One common VMware application is testing web pages on different web browsers running under multiple operating systems. With bridged and NAT network interfaces, you need to do no extra work for virtual machines to access a web server on an external network. However, you may not want (or be able) to use a bridged or NAT network, and moreover, your browsing performance may suffer due to replicated caches on your virtual disks.

You can set up a *proxy server* as a cheap way for guest systems to access web servers on external networks. A proxy acts as an intermediary between web browsers and web servers and does all the work of hostname resolution and caching. Because you don't need to run it as the superuser, you don't need any special access privileges on the host machine. And because you'll want to run it on a VMware host system, all of the cache files reside on the host's native filesystem and disk, so you can set the disk cache sizes on your browsers to zero, improving disk and memory performance on your guest systems.

10.9.1   Getting and Configuring Squid

The most popular web proxy server is called Squid, and you can get it from http://www.squid-cache.org/. Squid can proxy HTTP and FTP, and it can tunnel proxy HTTPS and other protocols. This section discusses the use of Squid on a Linux host machine, because Unix is Squid's primary platform. If you have a Window NT, 2000, or XP host, you can also run Squid—it compiles and runs under the Cygwin environment described in section 5.5. For more information, see the Squid website.

After you compile and install Squid on your host operating system, follow these steps:

1. Find your `squid.conf` file in the squid `etc` directory. Edit this file—it's very large, but you need to change only a few parameters (don't worry about messing up the file; there's a backup of the original in `squid.conf.default`).

2. If you want to change the default proxy port, change the `http_port` parameter (the default is 3128; in any case, make a note of the port number). Normally, you don't need to do this.

3. Skip down to the `cache_dir` parameter. This specifies where the cached files go. It looks something like this:

```
cache_dir ufs /scratch/squid/cache 100 16 256
```

The 100 means that this directory will hold at most 100 MB of data. If you aren't planning to make heavy use of your proxy server, it's probably a good idea to keep this setting as is. However, if you want to make the proxy server more generally available (to other users on your real network, not just on the VMware host-only network), you may want to increase this value or add more cache directories.

4. Verify that the directory listed in the `cache_dir` line has enough space to hold data of the configured data size. If not, change the directory.

5. Add an access control list (ACL) for your VMware host-only or NAT network. Skip down to the access control section, which consists of a number of `acl` and `http_access` parameters. Add an `acl` line for your host-only network; for example, if the address is 172.16.144.0/24, add the line

```
acl hostonly src 172.16.144.0/255.255.255.0
```

after the rest of the access control list.

6. Give the ACL you created in step 5 permission to use the proxy server. Go down to the lines that begin with `http_access`. The last one of these should read `http_access deny all`, and a note about inserting your own rules should appear above. This is where you'll put the permission. Add

```
http_access allow hostonly
```

just before the `deny all` line. *The order is important.*

7. Save your `squid.conf` file.

8. Run this command to create the cache directory structure (change `/scratch/squid/cache` to whatever you configured in the `cache_dir` line in steps 3 and 4):

```
mkdir -p /scratch/squid/cache
squid -z
```

9. If you plan to run `squid` as `root`, you must also run this command:

```
chown -R nobody /scratch/squid/cache
```

10. Run `squid -N` to test the proxy server. If you get an error message and your command prompt back, then there's a problem in your configuration somewhere (the error message should tell you exactly what the trouble is). If the test was successful, press CTRL-C.

11. Run `squid` (without any arguments) on the command line. `squid` should go into daemon mode, meaning that you'll get your prompt back. A process listing will verify that `squid` is running.

The most common problem is not being able to write to the `logs` directory, which may occur if you ran `squid` as `root` (see step 9); just run `chown nobody logs` if this is a problem. Squid normally dies right away if there's a configuration problem.

Now you're ready to use the proxy server from your guest operating system.

10.9.2   Guest System Proxy Configuration

After you have Squid to a point where it seems to work, you need to configure at least one of your guest systems to use the proxy. This process varies from system to system and browser to browser. For each of the following systems, we'll assume that the host operating system is at 172.16.144.1 and the proxy port is 3128.

Windows NT, IE: Open the **Internet Properties** control panel; it contains one tab. Check the **Use Proxy Server** box and enter **172.16.144.1:3128** in the **Proxy Server** box. Then click **OK**.

Windows 98/Me, IE: Select the **Connection** tab on the **Internet Properties** control panel. Check **Access the Internet using a proxy server**, enter **172.16.144.1** in the **Address** box, enter **3128** in the **Port** box, and click **OK**.

Windows 95, IE: As with Windows 98/Me, use the **Connection** tab on the **Internet** control panel. Then check the **Connect through a proxy server** box and click the **Settings** button. A new window appears; check the **Use the same proxy** box and enter **172.16.144.1** in the **HTTP Address** box, with **3128** as the port, and click **OK**.

Windows 2000/XP, IE: The process is similar to that for Windows 98/Me. Select the **Connections** tab on the **Internet Options** control panel. Click the **Lan Settings** button; a new window appears with the proxy server setting as described for Windows 98/Me.

All Systems, Netscape: Open the **Preferences** window and click the **Advanced** triangle; the item **Proxies** should appear. Click it, select **Manual proxy configuration**, and click the **View** button. In the **HTTP** and **FTP** proxy boxes, enter **172.16.144.1**, and use **3128** for the port numbers next to the boxes.

Unix, wget, and lynx: For wget, set your http_proxy and ftp_proxy (lowercase) environment or .wgetrc variables to http://172.16.144.1:3128/. The environment variables work for lynx as well as wget.

10.10   Considerations for Other Services

As mentioned many times before in this book, you can run any network service over a VMware host-only or NAT network. However, there are a few things that you should keep in mind when doing so:

Domain names. Is the service picky about domain names, like SSH and FTP servers? If you're running a bridged or NAT network and you tell your guest systems to look at a real DNS server to which you have continuous access, you shouldn't have a problem. However, if access is sporadic, or if you don't have a DNS server at all, you may run into delays while the guest times out on a nameserver request.

Security. While network services can be handy, they can also be serious security holes. Typical servers listen on all network interfaces, but you may want a particular service for only a host-only interface. If you have any doubt about a particular network program that you're installing, you shouldn't trust it, especially on a host system. One example is FTP servers; people continuously discover security holes in these.

Don't install any service on your host system without thinking about limiting access to other machines. It's generally easier to set up access control on a Linux host machine, because if you can't do it with /etc/hosts.deny, you can always fall back to a kernel-level firewall with ipchains or iptables. Windows hosts are a little tougher to configure, especially if you need to purchase firewall software.

Performance. Host-only and NAT networks are fairly quick, and you shouldn't have any trouble with performance. However, keep in mind that all host-only network traffic is internal to the host operating system. In particular, when traffic goes to and from the guest system, the operating system must perform several context switches inside and outside of VMware through the virtual network interface hardware, as well as go in and out of kernel mode. Short bursts won't hurt anything, but if you blast a continuous stream of data through a host-only network, your host system may slow down somewhat.

11

NON-NETWORKED FILE TRANSFER

Although the most convenient way to transfer files between host and guest operating systems is with VMware's networking features, sometimes you may not want to (or have the ability to) use the network.

As an alternative, you can use VMware's floppy, CD-ROM, and virtual disk devices, which are handy for transferring small files or making small changes to a guest operating system, especially when you're first setting one up (because you may not have networking support yet). Also, if you have to work with a DOS guest, you may find it preferable to work with VMware's virtual devices because you won't have to bother with the TCP/IP stack (or other network protocol software) that DOS requires for networking.

Most of this chapter deals with floppy disks and CD-ROM images. Because you can attach a file to a VMware virtual floppy, and all guest systems know how to read a FAT-type filesystem on a floppy disk, you can transfer a file from the host to a guest and back through a floppy disk file on the host operating system. The case is similar for CD-ROM images, except that while you can store much more on a CD-ROM image, you can transfer only from the host to the guest system.

11.1   Disk Images

A *floppy disk image* file is simply a file with an exact copy of all data that a floppy disk would contain, including the entire filesystem data structure.

The particular procedure for accessing floppy disk images depends on your host system. Due to the uniform block device mechanism in a Unix system, it's not unusual to have more flexibility on a Linux host. Block devices are a type of device driver; all disk utilities operate on block devices.

Single floppy disks don't hold much data, so if you need a way to transfer larger amounts of data from a host to a guest without networking, you should use a CD-ROM ISO9660 image file. VMware Workstation can attach an ISO9660 CD-ROM image to a VMware Workstation virtual CD-ROM drive. We'll talk about how to create CD-ROM image files in this chapter.

In addition, VMware Workstation for Linux includes a utility for attaching a virtual disk file directly to the host operating system as a filesystem; we'll cover that in section 11.5.

11.2   Disk Image Utilities (Linux Host)

The Linux kernel includes an extraordinary amount of filesystem support, making it possible to access files on almost any kind of media that you can attach to a PC, although you probably won't need all of this support when using Linux as a host or guest operating system. In fact, when using floppy disks, it's likely that you'll need only the Microsoft FAT-based filesystem family, though if you work with older Linux guest systems, you may find a Minix filesystem here and there. You need this filesystem support on your host system to be able to write an image onto the floppy disk that the guest system can understand.

The most convenient way to access a filesystem on a floppy disk image on your host operating system is through the loopback driver. This driver is a very simple device whose driver takes a file and maps its content to a block device in /dev, at which point you can attach the device somewhere on your current filesystem.

Here's an example of how to use the loopback driver to attach an example.flp image file (run this as root):

```
mount -t msdos -oloop=/dev/loop0 example.flp /mnt
```

After you run this command, the files on the floppy disk image from example.flp should be visible at /mnt. When you examine the files there, you should notice that some have somewhat odd names, like vmware~1.exe. This is called a *mangled* name—it's a truncated version of the actual file name. It appears this way because the real name is longer than seven characters, and the simple MS-

DOS filesystem can't handle that many characters in a file name. To see the whole file name, use `umount /mnt` to detach the image filesystem and then run the `mount` command just shown, but replace `msdos` with `vfat`.

IMPORTANT   *Always `umount` a loopback image as soon as you finish with it, especially before you connect it to a guest operating system running under VMware, because it's easy to forget about the image. You should detach the image because of the kernel's buffers: If you play around with the original image file before detaching it from your system, there's a good chance that you'll end up with inconsistencies. As soon as you use `umount`, all of the kernel's file buffers are flushed back into the original file. Even if you mount the image as read-only, the kernel won't be terribly pleased if you change the image's filesystem structure.*

NOTE   *You're not limited to the FAT filesystem on floppy disks, by the way. If you like, you can create a second extended filesystem on an image with `mke2fs`. Whatever works is the best solution—it's good if your host can create and your guest can read (or the other way around). You can also use the loopback device to attach an ISO9660 image to your Linux system; just use the filesystem type `iso9660`. This can be handy on a Linux host where you have a `.iso` image with some files for your guest system, but don't want to burn the image to a CD just for this purpose. We'll look at an example in section 11.4.*

11.2.1 Kernel Support for the Loopback Device

For loopback devices to work properly under Linux, you must have the appropriate kernel support, which most Linux distributions include. If you're compiling your own kernel, you'll find the option under `Block devices` on the main menu. You can compile the support as a module (`loop.o`); the automatic kernel module loader has no trouble figuring out that it needs to load the module when you access a device such as `/dev/loop0`.

To access more than one image at a time, you'll need to use separate loopback devices in `/dev`. To do so, use `/dev/loop1`, `/dev/loop2`, and so on for *device* in the `-oloop=device` part of the `mount` command.

11.2.2 Extracting Data from Floppy Disks

If you have a (real) floppy disk from which you want to extract all data for use under VMware Workstation, you can copy the entire disk directly from the floppy drive. To place the disk data from a floppy drive in a file called *image.flp*, use `dd` on the floppy drive's block device:

```
dd if=/dev/fd0 of=image.flp bs=512
```

Unfortunately, regular PC floppy drives and disks aren't very reliable, and the Linux drivers don't particularly like to deal with bad disks. If you get an I/O error, try ejecting and reinserting the disk a few times to see if there's some dust in the drive that you need to displace. If this doesn't work, try the superformat formatter on another disk to attempt to calibrate the drive. Finally, try another floppy drive or computer.

11.2.3 Creating New Floppy Images

If you just want to create a blank floppy image and put an empty filesystem on it, you don't need to bother with any real floppy disks or drives. With a reasonably new version of the mkdosfs command, you can create the image and put a DOS filesystem on it all in one shot with this command:

```
mkdosfs -C image.flp 1440
```

The 1440 is the block count. Since blocks are 1,024 bytes long, the mkdosfs command here is equivalent to these two commands:

```
dd if=/dev/zero of=image.flp bs=1024 count=1440
mkdosfs image.flp
```

Once the image has been created, you can do whatever you like with image.flp.

11.3 Floppy Disk Image Utilities (Windows Host)

If you have a Windows host system, you need to look for third-party solutions for floppy disk utilities if you want to create images for use under VMware Workstation's virtual floppy disk drives. One capable program is WinImage, which you'll find at http://www.winimage.com/. It's shareware, so you have to pay a nominal fee if you want to use it for more than 30 days (all upgrades are free).

Figure 11.1 shows WinImage in action on an example floppy image. The program behaves like any file browser. You can drag and drop items to and from the file listing, and several other options are available from the **Image** menu. For example, to create a new, empty image, use the **File • New** menu item; the program will prompt you for the floppy dimensions.

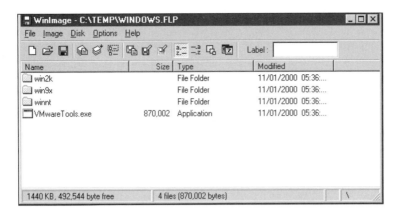

Figure 11.1: WinImage with a floppy image

NOTE *Make sure when you save a new image for the first time with WinImage that you select* `.IMA` *as the file type and extension to produce a plain, uncompressed image. The default is a compressed (*`.IMZ`*) format, which VMware Workstation can't map to a virtual floppy drive.*

In addition to manipulating images, WinImage can extract the contents of a floppy drive to an image file, write a floppy image, and browse (but not write) ISO9660 CD-ROM images.

If all you need to do is read disk images from a floppy, a free program called Floppy Image can do the job. You can get this program at http://www.rundegren.com/. To write a floppy image to disk, look for the `RAWRITE.EXE` program that comes with almost any Linux distribution.

11.3.1 Windows File Extensions

You may have noticed that there doesn't seem to be a consensus on what extension a floppy image file name should end with. VMware Workstation uses `.flp` for floppy disk images, WinImage uses `.IMA`, Floppy Image uses `.IMG`—and there are several others.

The right approach is to use whatever extensions your program accepts. VMware Workstation doesn't care about the extension except when file browsing. The only important thing to consider with VMware is file size: A 1.44-MB floppy image must be *exactly* 1,474,560 bytes long.

11.4 Creating CD-ROM Images

Because VMware Workstation 3 and higher allows you to attach a CD-ROM image directly to a virtual machine, you can move large amounts of data from a host operating system to a guest with a virtual CD-ROM drive. However, keep in mind that this assumes that you don't have use of the network; if you *do* have networking support on your guest system, it's much faster to use the network file transfer utilities described in Chapter 9.

Aside from file transfer, another application for CD-ROM image files in VMware Workstation is the testing of bootable CDs. You can create bootable CDs on your host operating system, attach them to a virtual machine, and test the boot process, all without leaving the comfort of your host operating system.

The most common type of filesystem on CD-ROMs is ISO9660. The following two sections describe how to create image files in this format for each host operating system.

11.4.1 Linux Host

The standard utility for creating ISO9660 images under Linux (and other Unix variants) is called mkisofs. It is free, comes with almost any Linux distribution, and works on the command line.

To create an image named *mycd.iso* containing the entire directory structure in *dir*, use

```
mkisofs options -o mycd.iso dir
```

where *options* can include the following:

-r: Use the Rock Ridge extension. Use this if you intend to use the image primarily with Unix guest systems; it enables the use of long file names.

-J: Use the Joliet extension. Use this if you want to use the image with Windows guest systems.

-b *boot_image:* Create an El Torito–style bootable ISO9660 image. The boot_image value must be a bootable floppy disk image within the dir hierarchy.

See the mkisofs manual page for more details.

11.4.2 Windows Host

There are many CD-ROM image utilities for Windows—so many that it's not feasible to mention how to use them all in a single section. Furthermore, since they are Windows programs, they're all fairly straightforward; all you need to do is drag a bunch of file and folder icons and click a Create button.

If you want a free program, you can use the same mkisofs program mentioned in the previous section. It requires the Cygwin package; see section 5.5. After you install Cygwin, you can compile the mkisofs source code and run the program just as you would on a Unix system.

One of the most popular commercial Windows-like CD-ROM image programs is CDEverywhere. Its primary strength is its support of many different formats. You can find it at http://www.i2rd.com/cdeverywhere/.

11.5   Accessing Guest Virtual Disks (Linux Host Only)

VMware Workstation for Linux includes a virtual disk access utility called vmware-mount.pl that attaches your guest operating system's virtual disks directly to your Unix directory tree. Here's an example of the utility in action:

```
vmware-mount.pl guestos.vmdk 1 /mnt
```

In this example, guestos.vmdk is the name of the virtual disk, 1 is the partition number, and /mnt is the mount point.

The vmware-mount.pl program responds to this command with a long message. If the operation is successful, the message reads as follows:

```
Using another terminal, you can now browse your
Virtual Hard Disk partition in /mnt. Hit Control-C
in this terminal when done.
```

At this point, you should be able to use cd /mnt and do anything you'd normally do with a regular filesystem. Just remember to leave the virtual disk's directory before you're finished with it. Then, press CTRL-C to detach the virtual disk from your host system.

If mount fails, you probably don't have network block device support in your Linux kernel. The vmware-mount.pl program tries to load this device support as a module, but if it can't find the module (nbd.o), it gives up. (As with the file loopback configuration, the network block device is in the Block devices category of the kernel configuration.)

NOTE *The vmware-mount.pl utility is meant for casual access, not heavy-duty use. It can handle moderate data transfers without a problem. However, do not try to pipe continuous streams of data into it (such as from /dev/zero–you may have thought to prepare a disk for VMware shrink operation this way). If you do, the data will get caught in the buffers while waiting for vmware-loop to write the data to the virtual disk file. As a result, all of the involved processes will be blocked while you wait for this write operation to complete (and you could end up waiting a long time). To move large amounts of data to a virtual disk regardless of the filesystem, consider setting up a small Linux guest system using a quick-booting distribution (like Debian) for the task. You can run the system in text-only mode with a small main memory–16 MB should do. Linux's particular advantage here is its ability to work with almost any type of filesystem.*

11.5.1 *vmware-mount.pl Options*

You may need three command line options when working with vmware-mount.pl. Two of them, -t and -o, are identical to the regular options in the mount program.

The -t option specifies a filesystem type. You may need to specify a type if the filesystem's kernel module isn't currently active.

You can also use any other mount options with -o. For example, you can use -o ro for read-only access. See the manual page for mount for a list of these options.

The -p option prints the partition table of a virtual disk, in case you don't know the partition number. Here's an example of what vmware-mount.pl -p linux.dsk returns (linux.dsk is a typical Linux guest virtual disk file):

```
Nr     Start       Size Type Id System
-- ---------- ---------- ---- -- -----------------------
1          63    3072321 BIOS 83 Linux
5     3072447    1020033 BIOS 82 Linux swap
```

12

TROUBLESHOOTING

In some respects, getting to the root of a problem with VMware Workstation isn't much different than finding a problem on a real PC. All computers have their own little operational quirks, and VMware is no exception. And just as the problems vary from system to system on real computers, you'll find that this is also the case with VMware. (Remember that a virtual machine is a hybrid of sorts—while its virtual hardware is uniform and well-documented, it uses your real processor, and any guest operating system acts as it would under that processor. Add your own special virtual hardware configuration and the guest system's driver characteristics, and you can see that there are a lot of variables.)

This chapter has three parts. The first part describes general troubleshooting procedures. This will give you a better idea of how to gather information about a problem with VMware Workstation and where to look for its solution.

The second, and largest, part of the chapter offers a list of common trouble spots and their solutions. We take the point of view that a problem isn't really fixed until you know why it occurred. Therefore, explanations accompany the fixes.

Finally, a small section details one way to recover from a virtual machine crash, using a guest operating system tuned specifically for that purpose.

12.1 General Troubleshooting Procedures

This section presents some general procedures you can follow to diagnose and fix a problem with VMware.

12.1.1 Try to Identify the Part of the System That's Causing Trouble

If one of your devices won't work, the problem has a large scope and may lie in the guest operating system's user interface, the guest's drivers, the VMware guest or host configuration, your host system's drivers, or the real hardware. Do the following to try to determine where the problem lies:

- As a sanity check, make sure the *host's* hardware and drivers work. Try to do something that's similar to what you'd do on a guest system. (For example, if your guest can't talk to the serial port, make sure that you can run a terminal program from the host.)

- Make a quick inspection of your guest system's virtual hardware in the VMware Configuration Editor. Make sure that the devices point to the right places, and perhaps more important, if Linux is your host, make sure that you clicked the **Install** button to bring the device into the configuration (this is an easy procedure to overlook).

- Try a known working guest operating system. Linux and Windows 98 are good for this purpose, because they install and boot quickly and have perfect device support. If the devices work under one of these systems, then the problem is almost certainly in the guest system.

- If you've isolated the guest as the trouble spot, try the simplest device access commands that you know of. For example, if you have trouble with parallel ports under a Linux guest, try redirecting some output directly to /dev/lp0.

If you have trouble booting a virtual machine, you'll need to figure out where your boot block is. Find the boot partition (see section 2.4 for more information on how a PC boots) and then find your guest system's main partition (C: on a Windows guest, and / (root) on a Unix-like guest).

12.1.2 Diagnostic Messages and Errors

VMware Workstation may display a diagnostic message or abort with an error. The diagnostic messages usually aren't fatal (like what you get when the guest system sends an unsupported CD-ROM command). These messages won't stop VMware or its guest system, but they may become annoying after a while.

On the other hand, aborts (also labeled PANIC) stop your virtual machine in its tracks. If you get an abort, pay close attention to the message. Some aborts result from known bugs and include a message containing the text bugNr=n, where n is some number. This message means that the bug is already in VMware's database, and if a newer Workstation release is available, it may fix this bug.

You may also get an "Unimplemented" abort message, which usually means that one of the guest system's device drivers tried to do something with the virtual hardware that VMware can't handle. You can usually deduce what the hardware is by the message (and, in some cases, by what the guest was doing right before the crash). If you get one of these aborts, you may be able to avoid it by disconnecting the device in question.

In the worst kind of crash, VMware trips over itself so badly that it can't catch its own error, and the host operating system has to take over. Fortunately, crashes of this type are rare, and they're usually related to a condition on the host system. (Broken VMware kernel modules on a Linux host may cause this kind of crash.) If you encounter a problem like this, first check your host system configuration to see if it's known to work well with VMware Workstation, or whether there are issues listed in the documentation.

Where to Find Diagnostic Messages

One of the best places to look for VMware diagnostic messages is in your virtual machine's log file. On a Windows host, this file is in your virtual machine's configuration directory as `VMware.log`. On a Linux host, you'll find it in the same directory as your configuration file; the file name ends with `.log` (for example, `freebsd.log`).

Normally, VMware removes a virtual machine's log file when it switches configurations or exits, so if you want to look at the file, you must keep the VMware application running with the same active configuration (it doesn't matter if you turn off the virtual machine, though). However, the log file remains if VMware aborts abnormally.

12.1.3   Other Resources

If you still haven't isolated the problem, try to locate a solution in this chapter. The chapter discusses problems related to the host and guest operating systems, general configuration, VMware Tools, and networking. Also be sure to check this book's index or table of contents for the appropriate subject.

In addition, VMware's support page at http://www.vmware.com/support/ offers other, up-to-date solutions. In particular, the online troubleshooting documentation includes information about many obscure hardware bugs that affect a very small percentage of systems.

Your guest operating system's support area also may have something of note regarding your processor and the hardware that corresponds to VMware's virtual hardware. And keep your motherboard in mind; some issues regarding a motherboard's chipset or BIOS may cause trouble. (You can find information on these issues on VMware's support pages as well.)

Finally, if you're a registered VMware customer, you can always contact VMware's technical support people directly.

12.2 Problems and Solutions

This section describes some common problems and their solutions. The problems are categorized as follows: host operating systems, general configuration, guest operating systems, VMware Tools, and networking. The following information is presented for each problem:

Problem: A description of the symptoms.

Fix: An explanation of the problem and possible remedies.

12.2.1 Windows Host Operating System Problems

Problem: Sound doesn't work: "Error 32 opening output sound device." You have more than one sound card.

Fix: One of your sound cards probably isn't working correctly. Try adding

```
sound.device = -1
```

to your virtual machine's configuration file. (This parameter setting tells VMware to look for a properly functioning sound card; if you set it to a number greater than or equal to 0, you're directly picking a sound card.)

12.2.2 Linux Host Operating System Problems

Problem: When you try to run the installer, it says that it can't find an `uninstall` script (or some other script). You ran the installer script to upgrade or install VMware Workstation for Linux, but accidentally pressed CTRL-C during the process.

Fix: If `/etc/vmware` exists, the installer assumes an upgrade and removes your old version with the `vmware-uninstall.pl` script before installing the new version on an upgrade. However, if this directory is incomplete, the script can't find the uninstaller and exits. Run the following to rename the `/etc/vmware` directory:

```
mv /etc/vmware /etc/vmware.orig
```

You may want to delete the old directory, but be careful: you may want to copy some configuration files from it. Furthermore, if you remove it, it won't be easy to remove your old version if you want to put the new one in a different location. First see whether the `locations` file exists and save a copy if it does.

Problem: Your Linux machine routes packets to and from your host-only network, but you don't want it to.

Fix: If you don't want your Linux host to route anything at all, just enter this command:

```
echo 0 > /proc/sys/net/ipv4/ip_forward
```

However, if you do want the host to route packets (just not the host-only packets), then you should use a firewall to keep the packets out. For Linux kernel series 2.2, use `ipchains`:

```
ipchains -A forward -i vmnet1 -j REJECT
```

For 2.4.*x*, use `iptables`:

```
iptables -A FORWARD -o vmnet1 -j DROP
iptables -A FORWARD -i vmnet1 -j DROP
```

(For `iptables`, you can use `REJECT` instead of `DROP` if you have this support in your kernel or as a module.)

Problem: When you power on the virtual machine, VMware pops up a dialog saying that it can't open `/dev/rtc`. How can you fix this, and is this really a problem?

Fix: The `/dev/rtc` special file is the real-time clock on your PC's motherboard (the one that's backed up by the battery). There are a few possible reasons for this warning:

- You may not have permission to read `/dev/rtc` on your host system. This is easy to fix; just enter `chmod go+r /dev/rtc` as `root` on your host. (You need only read permission; don't give everyone on your system write access to `/dev/rtc`, because that would allow everyone to set the hardware clock.)

- Some other program (such as another instance of VMware) may have the device open.

- You don't have RTC support in your kernel. You'll find it on the `Character devices` submenu of the kernel configuration (`CONFIG_RTC`). It's fine to compile the RTC driver as a module; the automatic kernel module loader knows about it. If `/dev/rtc` doesn't exist on your system, enter the following:

```
mknod /dev/rtc c 10 135
chmod 644 /dev/rtc
```

If you can't get VMware to connect to the real-time clock, there may be no reason to worry. However, some guest operating systems want it—Windows 98, in particular, uses the real-time clock more than most systems, and it may perform irregularly without access.

If you want the warning to go away, put this in your virtual machine configuration file to disconnect the RTC when you power on the virtual machine:

```
rtc.startConnected = FALSE
```

Problem: Something goes wrong with the module compilation when you run `vmware-config.pl`.

Fix: You need a working C compiler and matching header files. The header files are in the `include` directory of a Linux kernel distribution.

A few things can go wrong with a module compile operation:

- You see a message similar to `make: not found`. You have no development tools installed. (See the next bullet point for what to do.)
- The message `make: gcc: command not found` means that you have `make`, but you don't have the C compiler on your system. Look for it in the development series of your distribution's packages. Make sure that you install `gcc` version 2, not 3. Red Hat sometimes calls this `kgcc`.
- The `vmware-config.pl` program tells you that your header files don't match your current kernel version. If you're running a special distribution kernel, install the kernel source package for that version (run `uname -a` for your version). Otherwise, go to http://www.kernel.org/ and pick up your version, unpack it, and point `vmware-config.pl` at the header files there (the `include` directory).

If a module compile operation fails, look in `/tmp/vmware-config0`. This directory contains the source code that the compiler couldn't handle. You can go into one of the subdirectories of `/tmp/vmware-config0` and use `make` to try the compile operation by hand. This may give you more diagnostic messages. (Note that if you try `vmware-config.pl` more than once, you'll get `vmware-config0`, `vmware-config1`, and so on as compile directories—one for each try.)

Problem: Something goes wrong with the modules after you run `vmware-config.pl` and try to load them. (This happens most often with SMP systems.)
Fix: Even though the version numbers are the same, your header files may not match your kernel's configuration. Make sure that you run `make mrproper` in your kernel source directory; then use a command such as `make menuconfig` with the same parameters as your current kernel. In particular, pay attention to the processor options, such as SMP.

Problem: The display is corrupt in full-screen mode. The most common symptom is a black window.
Fix: If you're running XFree86 4.0.*x*, the direct graphics access (DGA) driver may have some bugs. Try upgrading to a newer version of XFree86 to see if this fixes the problem, or downgrade to XFree86 3.3.*x*. The newest and fastest cards on the market are most likely to have problems like this.

You can also try putting this line in your virtual machine's `.cfg` file:

```
xinfo.noDGAAccel = TRUE
```

Problem: No matter what settings you use in your host's `XF86Config` file, full-screen mode doesn't seem to work.
Explanation: Some X servers don't adequately support DGA, and full-screen mode requires DGA. There's no solution here; you'll have to live with window mode.

Problem: Various Linux kernel incompatibilities exist. (See the following list for specific kernel versions.)

Fix: The best way to fix these problems is to upgrade your kernel. You can either get an update for your distribution (probably the best solution if you're running Red Hat), or compile your own kernel. Remember that once you change your kernel, you must run `vmware-config.pl` again to put the appropriate VMware kernel modules in place.

You might run into trouble with these versions in particular:

2.2.3 and earlier: These versions have a few CD-ROM problems. For example, the tray may continuously open and close when you start VMware. This problem manifests itself most often when a guest system wants to do something automatically with a CD as soon as you insert it.

2.2.16: This version has some bugs in the Linux CD-ROM driver. VMware has trouble detecting a CD when you insert it, and you'll see a warning dialog box when you power on the virtual machine. Windows 95 and 98 guest systems will see data CDs as audio CDs.

2.4.0 – 2.4.8: Various issues come up with these earlier production-release kernels, in particular in compiling the `vmmon` and `vmnet` modules. Try to use a later version of the kernel if you can, and make sure that your VMware build is reasonably up-to-date.

Problem: Your virtual machine can't access a device.

Fix: There are two main solutions to this problem. First, check to see if you have permission to access the device; VMware won't allow you to use a device in a virtual machine that you can't touch on the host side. If the permissions are okay, see if some other program on your host system has the device open or locked.

NOTE *You're better off not directly sharing certain devices between the host and guest systems because of possible conflicts; instead, you should use host-only networking features. For example, use SAMBA or* `lpd` *to make your printer accessible to your guest.*

Problem: VMware doesn't work after a major host operating system upgrade. When you run the installer again after a host operating system upgrade, it tells you that it found a previous installation, but it aborts after telling you that it was unable to stop the VMware services.

Fix: After a major system upgrade, the VMware Workstation services probably won't start at boot time. Instead of running the installer again, run `vmware-config.pl` to install the appropriate kernel modules.

If this doesn't work, try to replace VMware by removing the old version by hand with `vmware-uninstall.pl`; then reinstall VMware Workstation, using a newer version. If you get the same error as before, obtain a process listing for your system and look for all of the VMware-related processes (`ps auxww | grep vmware`) and kill them. Then use `lsmod` to locate any VMware kernel modules and use `rmmod` to remove them.

Now run `mv /etc/vmware /etc/vmware.orig` and note where you installed VMware the last time. Run the installer again and give the same answers that you gave when you first installed VMware (if you can't remember, look at `/etc/vmware.orig/locations`). When you're done with the installation, you can copy some of your old configuration data back from `/etc/vmware.orig`—for instance, the host-only networking settings in the `config` file and the entire `vmnet1` directory.

Problem: Your system includes a package called `libsafe`, and VMware aborts when you try to start it.
Fix: Remove this library package; VMware requires the `brk()` system call, and `libsafe` doesn't let programs issue it.

12.2.3 General Configuration Problems

Problem: Your guest system doesn't seem to boot, and the disk settings seem incorrect. The virtual BIOS beeps a lot after you power on the virtual machine.
Fix: In rare cases, the NVRAM file that VMware uses to store BIOS settings becomes corrupt. This file contains configuration data such as the floppy drive setup and boot sequence data. If the BIOS reads the NVRAM file incorrectly, you may have trouble allocating IRQs in the virtual machine, reading disk geometry, and so on.

The easiest way to fix these problems is to shut down the virtual machine and quit VMware, then delete the NVRAM file. (Remember that the file is called `nvram` on a Windows host, and the file name ends with `.nvram` on a Linux host.) When you power on the virtual machine again, VMware creates a new NVRAM file.

Problem: You deleted or corrupted your virtual machine configuration (`.vmx` or `.cfg` file).
Fix: Use the Configuration Wizard to create a new configuration file and then copy it over your old one. Everything probably won't work perfectly initially because you'll likely leave out some virtual hardware. To solve that problem, use the Configuration Editor until you get the results you want.

NOTE *If you think your configuration file is corrupt, try deleting the NVRAM file first, as outlined in the discussion of the previous problem.*

Problem: Your guest system doesn't recognize the second virtual floppy drive, even though you added it with the VMware Configuration Editor.
Fix: The VMware BIOS doesn't automatically pick up changes made to floppy drives with the Configuration Editor; you must go into the BIOS setup utility and add them manually. (See section 4.14 for more information on the BIOS.)

To do so, press F2 when the guest system boots, move the cursor down to `Legacy Diskette B:`, and press ENTER to bring up a list of floppy drive choices (usually what you want is the `1.44/1.25 MB` drive). Then press F10 to save and exit the BIOS. Make sure that you go into the BIOS and disable the second floppy if you ever decide to remove the virtual floppy device in the Configuration Editor.

Also, if you have a Linux host system, make sure that you clicked the **Install** button in the Configuration Editor when you entered the virtual floppy's information.

Problem: You can't seem to make certain changes with the Configuration Editor; the items you want to alter are dimmed.

Fix: You can't change certain options when a virtual machine has power or is in a suspended state. To make changes, you must power off the machine and then open the Configuration Editor. Think of these parameters as hardware you wouldn't be able to change on a real machine if it were running—for example, you can't remove hard disks and regular expansion cards when a computer is up.

12.2.4   *General Guest Operating System Problems*

Problem: When you suspend certain guest systems with VMware's suspend-to-disk feature, your host system freezes for a little while.

Fix: When you suspend a system, VMware Workstation writes all of the virtual machine memory state out to the disk and fixes any changes to the virtual machine's disks. This can send a great deal of data to your host machine's disk, and the host's disk memory buffers may fill up, causing a flood of real disk writes. During the writes, all system calls to the disk are blocked.

You can improve things in two ways. First, you can try to reduce the amount of memory in the virtual machine configuration so that a suspend operating system has less memory to write out. Otherwise, you can try to put the virtual machine configuration file and directory on a different disk. VMware writes a machine's state data to the same directory that contains its configuration file. If that also happens to be your system disk, any system activity involving that disk will freeze while the write buffers flush.

Finally, you can try to improve your disk performance. If you have special drivers for your disk hardware on a Windows host, install them. Make sure that any DMA and multiple-sector transfer modes are on. On a Linux host with IDE disks, you can try running hdparm to enable special modes. The most significant of these are usually multiple-sector transfers (for example, hdparm -m 16 /dev/hda). See the hdparm manual page for a full list.

If none of these options works for you, you can always just grin and bear it.

Problem: When you try to suspend your virtual machine, VMware tells you that the guest doesn't want to do it.

Fix: Turn off the **Use APM features of guest OS when suspending** option in the Configuration Editor. This is generally a good idea anyway, because your guest system may want to do something rude, such as write its state to a partition on a raw disk. Not only is this likely to result in corruption to or by another operating system, but the system may just not work at all due to raw disk permissions, BIOS incompatibilities, the phase of the moon, or something else that you really don't want to get involved with.

Problem: When you perform a real suspend operation on your notebook host, VMware crashes.

Workaround: Click the VMware **Suspend** button *before* performing the real suspend operation. Also, as stated in the discussion of the preceding problem, don't use APM for your guest's suspend operation.

Problem: You can't boot your guest system from the CD.
Fix: It's likely that the boot sequence in the VMware BIOS is set to search for an operating system on the hard disk before the CD-ROM. See section 4.14 for more information on the VMware BIOS.

Problem: Your host system performs horribly when running certain guest systems or the VMware BIOS on Windows host systems in particular.
Fix: Your guest system doesn't release the CPU when it should, as explained in section 8.1. If your guest has a processor idle utility and/or APM support, use it.

This problem manifests itself more often on Windows host systems because the scheduler on these hosts tries to optimize itself for active and inactive windows, whereas Linux systems generally give equal priority to everything (even if you run a CPU-intensive screensaver with one of the guest systems running in the background, a Linux system still won't grind to a halt). You can give a Windows host some hints in the **Priority** section of the VMware **Global Settings** or the Configuration Editor by using the lowest possible setting.

If you're having serious CPU performance problems on a Linux host, use renice on the VMware process.

Problem: Your IDE drive settings don't seem to work; you're trying to configure a drive on the secondary slave.
Fix: You can't configure a slave drive without a master under VMware Workstation. Either install a master (anything will do) or move the drive to the master.

Problem: You need a certain bit depth, but no matter what you do, your guest system's VMware video drivers don't want to change.
Fix: For the SVGA drivers, the guest's bit depth is always the same as the host's. So to change the guest's bit depth, set the host bit depth first.

Problem: You want to use 8-bit (256-color) mode, but VMware Workstation doesn't allow it.
Fix: Set the host to this bit depth. If your host happens to be Windows, add

```
draw.allow8Bit = TRUE
```

to the virtual machine's configuration (.vmx) file.

NOTE *Not all of the VMware SVGA drivers support 8-bit mode.*

Problem: Your guest operating system loses time.
Fix: If you can, install the VMware Tools and select **Time synchronization** on the **Other** tab. For Linux and FreeBSD systems, run vmware-guestd.

NOTE *Using the **Time synchronization** setting can degrade system performance somewhat.*

Problem: Sometimes the VMware guest display looks funny, like someone smeared it.
Fix: The scroller can occasionally cause trouble, especially if you have Autofit turned off. To solve this problem, turn on the Autofit option (on the **View** menu) to eliminate the scrollbars.

Problem: You're trying to mount a disk on both your host and guest systems at once (for example, a dual-boot and dual-configuration system), with Linux as the host and Windows as the guest, and you have the Windows partition mounted at /dos. However, when you write changes to the host system, the guest doesn't see these changes unless you power the virtual machine off and on.

Fix: Use network file sharing (described in Chapter 10) rather than trying to share your partitions directly like this. Because all modern operating systems cache reads and writes to disk, unless they're synchronized one system won't know what the other is doing. Thus, only one operating system should have direct access to a disk partition at any one time; if you give two systems direct write access to the same partition, you'll eventually corrupt the partition because there is no synchronization.

Problem: You made some changes to the global configuration, and when you try to resume a suspended virtual machine, things don't come back correctly.

Explanation: What you've done is tantamount to suspending an operating system running on a real computer, changing its hardware, and then resuming execution. The system's device drivers won't react favorably to that sort of change. It is true that there are some things you can get away with, but you'll have to be daring to find out what those things are.

Recommendation: Don't do that.

12.2.5   Windows Guest Operating System Problems (All Versions)

Problem: You added a new piece of hardware to your dual-boot, dual-configuration machine, and now Windows won't boot as a VMware guest system.

Fix: Windows likes to add certain pieces of hardware (such as video cards) to all hardware profiles. The easiest way to fix this problem is to boot Windows in safe mode, bring up the hardware profiles and Device Manager, and remove your new device from the virtual machine configuration.

Problem: Some (or all) virtual hardware doesn't work when you install from the Windows CD that came with your computer, or the Windows CD won't let you install under VMware at all.

Fix: PCs often come with OEM versions of Windows that assume a particular kind of hardware. If you encounter this problem, view the Windows Device Manager and try to remove all special drivers, including IDE drivers; then reboot the guest system. Windows will automatically detect anything you might have accidentally deleted, other than the sound card.

In their most draconian form, OEM versions of Windows look for a particular kind of BIOS, and if they don't find that BIOS, the installer program on the CD refuses to work. Since the VMware BIOS is in no way like your real machine's BIOS, there's really no way around this problem unless you get a Windows release that doesn't assume any hardware.

12.2.6 Windows 95 Guest Operating System Problems

Problem: Windows 95 fails to boot and reports a fatal error or an error that mentions IOS:. This problem is sporadic: sometimes the machine boots, and sometimes it doesn't.

Fix: If your host machine's processor is an AMD K6-2, AMD Athlon, or Intel Pentium 4, install a small upgrade to Windows 95. Look for the amdk6upd.exe update (search for it at http://microsoft.com/). Use the same patch for the Pentium 4.

NOTE *AMD also has a patch, but it has problems with the VMware BIOS. Don't install it.*

Problem: Your Windows 95 guest system takes up all available CPU time on your host.

Fix: The first releases of Windows 95 did not properly idle the processor. Upgrade to version OSR2 of Windows 95 or install an idler utility such as CPU-Idle (http://www.cpuidle.de/), Rain, or Waterfall. See section 8.1 for an explanation of why your guest operating system is monopolizing your host system's CPU.

Problem: DHCP and other networking functions don't work on your Windows 95 guest system.

Fix: Upgrade your version of Windows 95 to a release that includes Winsock 2.0.

12.2.7 Windows 98 Guest Operating System Problems

Problem: You have big trouble installing certain versions of Windows 98 (such as the Japanese Windows 98 SE).

Fix: This is likely due to EMM386; VMware Workstation doesn't support EMM386, so you'll need to remove it somehow. Just after you install the operating system, boot from a floppy disk, or press F8 as soon as Windows starts, and edit your CONFIG.SYS file. Look for the line that says something like this:

```
DEVICE=C:\WINDOWS\EMM386.EXE RAM
```

Comment this line out (with rem) or just delete it. You may also have to modify a line in the JDISP.SYS file to read as follows:

```
DEVICE=C:\WINDOWS\JDISP.SYS /HS=LC
```

12.2.8 Windows NT, 2000, and XP Guest Operating System Problems

Problem: The sound on your Windows 2000 or XP guest system is scratchy, or it pops.

Fix: Windows 2000 and XP require more processor time and power than most other guest operating systems (try running top on a Linux host when the Windows guest is powered on sometime). Because its sound support may want a bigger processor slice than the host operating system is willing to give up, the Windows 2000/XP sound driver may drop sound fragments.

There are a few possible workarounds. First, if the problem isn't too bad, you can try adding this to your virtual machine's configuration file:

```
sound.maxLength = 512
sound.smallBlockSize = 512
```

You may have to play with the numbers a bit (try pushing them up or down until something happens). You can also try to make Windows take up less CPU time by turning off animations, unwanted services, and so forth. You can also check your host system to see if it has an unusually high load.

Normally, you have just two choices: either get a faster processor or turn off sound.

Problem: Your COM1 serial port doesn't work right on a Windows 2000 guest system with a Linux host system.
Fix: Do the following for the first serial port (COM1):

1. Install the serial port on the virtual machine with the Configuration Editor, and turn on the virtual machine.
2. Open the Device Manager, and look under **Ports.** Find out how many serial ports there are.
3. If there are less than six ports, right-click on COM5 and COM6, **Uninstall** them, and then reboot your guest system. Otherwise, skip to the next step.
4. If there are six ports, right-click on COM3 and **Uninstall** the port. Then do the same for COM2 and COM4, in that order.

Problem: On your Windows 2000 or XP system, you get a blue screen on installation or after installation. The error message includes something about INACCESSIBLE_BOOT_DISK.
Fix: Unfortunately, there are a number of possible problems here, but the basic problem is that Windows can't access its boot filesystem for one of the following reasons:

- Malfunctioning IDE device driver: This is like the problem on page 219; the driver for your particular IDE chipset may be unable to access the VMware virtual hardware. You can remove the IDE devices and any others that don't correspond to your virtual hardware. If that doesn't work, try replacing the IDE driver:

1. Make two hardware profiles as described in section 5.4.3.
2. Boot the machine with the virtual profile.
3. Go to the Device Manager and bring up the **Properties** screen for your IDE controller.
4. On the **Driver** tab, click the **Update Driver** button to run the Add/Remove Hardware Wizard.
5. Pick the driver from the list of known drivers for Windows 2000/XP. Use the **Standard Dual Channel IDE Controller** selection.

6. Shut down Windows 2000/XP.

7. Boot your system into whatever you want to use as a host system and then try to boot the machine from within VMware.

- No write access to the partition: Go to the disk setup in the Configuration Editor and click the **Partitions** button to see if the virtual machine has access to the target partition.

12.2.9 DOS Guest Operating System Problems

Problem: FDISK can't see more than one hard drive under DOS when you configure SCSI drives on the system.
Fix: The SCSI drives interfere with the VMware BIOS. If you need to partition IDE disks under DOS, temporarily remove your SCSI drives in the Configuration Editor. Also, FDISK doesn't work on SCSI drives; use the BTFDISK tool in the SCSI drives instead. (This applies to DOS only; use FDISK at a command prompt to partition any kind of disk in Windows 95 or 98, including SCSI devices.)

Problem: Your CD-ROM doesn't work under DOS, even though your drivers are for ATAPI drives.
Fix: There are many different DOS CD-ROM drivers, but not all of them function properly under VMware Workstation. Use the Mitsumi driver described in section 5.6.3.

12.2.10 Linux Guest Operating System Problems

Problem: The LILO boot loader doesn't work under VMware with a raw disk; it never gets past the L keyword.
Fix: The linear option in /etc/lilo.conf may not work under VMware. Comment it out and rerun /sbin/lilo.

If this causes problems in booting Linux, then forget about LILO and make a boot floppy under your guest system. Copy these boot floppies to image files (see Chapter 11 for more information) and attach them to your virtual floppy drive in the VMware Configuration Editor.

Problem: You messed up your Linux guest system in some way, and you can't boot it to a usable state.
Fix: Try text mode or single-user mode. In Red Hat, use linux 3 at the LILO boot: prompt to boot to runlevel 3 (the one that doesn't start an X server). For single-user mode, try linux -s at the boot prompt in other systems. Your system may not recognize the linux boot label; press TAB to see a list of valid labels.

(If you get LILO and not LILO boot:, press SHIFT to bring up the boot: part. If you get graphics instead of the prompt, press CTRL-X to bring up text mode.)

Problem: Your system doesn't boot; you get a kernel panic, saying that it can't mount root fs on $x:y$. You're using a raw disk.
Fix: The error means that the Linux kernel can't find its root (/) filesystem, and without that, it stops.

To solve this problem, first find the partition number (in the $x:y$ mentioned in the problem description, the y is the partition number. x is usually 03,

/dev/hda. So if the number were 03:02, your root device would be /dev/hda2, or the second partition on the primary master device.)

Your fix depends on the specific problem:

- If your raw disk setup denies the guest access to root partition, go to the disk setup in the Configuration Editor and see if the guest system has read-write access.

- You may be using the wrong partition or disk. Run fdisk on the disk and print the partition table. At the LILO boot: prompt mentioned in the previous problem, try using root=/dev/hd*x*n, where *x* is the drive name and *n* is the partition number. If this works, change your /etc/lilo.conf file and run lilo, but *only* if your system isn't dual boot.

- For dual-boot systems, you may have misconfigured the disk. In the Configuration Editor, inspect the disk's location to see whether it corresponds to the disk's actual location on the real system. If you can't inspect the disk (for example, if the real device is on an IDE interface that VMware doesn't provide), make a boot floppy image.

- If you're trying to boot from a floppy disk (or floppy image) because the BIOS can't access a LILO boot block for some reason, use rdev /dev/fd0 */dev/rootdev*, where *rootdev* is your root filesystem's device.

- Your kernel may be able to find the partition but may not support the filesystem and/or device. This problem is commonly encountered just after you compile and install a new kernel. If you have a SCSI virtual disk, you must compile SCSI support directly into your kernel or have an appropriate initial RAM disk image that loads the module (your distribution should be able to set up such a disk for you). Also, you *must* directly compile the root filesystem's partition type (usually ext2) into the kernel; a module will not do.

Problem: Your system doesn't boot; you get a protection fault almost as soon as the kernel loads.

Fix: This problem is probably due to a memory misconfiguration. On some hardware, the kernel won't see all available memory unless you give it a mem=*n* MB option, where *n* is the number of megabytes in the system. However, if this is a dual-configuration system, your real memory size won't be the same as the virtual machine's, and when the Linux kernel tries to address more memory than is actually available (in the Linux guest system), the system crashes.

To see whether this is the problem, find your virtual machine's memory size in the Configuration Editor (we'll call it *n*) and power on the virtual machine. When you get the LILO boot: prompt (discussed two problems back), type linux mem=*n* M. If the system boots correctly, you've found your problem.

There are a few ways to fix this problem for good. If possible, look in /etc/lilo.conf and make the appropriate changes. Normally, you just comment out the append=.. line and run lilo. However, if yours is a dual-configuration system, make sure that you boot the guest operating system in native mode to verify that the change didn't cause the system to get the wrong amount of memory in real mode. If it did, you have two options: try a newer kernel version or learn to live with typing in the memory size at the boot prompt.

Problem: You created a virtual machine for a Linux guest. After the system boots to the log-in prompt, the screen flashes between a blank screen and the log-in prompt. (This problem is most common in dual-boot machines with raw disks, but may also occur after installation on virtual disks with any system where you are unable to create a working XF86Config file.)

Fix: Your system's display manager is trying to start the X server, but it's configured for the wrong hardware. Turn off the server or display manager or use the server that comes with VMware Tools for Linux. (See section 6.4 for more information on how to turn off the display manager before you install the Tools.)

Problem: Your mouse behaves erratically.

Fix: You're probably not using the correct PS/2 mouse protocol. For X servers, look in your XF86Config file for the mouse setting; it should have a line like this in the Pointer section:

```
Protocol        "IntelliMouse"
```

If you have gpm running, confirm that you are using the -t imps option.

The gpm program can also get in your way if it's using repeater mode (where gpm echoes mouse events to another device). To see if this is the case, display a process listing and look for gpm with the -R or -M option. If you find it, see whether your XF86Config file's mouse device is /dev/gpmdata—change it if you need to. Now, with the XF86Config file still open, change the protocol to mousesystems. (Remember, though: do this *only* if the mouse is in repeater mode.

Problem: Red Hat 6.2 doesn't install correctly on your Pentium 4–based host under VMware; the installer displays a lot of anaconda error messages.

Workaround: Even outside a virtual machine, these processors cause trouble for Red Hat 6.2. Try a newer version.

Problem: Even though you have several resolutions defined for your display, the VMware X server doesn't let you use CTRL-ALT-Plus to switch between them.

Fix: You'll have to work around this. VMware's server doesn't support resolution switching. See the following problem for a possible fix.

Problem: You want to use two XF86Config files on your notebook: one for your screen resolution and the other for your external monitor. How do you do this?

Fix: Make one file your primary XF86Config file and name the other something like XF86Config-alt. Make sure that both are in the configuration file search path (/etc/X11 is usually the best place). To use the alternate file, use the -xf86config XF86Config-alt server options. To do so with the startx or xinit commands, use these forms:

```
xinit -- -xf86config XF86Config-alt
startx -- -xf86config XF86Config-alt
```

It's important to use only the name of the file, *not* the full pathname (/etc/X11/XF86Config-alt doesn't work). Also, note that in this situation, it's very inconvenient to use a display manager such as gdm, kdm, or xdm, because these don't provide a simple way to switch between server configuration files.

Problem: Linux kernel version 2.4.3 doesn't work under VMware.
Fix: There are bugs in this release. If you want to run the 2.4 kernel series, use version 2.4.4 or higher.

Problem: You installed VMware Tools for Linux, but you can't start the X server.
Fix: If you get an error message complaining about undefined symbols or references, update your Linux guest system to get newer versions of the C library (glibc). Red Hat 5 is one such distribution where this problem is known to occur.

If you get some other message, you probably have a configuration file problem. The easiest way to check this is to run

```
X > /tmp/x_log 2>&1
```

and examine /tmp/x_log. Look for anything that shows up as an error (you can often ignore warnings). Usually, the problem is something trivial like a mouse device problem, but some other common problems include the following:

- An incorrect XF86Config file. The server checks in several places for this file and uses the first one it finds. If that's not the one the VMware Tools installer set up for you, it probably won't work.

- An incorrect X server (XWrapper or X). Check the symbolic links in /usr/X11R6/bin and the files in /etc/X11 for this setting.

- An attempt to run the server at an unsupported bit depth.

12.2.11   VMware Tools Problems

Problem: You installed the VMware Tools, but you can't move the mouse off the edge of the VMware screen to get back to the host system; you still have to press CTRL-ALT.
Fix: To get the VMware Tools' mouse features to work, you must run the VMware Toolbox.

On a Linux or FreeBSD guest system, you have to run the vmware-toolbox command in some form within the X Window System (it won't work at the console). It's fine to run the Toolbox before log-in, for example, while an xdm log-in box appears, but make sure that the Toolbox continues to run after log-in.

Problem: Your VMware Tools don't seem to have all of the features mentioned in the documentation, but you downloaded the most recent version from the VMware website.

Fix: Don't download the Tools from the website; the most recent (and appropriate) version comes with the VMware Workstation distribution. Mismatched Tools packages may not function properly.

Problem: You're trying to upgrade your Tools, but without success.

Fix: You can't run the Toolbox or Tools/Properties during the upgrade, so exit them before installing the Tools. (Windows guests: Exit the tools icon in the taskbar. Unix guests: Bring up a virtual console and kill your display manager if it's running, which will kill `vmware-toolbox` and the X server.)

12.2.12   Networking Problems

Problem: Networking doesn't seem to work under Windows 95 just after installation.

Fix: For some reason, the Windows 95 installer doesn't always get the network card settings right. To solve this problem, bring up the **System** control panel and look at the Device Manager. Remove any visible network adapters; then reboot the machine. When the system reboots, it automatically detects the network card, and this time it should work properly.

Problem: You're trying to use bridged networking on your guest operating system, but it's not working. You know you're using the right driver for your host's Ethernet card.

Fix: Don't use your host machine's driver on your guest system; the virtual hardware is an AMD PCnet32 in a virtual machine with a bridged network interface (just as it is with a host-only network).

Problem: When you try to connect to a network service on your host from your guest system (or vice versa), the connection hangs for a while or times out.

Fix: The server is probably attempting to perform a reverse name lookup on the IP number of the guest system. To solve this problem, put the guest's IP number and name in your `hosts` file (see section 9.6).

Problem: You're trying to connect your guest system to your cable or DSL service with bridged networking, but your ISP's software isn't working.

Fix: Service providers generally only allow one connection or IP address on a line at a time, and their DHCP server may even refuse to talk to your bridged interface because the MAC address isn't the same as your host's. (There may be other issues with the software and the bridged network as well.)

It's much easier to put your virtual machine on a VMware NAT network in cases like this.

Question: You're using bridged networking in your guest system to talk to your host system. Is this a problem?

Fix: Not necessarily, but there are a few things to watch out for:

- If you're using a notebook, this isn't a terribly good idea, because you generally won't be able to perform host-guest communication when disconnected from a local area network.

- If your local area network has some sort of trouble (affecting performance or whatever), that trouble will affect the VMware bridged network's performance.

- If you're running VMware Workstation for Linux, the accompanying SAMBA server isn't set up for interfaces outside the host-only network.

- You may be vulnerable to security holes in your host and/or guest systems' services if you aren't careful.

12.3 Setting Up a Recovery Guest Operating System

One frustrating problem that you may run into is a guest system that won't boot due to a problem with some system startup file. However, since you can't boot the system, you can't make any changes. As mentioned in Chapter 11, you can use some guest operating systems to work on a filesystem on a raw, virtual, or plain disk. However, installing a full-blown guest system is overkill for this purpose. Here are some things to keep in mind when setting up a recovery system:

- When choosing a guest system for recovery purposes, keep two things in mind: what the operating system can talk to and how well you know the guest system. For example, although Linux can attach almost any kind of filesystem and has no problems with VMware's networking, you may not be very familiar with Unix. Windows systems, on the other hand, could be easier for you to work with, but they don't have as much filesystem support, and you don't have terribly fine control over the system's mount points.

  Linux works for most Unix-like guest systems and Windows 95/98. However, its support for the Windows NT Filesystem (NTFS) is currently read-only, which could be a problem.

- Consider the size of your system and how long it takes to boot. When doing this kind of work, you may have to reboot (and possibly alter) the virtual machine often. One good choice for a Linux recovery system is Debian, stripped down to a minimum configuration (because you won't have to sit through things like Red Hat's hardware detection scripts). As for Windows, consider Windows 98 if you don't need NTFS; it generally does a decent job of detecting new hard disks (which is all you care about).

- Install the system on a virtual disk with a minimum of packages. Once you have it working the way you want it to, power off the virtual machine and make a copy of the virtual disk file. This may take up a bit of disk space on your host system, but if you accidentally corrupt the recovery system's own disk, you'll save a lot of time if you have a backup.

LINUX DISPLAY PARAMETERS

To really get a handle on your host system's X configuration, you need to edit the `XF86Config` file by hand. It's normally in `/etc/X11` or `/etc`, but it may also be in `/usr/X11R6/lib/X11` on your system. If you're running XFree86 version 4, the configuration file may be `XF86Config-4`.

Assuming that your `XF86Config` file has the proper settings for your video card (most configuration tools handle this correctly), you need to worry about only the video modes. These depend on your monitor, as well as your version of XFree86.

This appendix doesn't go into great detail about how to set up an X configuration file; it only points out certain areas and parameters of interest. You should look at the `XF86Config` (5) manual page if you need more information than what is presented here.

A.1 XFree86 Version 3

Find out which X server you're running. Depending on your system, one of these commands should show it to you:

```
ls -l /etc/X11/X
ls -l /etc/X
ls -l /usr/X11R6/bin/X
cat /etc/X11/Xserver
```

The output from one of these commands should contain something like this:

```
/usr/X11R6/bin/XF86_SVGA
```

In this particular case, we're using the SVGA driver. Skip down to the end of the XF86Config file and look for a section that begins with these lines (be careful; there may be several that look alike):

```
Section "Screen"
    Driver          "SVGA"
    Device          "Primary Card"
    Monitor         "Primary Monitor"
    DefaultColorDepth 32
```

The definitions for Primary Card and Primary Monitor appear earlier in the XF86Config file. The DefaultColorDepth value is your bit depth and should be set as high as possible. If you don't see this property in this section, it's likely that your display is running in 8-bit mode (and as a result, your colors won't look so great, especially on your web browser). If you want to change this, change the DefaultColorDepth line (or add it if it's missing), go down a little in the section, and look for a subsection like this:

```
    SubSection "Display"
        Depth       8
        Modes       "1280x1024" "1024x768"
    EndSubSection
```

Let's say you want to go from 8 bits to 24 bits. First, check to see if a similar subsection appears with 24 instead of the 8. If so, you shouldn't need to do anything; if not, copy the 8-bit subsection and change the 8 to 24 in the copy.

Now, verify that the resolutions on the Modes line are what you want. The first is the initial mode, and you normally want to set it to the highest value. If all of your desired resolutions don't appear (or you're otherwise unhappy with them), you can't just add modes and expect them to show up—you need to go up to a Monitor section. In the case here, the monitor has the Primary Monitor label, so go back in XF86Config file and look for a section that starts with these two lines:

```
Section "Monitor"
    Identifier      "Primary Monitor"
```

There are two lines in this section that define the monitor's capabilities:

```
    HorizSync       30-94
    VertRefresh     48-160
```

These *must* match your monitor's horizontal and vertical scan frequency ranges. This information should be in your monitor's manual, but if it isn't, the vendor frequently has the information online. Assuming that these settings are correct, look for the actual video mode definition line, which looks like this:

```
Modeline  "1280x1024" 157.50 1280 1360 1520 1728 1024 1025 1028 1072
```

Or you may find a more verbose version:

```
Mode "1280x1024"
    DotClock 157.50
    HTimings 1280 1360 1520 1728
    VTimings 1024 1025 1028 1072
EndMode
```

Any mode that you want to place in the `Display` subsection just described must have a `Modeline` or `Mode` definition in the `Monitor` section. The numbers are precise timings, and you can't randomly guess them. There was a time when you had to calculate these by hand for each video card and monitor (and you ran a risk of destroying your monitor if you got it wrong!), but display technology has improved somewhat since then. Your `XF86Config` file may already have a number of timing sets for each mode—some X configuration programs provide these. In that case, all you need to do is pick out the ones that you like and see if they work. Otherwise, you can search for some VESA standard display modes. Most monitors work well with these, unless the timings are outside of the monitor's capabilities.

A.2 XFree86 Version 4

Rather than provide a different X server executable for each type of display device, XFree86 version 4 has one X server that loads the drivers dynamically. First, hunt down the `Screen` section in your `XF86Config` or `XF86Config-4` file. Here's the start of one from a 16-bit LCD notebook display configuration:

```
Section "Screen"
    Identifier "Screen0"
    Device    "Card0"
    Monitor   "Monitor0"

    DefaultDepth 16
```

Then there's a `Display` subsection inside, showing the currently available modes. Add more `Modes` lines for more modes. As in XFree86 version 3, the mode must be in the `Monitor` section.

```
SubSection "Display"
     Depth     16
     Modes     "1024x768"
EndSubSection
```

The `Monitor` section in XFree86 version 4 looks like the one in XFree86 version 3, described in the previous section.

UPGRADING FROM VMWARE WORKSTATION 2

If you upgraded from a previous version of VMware Workstation, there are a few changes to your guest systems that you need to make. Specifically, you need to upgrade your virtual hardware. If you choose not to upgrade the virtual hardware, you can still use the virtual machine, but you won't be able to use all disk modes, and the guest operating system won't have access to the new hardware in VMware Workstation 3: USB devices, generic SCSI devices, and so on.

This appendix applies *only* to virtual machines and virtual disks that you created under the previous Workstation version (if you create a new virtual machine but use an old virtual disk image, Workstation 3 treats the virtual machine like an old one). Any new configurations you create with new disks and fresh operating system installations have full access to all new Workstation 3 features.

B.1 Upgrading the Virtual Hardware

The virtual machine upgrade process is somewhat involved, but if you understand why each step is important, you can avoid unnecessary trouble and wasted time.

1. If you're using a virtual disk, make a backup copy of your virtual disk file.

2. Boot the virtual machine. If **Upgrade Virtual Hardware** in the **Settings** menu is dimmed, then you don't need to upgrade your virtual hardware (don't select this menu item yet).

3. Install or upgrade to the VMware Tools on your guest operating system. This step is important because the Tools include drivers that work under the new VMware Workstation 3 hardware.

4. Shut down the guest operating system and turn off the virtual machine's power. VMware Workstation should notify you that you installed the VMware Tools.

5. Select **Upgrade Virtual Hardware** from VMware's **Settings** menu. You can perform this step only after upgrading VMware Tools on your guest system.

6. A new window appears, telling you what you are about to do. When you confirm this screen, another window comes up with special instructions for your guest operating system. Take careful note of these (writing them down if necessary).

7. Turn on the virtual machine's power. The **Upgrade Virtual Hardware** item referred to in steps 2 and 5 should now be dimmed.

8. Carry out the special instructions you obtained in step 6.

B.1.1   Upgrading Windows Guest Systems

When you boot a Windows guest system for the first time after upgrading the virtual hardware, the system automatically detects any new hardware, such as USB devices. Let Windows go through this process until it calms down.

However, if the upgrade in step 6 of the previous section didn't go smoothly, your virtual machine won't behave the way it should. In particular, the video drivers won't work right: you won't have full resolution or as many colors as you used to. This is easy to fix—it's just a matter of one too many active drivers.

If your guest system is anything but Windows NT, do the following:

1. Go to the Device Manager (described in sections 5.2.1 and 5.3.2) and look for the video card. More the one card should show up (at least one should have a small error icon). Right-click the video cards one at a time and choose the **Uninstall** or **Remove** option. Don't reboot your system until you've gotten rid of all of the cards.

2. Reboot your guest system. The Windows guest system will detect the video card and install the driver correctly (possibly making you reboot once more).

3. Open the **Display** control panel and choose a new resolution if you want to.

Windows NT is a little different:

1. On the **Display** control panel, select the **Settings** tab. Click the **Display Type** button; a new **Display Type** window should appear. If the **Adapter Type** shown is **VMware SVGA II**, you don't need to do anything. Otherwise, click **Change**.

2. A new window, **Change Display**, should appear. Scroll down the **Manufacturers** list and select **VMware, Inc.**

3. Select **VMware SVGA II** in the **Display** list and click **OK**. Click **Yes** on the warning message that follows.

4. Close the **Display** panel and reboot your NT guest system.

B.2 Upgrading Virtual Disks (Windows Host Only)

When you upgrade VMware Workstation for Windows, you have the option to search for old virtual disk files with the `.dsk` extension and replace them with `.vmdk` files. If you choose not to, you may still do so at any time without reinstalling VMware Workstation. Run the `dskrename.exe` program in the VMware Workstation program folder to perform a filename update.

INDEX

C

D

F

FDISK

    DOS, 16, 90–91, 222

    FreeBSD, fdisk, 127

    FreeDOS, 151

    Linux, fdisk, 108–109

    replacing MBR with, 16

    Windows 95/98/Me, 80

file sharing

    Linux guest, 186–187

    Linux host, 180

    Windows guest, 184–186

    Windows host, 184

file transfer, with SSH, 194

filesystem

    creating, 108–109

    FreeBSD kernel configuration, 133–134

    FreeDOS, 151

    ISO9660, 60, 203, 206

    Linux, 116

    Minix, 202

    MS-DOS, 110, 202–205

    on floppy disk, 203

FIPS, 144

floppy drive, 11, 61

    booting from, 15

    configuration wizard, 36

    dd, 118

    DOS guest, 91–92

    FreeBSD guest, 129

    FreeBSD kernel configuration, 135

    image, 202

    Linux boot, 118

    Linux guest, 110

    Linux kernel configuration, 114

    NetBSD guest, 142

    OpenBSD guest, 142

    problems, 216

    reliability, 204

    Solaris 2.7, 151

    Solaris guest, 150

    Windows guest, 75

FloppyImage, 205. *See also* disk image

formatting, disk. *See* disk, partitioning

FreeBSD guest

    ATAPI CD-ROM, 129

    booting, 124–125, 133, 136

    devices, 125–131

    disk partitioning, 125–128

    dual configuration, 123–125

    Ethernet interface, 124, 129

    floppy drive, 129

    IDE disk, 125–128

    installing, 120

    mouse, 122–122, 130–131 (*see also* moused)

    network configuration, 164

    parallel port, 130

    SCSI, 129

    serial port, 130

    sound card, 131

    USB, 130

    VMware Tools, 121–122

FreeBSD kernel

    building, 132

    configuration, 132–135

    testing, 133

FreeBSD system information, 136. *See also* dmesg

FreeBSD, Linux binary compatibility, 120

FreeDOS guest

    devices, 152

    filesystem, 151

    installing, 152–153

VMware GSX Server

VMware™ GSX Server™ is virtualization software for partitioning servers. By isolating server resources and applications in virtual servers, VMware GSX Server lets you run multiple applications on the same physical server, ensuring each application's peak performance and scalability. Use VMware GSX Server to:

- Increase server capacity without buying new servers.
- Provide a secure, stable platform to deploy new solutions faster and more efficiently.
- Maximize server management efficiency and minimize costs across server infrastructure.

VMware ESX Server

VMware ESX Server™ is virtualization software for partitioning servers in high-performance environments. Ideally suited for corporate IT and service provider data centers, VMware ESX Server offers high performance, scalability, and advanced resource management. Use VMware ESX Server to:

- Provide a secure, uniform platform for rapidly deploying, easily managing, and remotely controlling more servers at a lower cost.
- Deliver cost-effective high availability.
- Reduce total cost of ownership across your IT infrastructure.

VMware Workstation

VMware Workstation is virtualization software for software developers, QA/test engineers, help desk and technical support teams, corporate trainers, and sales/marketing professionals. VMware Workstation improves productivity by letting you run multiple operating systems in secure, transportable, and high-performance virtual computers on physical computers. VMware Workstation lets you:

- Spend less time installing operating systems, rebooting, or reconfiguring hardware.
- Spend more time developing, testing, and deploying applications.
- Shorten time-to-market, improve product quality, and enhance your competitive advantage.

VMware, Inc. 3145 Porter Drive, Bldg. F Palo Alto, CA 94304 USA Tel: 877-486-9273 Fax: 650-475-5001 www.vmware.com

To find out more about VMware software products, visit us on the Web at http://www.vmware.com/products/

LINUX IN THE WORKPLACE

by SSC, PUBLISHER OF *LINUX JOURNAL*

Linux in the Workplace introduces Linux users to the desktop capabilities of Linux and the K Desktop Environment (KDE) graphical user interface, a powerful Open Source graphical desktop environment for UNIX workstations. Includes information on how to use email and surf the Internet; perform general office-related tasks; work with the command line; and much more.

MAY 2002, 400 PP., $29.95 ($44.95 CDN)
ISBN 1-886411-86-7

THE LINUX COOKBOOK
Tips and Techniques for Everyday Use

by MICHAEL STUTZ

This is a complete reference to all of the free software that comes with Linux, with sections on printing, converting and managing files, editing and formatting text; working with digital audio; creating and manipulating graphics, and connecting to the Internet.

2001, 396 PP., $29.95 ($44.95 CDN)
ISBN 1-886411-48-4

THE BOOK OF ZOPE
How to Build and Deliver Web Applications

by BEEHIVE

Zope, the leading Open Source web application server, helps teams of developers create and manage dynamic, web-based business applications like Intranets and portals. *The Book of Zope* is a complete introduction, covering installation; DTML programming; users, roles, and permissions; ZClasses; ZCatalog; databases; programming Zope with Python; debugging; and the use of external data sources.

2001, 400 PP., $39.95 ($59.95 CDN)
ISBN 1-886411-57-3

PROGRAMMING LINUX GAMES
Building Multimedia Applications with SDL, OpenAL™, and Other APIs

by LOKI SOFTWARE, INC. WITH JOHN R. HALL

Programming Linux Games discusses important multimedia toolkits (including a very thorough discussion of the Simple DirectMedia Layer) and teaches the basics of Linux game programming. Learn about the state of the Linux gaming world, and how to write and distribute Linux games to the Linux gaming community.

2001, 416 PP., $39.95 ($59.95 CDN)
ISBN 1-886411-49-2

THE LINUX PROBLEM SOLVER
Hands-on Solutions for Systems Administrators

BY BRIAN WARD

This book is a must-have for solving technical problems related to printing, networking, back-up, crash recovery, and compiling or upgrading a kernel. The CD-ROM supports the book with configuration files and numerous programs not included in many Linux distributions.

2000, 283 PP. W/CD-ROM, $34.95 ($53.95 CDN)
ISBN 1-886411-35-2

Phone:

1 (800) 420-7240 OR
(415) 863-9900
MONDAY THROUGH FRIDAY,
9 A.M. TO 5 P.M. (PST)

Fax:

(415) 863-9950
24 HOURS A DAY,
7 DAYS A WEEK

Email:

SALES@NOSTARCH.COM

Web:

HTTP://WWW.NOSTARCH.COM

Mail:

NO STARCH PRESS
555 DE HARO STREET, SUITE 250
SAN FRANCISCO, CA 94107
USA

Distributed in the U.S. by Publishers Group West

UPDATES

This book was carefully reviewed for technical accuracy, but it's inevitable that some things will change after the book goes to press. Visit **http://www.nostarch.com/vmware_updates.htm** for updates, errata, and other information.